The Very Nearly Man

An Autobiography

ROBERT HOUNSOME

The Very Nearly Man

An Autobiography

Matador
9 De Montfort Mews
Leicester LE1 7FW, UK
Tel: (+44) 116 255 9311 / 9312
Email: books@troubador.co.uk
Web: www.troubador.co.uk/matador

ISBN 1 905237 72 3

Front cover: Robert Hounsome in his news agency office, late 1960s
Back cover (top right): Sylvia and Robert Hounsome at their Golden Wedding Anniversary (April 1993)

Typeset in 11pt Bembo by Troubador Publishing Ltd, Leicester, UK
Printed in the UK by The Cromwell Press Ltd, Trowbridge, Wilts, UK

Matador is an imprint of Troubador Publishing Ltd

Dedicated to the memory of my late wife, Sylvia, and to the three daughters she gave me.

For in and out, above, about, below,
'Tis nothing but a Magic Shadow-show,
Play'd in a Box whose Candle is the Sun,
Round which we Phantom Figures come and go.

The Rubaiyat of Omar Khayyam

Acknowledgements

Advancing age tends to play tricks with the memory. Existing records have helped in compiling this autobiography, but I am indebted to my family and other relatives, to fellow journalists and other long-standing friends, to military establishments and to municipal Local Study and Record Offices in Brighton, Chichester (West Sussex CC) and Lewes (East Sussex CC) for their generous help in achieving factual and chronological accuracy. I should also like to thank ex-colleague Sally Cline, now an established author and Royal Literary Fund Writing Fellow, for her advice and guidance.

Prologue

Dawn on 1 July, 1916: an empty blue sky and an early mist hovering along the river heralded a perfect summer's day. But it was the silence that struck the waiting infantrymen. For six days they had been stunned by the relentless gunfire of their own artillery. Now, suddenly, they could hear the larks singing.

It couldn't last and, at 7.30 am, another barrage erupted. Whistles shrilled across the Flanders' trenches and the first assault troops poured into No Man's Land. The Battle of the Somme had begun; the Big Push that would finally drive the Germans into the ground and end the war, so it was said.

On the right of the line, flanking the French Army, the men of the 16th, 17th and 18th Battalions of the Manchester Regiment waited to launch the second attack, timed for 8.30 am. They were better known as the lst, 2nd and 3rd Pals from the time when, as colleagues and workmates they had, together, answered Lord Derby's call to arms.

Among them was my cousin and namesake - and even perhaps my alter ego - 25-year-old Salford schoolteacher Robert Hounsome Allen, a member of IX Troop, 'C' Company of the 18th Manchesters - the 3rd Pals.

The three battalions, along with the 2nd Royal Scots Fusiliers, formed 90th Brigade. They had been in France for some months but this was their first battle. Morale was high despite the huge British casualties of the first two years of the war. For the past week nearly 1,500 guns of the 4th Army had blasted 1.5 million shells into the German lines. The enemy couldn't survive such a bombardment could it? Their generals had told them so. All that was needed now was for the infantry to stroll over No Man's Land and mop up the demoralised stragglers.

The reality was starkly different. The Germans held the high ground and, because of their elaborate trench system, casualties were far fewer than estimated. Their artillery and machine guns, too, remained largely intact. Far from being a stroll the British advance turned into a shambles. Crossing the open ground they were cut to pieces. Any territorial gain was minimal.

The 90th Brigade had some success. Their objective was the French village of Montauban. The 17th Manchesters led the assault on the right and the 16th on the left. The 2nd Royal Scots Fusiliers followed in support with the 18th Manchesters providing carrying parties. Their orders: 'After the first bombardment has been completed they will come and go to Montauban by the communication trenches, moving on top of and beside the trench (sic) and continue to move as fast as possible…Carrying parties must not halt on account of enemy fire.'

Two groups finally broke through to the village. But all along the 4th Army front the casualties were astronomic – nearly 60,000 killed, wounded and missing. It was the greatest one-day loss in British military history.

The Manchesters suffered their own extensive mauling. The 18th – the 3rd Pals – had one officer killed and four wounded, with 170 other rank casualties. Significantly, one hundred of those belonged to Robert Hounsome Allen's 'C' Company.

The scale of the casualties overwhelmed medical and transport resources. Many of the dead and wounded could not even be retrieved from the battlefield. So Robert must have been an early casualty. He was carried in and evacuated fifteen miles back to the Main Dressing Station in the French village of Sailly-le-Sec, two miles east of Amiens in the valley of the Somme.

He never regained consciousness. At some time on 2 July, 1916, No.10589 Private Robert Hounsome Allen, former schoolteacher and graduate of Chester College, died of his wounds. He lies buried in Grave 25, Plot 2, Row 'C' in Dive Copse Military Cemetery, a mile from Sailly Church.

Three other Manchester Pals battalions lost more men in later stages of the Battle of the Somme. Among the hundreds left to mourn was Robert's mother Mary Allen, known as Mollie, who had been born

Mary Hounsome in the tiny West Sussex village of East Marden. She had three sons and four daughters (another son had died at birth), but she had a special affinity with Robert. He was the youngest son and she, too, had been a schoolteacher.

As she wrote to her sister Hilda: '...We have heard that poor Bob has been killed in France... It came through first of all that he was wounded and then we heard from an RAMC man attached to the hospital that he died of wounds while still unconscious... I had a letter from him on 27 June, just a month ago last Sunday, and not a word since. The silence has been awful and I can hardly realise that the poor lad has gone under... The Manchesters have been in the thick of the fighting and have suffered heavily. Lots of boys from just about here have either been killed or wounded. Oh it's a terrible war. It is too dreadful for anything...'

Mollie's brother, Owen Hounsome, and his wife Emma also mourned Robert's death. He and his girlfriend had spent part of his embarkation leave at the couple's terraced house in Brighton. So, when I was born in 1919, they named me Robert in his memory.

It was to be another eight years before my mother suddenly produced Robert Allen's silver watch chain and explained its significance to me. His mother had sent it to me as a memento.

In the end his death was in vain. This was supposed to have been the war to end all wars. But twenty years later Britain and Germany were at war again; and this time it engulfed my own generation.

CHAPTER 1

An Unplanned Birth

I was a lunchtime baby, born on 8 October, 1919, in the front bedroom of 37 Cobden Road, Brighton – the same house where Robert Hounsome Allen had spent his embarkation leave. My mother would be 39 the next day, my father already 47. Both had led hard, disadvantaged lives. They already had three other children – Ethel, born on Boxing Day, 1902, Reginald following in 1905 and Eva in 1909 – so my conception ten years later could hardly have been welcome news. I was a mistake, so it was supposed. Or was some other force at work? Was my life in some way inextricably linked with the spirit of Robert Hounsome Allen?★ We were both Librans, our birthdays only five days apart, and we shared similar characteristics.

It was five years since the First World War had broken out and Robert had joined the Army. Now my own life would take a crucial turn every five years, as if manipulated by his guiding spirit.

There would be many examples of his possible influence. Was it coincidence, for example, that, after completing my training in the Second World War, I was posted from the south coast to the far north to join my first active service unit? The 52nd Field Regiment RA had just returned from Dunkirk and empty places had to be filled. But the unit strength was made up mostly of a new generation of Manchester volunteers. For the 52nd turned out to be a Manchester Territorial Army regiment. So it would continue throughout my wartime service; eventful but with some protective influence seemingly shielding me from potential hazards.

★Robert had a nephew, now dead, also named Robert Hounsome Allen, probably also named after him. Perhaps we shared him as a guiding spirit.

But such considerations formed no part of my consciousness in the early years. My first remembered experience dates back to the age of 20 months. It was one of those snapshots, some important, others of no apparent consequence, which become imprinted forever in the memory like a frozen frame from a film sequence.

I am sitting in one of those old-fashioned high chairs that converted into rocking chairs. My mother is feeding me. There is a round table with a white tablecloth bearing the wreckage of hastily consumed breakfasts. My older sister, now aged 18, is on the other side of the table, late for work and exchanging departing words with my mother.

Just about at that time young Rose Heise, nee Killick, living in two rooms about a mile away in Stanley Street, gave birth to her only child, a girl. They named her Sylvia and she was destined to drift in and out of my life until we were married twenty-one years later. It was an occasion Rose Heise never lived to see, however. Seventeen months after her baby's birth she died from that scourge of the time, tuberculosis – or consumption as it was known.

This was how life began for both of us; trapped in an unrelenting working class sub-culture, a social basement from which escape appeared a remote hope. Yet many of us did escape. For Sylvia and me the escape route came through the unlikely medium of journalism by way of the encouragement of dedicated schoolteachers. But in those struggling 1920s and early Thirties it never occurred to either of us that one day we would mingle with the stars, from Tom Mix and Max Miller to Marilyn Monroe and John Wayne, or that we would follow Royalty around and drink champagne cocktails at the Ritz.

All that lay in the future, however. In those early years survival was the priority. In my case life revolved round our home and its immediate environment. Cobden Road ran at right angles to the lower end of Elm Grove, a main artery that led ultimately, by an increasingly steep gradient, to the Race Hill and Race Course. We considered it to be at the better working class end of the town. We were poor but not destitute.

Steps led up to the front door and a narrow apology for a front garden supported a Virginia creeper, which clambered up the cement-rendered front elevation, and a row of privets colonised by caterpillars, chrysalises and butterflies in the spring and summer.

There was a front room – never the lounge or sitting room, a living room – never the dining room, and a brick floored scullery too dismal to be considered a kitchen. Upstairs there were three bedrooms, the rear one of which was referred to, for some obscure architectural reason, as 'the slip room'.

The life-support fittings were of the more primitive variety. The front room and living room depended for illumination on gas mantles operated by chains. The two front bedrooms – the slip room was excluded – had to make do with gas jets on the wall. Along with the iron-barred fireplaces they were lit only in the event of illness. Otherwise one groped one's way to bed by spluttering candlelight.

The living room was heated by a Victorian range with hobs and adjoining oven which were much used by my mother in preparing our meals (it was also ideal for toasting bread and roasting chestnuts at Christmas). Coal was kept under the stairs and delivered, a couple of hundredweight at a time, on the bowed back of the coalman.

The scullery was a depressing place, darkened by a high wall which separated us from our neighbours and against which my father later built a rickety lean-to. A long deal table stood under the window opposite a cast iron gas stove which, along with the living room range, was scrubbed and burnished regularly with metal polish. One corner was occupied by that essential of every working class home, a concrete copper, into the centre of which was embedded the metal container to accommodate the week's wash. The fire for heating the water was located in an orifice at the bottom of the copper. Another frozen snapshot is of my mother on hands and knees inserting a faggot of sticks, scraps of newspapers and a shovelful of cinders into the orifice and encouraging them to ignite with the aid of a mounting pile of burnt out matches. The scullery also accommodated a massive mangle, used to extract cascades of water from the dripping laundry.

Our bathroom comprised a galvanised bath, the shape of a canal narrow boat, which hung from a nail in the backyard. It was retrieved on Friday nights and filled with cauldrons of boiling water from the gas stove, tempered by saucepans of cold water.

A backyard ran alongside the scullery to an outside toilet with a high-level cistern that sometimes froze up in winter. Next to it an outhouse contained various garden implements and, from time to time, three or four demented chickens or hutches of docile rabbits destined as future supplements to the household diet.

Steps led up to a long raised garden ending in a high flint retainer wall behind which loomed the backs of houses in Luther Street, the next road up and therefore built at a higher level. Only the back bedroom windows were visible to us. But from our garden we could hear the Colour Sergeant voice of Mrs Preston quelling her raucous brood. In fair weather her bedroom window remained permanently open, the sill sometimes holding a variety of mats, which were beaten with vicious abandon, and at other times supporting her generous bosom as she leaned out to gossip with unseen neighbours in the gardens below. This was 37 Cobden Road, the temporary maternity ward into which I was born, and which was to be my home for the next twenty years.

That single imprinted moment round the breakfast table was followed only by vague impressions; my mother gossiping with the neighbours, being sick (I was a frail baby and a frequent visitor to Dr Paul Kirby's surgery).

Another frozen frame belongs to 1924. I am 4 years old and sitting with my mother in a cool, stone-floored room of a distant cottage. A stooping old lady shuffles across the floor, disappears into a cavernous larder and re-appears with food and drink. I still recall the aroma of home-cured ham and oven-baked bread.

The old lady is my maternal grandmother, Martha Woods, 79, wearing traditional widow's black and living in retirement at Oak Cottage in Nyewood village near South Harting, West Sussex.

She was the first and only grandparent I ever met – the other three were already dead when I was born. Until then I had never heard of grandparents.

My mother had visited her mother once or twice after leaving home more than twenty years earlier but my father never, as far as I know, saw his parents again after leaving the family home. This lack of contact had nothing to do with family discord but reflected the disruption of country life in the final years of the nineteenth century.

My father's forebears had remained within about a twenty-five mile radius of their origins for some 650 years, rising to be farmers and smallholders with diversions into other rural callings such as blacksmiths and gamekeepers.

By the 1800s my father's branch had settled in East Marden. Born on 17 June, 1872, he was one of twelve children. A family of eight surviving cousins and a few other relatives also lived in the village.

My mother's family, the Woods, were rooted in Forestside, another downland village across the valley from East Marden. Her father, William Woods, followed his father as gamekeeper on the Stansted estate but he had to give up in 1889 after being injured in a night attack by poachers. Strings were pulled and as compensation he was granted the licence of the Royal Oak, at Hooksway, up the road from East Marden. It is a popular inn these days but was then a beer house serving villagers and passing farmworkers. With it went seven acres of woodland and here my grandfather made hurdles and kept a few livestock while his wife Martha ran the pub. She did so with determination, setting her own opening hours by bribing the local Bobby with a regular supply of free beer and wild rabbits. Among the customers were the Hounsome boys. This is when my mother first met my father, though she was barely more than a schoolgirl at the time.

She had been born in a cottage in Woodberry Lane, Cockbush, alongside the Stansted estate on 9 October, 1880, one of nine children – eleven if you count two from a set of triplets who died in babyhood.

By now the pattern of life was already changing. The exodus from the countryside had begun as early as the 1840s when two of my mother's aunts, Charlotte Woods and her sister Caroline Safwell, opened boarding houses in London. Another sister, Eliza Shellock, and her husband ran a greengrocer's shop in Pimlico. By 1910 all the Woods children, except two, had left the locality and only one Hounsome remained. Two of my father's cousins emigrated to Canada at the beginning of the 1870s followed by another in 1909.

The drift away was understandable. Large families continued to proliferate but farm work – the main source of employment – declined due to what became known as the Great Depression of the rural economy. It was accompanied by increasing mechanisation with the introduction of the traction engine, the combine harvester and the threshing machine.

Simultaneously the spread of formal education brought greater literacy and numeracy to the working classes (the village school in East Marden opened in 1845) while the coming of the railways suddenly offered fast, cheap travel. For the impoverished villagers new horizons beckoned with the means to reach them.

Some men turned to the colonies. Others enlisted in the services where there was a constant demand for manpower to maintain the Empire and prosecute the Crimean and Boer Wars. Still others worked on the expanding railways or headed for new opportunities in the towns.

For most girls there was only one destination – domestic service, with its attendant hazards; exploitative employers and lecherous sons.

Education remained patchy in the villages. Schooling for all 5 to 10 year olds was introduced in 1870 and became compulsory in 1881 but parents were still required to contribute towards the cost (it was not until 1891 that education became free of charge). My mother's family did not fare too badly. However, my mother had to leave school at 12 and so she was never able to realise her secret ambition of becoming a teacher.

My paternal grandparents, with twelve children, were forced to discriminate. Mollie Hounsome, regarded as 'the clever one', was encouraged to stay at school and money was found to send her to the Bishop Otter teacher training college in Chichester. After qualifying she taught in Sussex until her marriage and her move to Manchester.

The Hounsome boys' education was varied but my father seems to have drawn the short straw. His schooling ended at the age of 9, after which be became a shepherd boy. He probably left home for the bright lights of Brighton in his early twenties but, as with most others, the move from village to town brought no great material improvement.

The transition was probably less of a culture shock for my mother. She at least had been introduced to town life by spending some months with Great Aunt Caroline Safwell, by then a widow, at her boarding house in Kensington. That was probably after she left school so it is likely that she had entered service as an undermaid by the time she was 14. After serving the gentry, first in Emsworth and then in Haywards Heath, she reached Brighton sometime around 1900 when she was still only 19. There, on a Sunday afternoon off duty, she re-met my father by chance on Brighton seafront.

They were married at St John's Church, high up among the town's back streets, on 8 February, 1902. It was a Spartan affair. The only relatives known to have attended were my mother's brother Frederick and her sister Martha (the surviving triplet, known as Marnie).

I uncovered the bulk of this ancestral history many years later with the help of contemporary relatives. My sisters, I discovered eventually, were better informed than me. My parents revealed only limited details during my childhood, their family links having weakened probably still further by then.

Setting up home far from their families must have been accompanied by a sense of insecurity, particularly as they were limited to two rented rooms in Lennox Street hard by the church where they had wed. Whether it was a marriage of love or convenience is hard to tell. My mother never accustomed herself to the humiliation of domestic service and my father was no doubt weary of living in lodgings for several lonely years.

Life was always tough. My sisters told me that my brother, before going to school, would walk down to the then beachside fish market two miles away and to the wholesale vegetable market and filch whatever discarded or overlooked items he could to contribute to the family fare. When Eva contracted scarlet fever, my mother had to wait for five days before saving up the half-a-crown – 12p in today's money – needed to summon the doctor.

I don't recall the contact between children and parents being either tactile or intimate. It was an undemonstrative relationship reflecting the economic restraints of the marriage and our parents' harsh upbringing.

But in their own way they had, I later realised, the utmost affection for us.

My mother was the dominant influence and driving force within the partnership. My father remained a less definable figure. Arriving in Brighton, he had landed, through his rural experience of handling horses, a job with Durtnalls, the leading furniture removal company in the town, which was still using teams of Shires to tow its pantechnicons. In those early years he was sometimes away for days at a time, driving around southern England. One problem was that he had become over partial to strong drink. It had no doubt taken hold during his lonely time in lodgings. But it imposed a further strain on the already-stretched domestic finances.

My mother, resorting to the resourcefulness she had learnt as a girl at the Royal Oak and in service, eased the family's straightened circumstances by earning a reputation as a dressmaker and by taking in occasional holidaymakers.

CHAPTER 2

Working Class Morality

My fifth birthday in 1924 signalled the first of those five-yearly cycles that were to highlight the rest of my life. It brought new experiences straight away.

A month earlier I had been introduced to the infants' department of Elm Grove School, a tall, red brick, high-railinged Victorian building typical of educational institutions of the period.

I was determined not to join those other newcomers who dissolved into tears when their parents left. The classroom was crammed with so many children that I sat cross-legged on the floor. Halfway through the morning screens were wheeled into place dividing us into two classes. My group then savoured the undivided attention of Miss Bailey, a smiling lady of marriageable age, whose golden complexion and hair colouring matched her sunny personality. For the rest of the morning she struggled to impart knowledge to us against an intrusive hubbub escaping from the other side of the screens.

Soon afterwards my schooling was temporarily interrupted by the onset of diphtheria, another of those medical scourges of the day. It necessitated a five-week sojourn to Bevendean Isolation Hospital, remotely sited, as a precaution, at the top of Bear Road but ominously on the opposite side of the road from a cemetery.

My parents appeared occasionally, mouthing inaudible endearments from the other side of a transparent screen. Diphtheria was a serious, often fatal, illness; a girl living nearby, whose parents refused hospital treatment was crippled and left permanently confined to a wheelchair. In my case it was a turning point, leaving me more robust and confident. That genie was watching over me.

Back home, unaccustomed signs of affluence baffled me. Doors and scuffed skirting boards had been repainted and there was some new lino brightened by new rugs. I thought I had entered Mrs Gates's house next door by mistake. Her family was always regarded as more comfortably off. Her home was in better decorative order, she was the one who always had the cup of sugar to lend and her daughter had a posh job – possibly a buyer it was thought – with Barrance and Ford, an up-market fashion house on Brighton seafront.

Many years later I discovered that the display of comparative wealth was the result of a bequest of £109 to my mother under the will of Great Aunt Caroline Safwell. It was this that had also, probably, financed the visit to grandmother Martha Woods. The money must have come as a relief to my mother. After years of scrimping she could be excused a bit of a spending bonanza.

In May, 1925, we headed once more for Oak Cottage, Nyewood, where I was marched upstairs to see my grandmother again. This time she was lying in her coffin – another of those frozen frame moments, memorable because she was the first dead person I had seen and because she looked remarkably like my mother in repose.

A horse-drawn carriage carried the cortege to the cemetery. Back at Oak Cottage I recall a flurry of aunts bickering, I was told, over the division of grandma's chattels. Her death brought my mother another legacy of £100.

By now my two sisters were working and my brother was an engineering apprentice at Allen West, the town's largest engineering company. There was a comforting sense of financial security. But my mother, conditioned by the past, never ceased to worry about money – and with good cause.

By 1920 the immediate post-war boom was already sliding towards depression. Wages plummeted and unemployment reached a million. On the other hand, the better off were acquiring their first motor cars and installing candlestick telephones. The debutantes were back and the Bright Young Things were living it up in nightclubs, celebrating the arrival of the Jazz Age, dancing the new-fangled shimmy and Charleston and experimenting with heroin.

In our neighbourhood the depression bit deep, embittered further by still-vivid memories of the war. It had left empty chairs, sad widows and fatherless children struggling to survive. Groups of disillusioned ex-servicemen, promised 'a land fit for heroes', found themselves singing in the streets. Boys went absent from school because they had no shoes. The pawnbrokers at the bottom of Islingwood Road were never short of customers. Out-of-work husbands, their National Insurance – or dole as it became known – terminated after six months, sidled shamefacedly off to 'the Parish'.

Mounting resentment at this inequality found expression in January, 1924, with the election and brief reign of the first Labour Government. As a minority government, however, it had no chance and by October the Conservatives were in office again on the back of the fraudulent but effective Zinoviev 'Reds under the bed' Letter scare.

Six months later Winston Churchill, the Chancellor of the Exchequer, made the disastrous, if reluctant, decision to return Britain to the gold standard. It simply added to the pressure cooker of discontent which finally blew its safety valve in 1926. The miners, told to work longer hours for less money, initiated the General Strike, backed by the Trades Union Congress.

Instead of negotiating a compromise settlement – which might well have produced a more positive long-term worker-employer relationship – the new Government set about not only breaking the strike but also emasculating the trade unions. One of the more dedicated strikebreakers was, again, Winston Churchill.

Superficially, the Socialist movement seemed down and very nearly out. The Labour Government had lasted only eleven months and the General Strike five days – though the miners held out for another six months. In fact it marked the stirring of an underlying change in social attitudes that gathered strength throughout the Thirties and found final expression in the political aftermath of the Second World War.

I was unaware of the upheaval. My only memory of the General Strike is being taken by my father to the bottom of Elm Grove to see the first strike-busting trams emerge along Lewes Road, their windows protected from protesting stone throwers by rope meshes.

The depression had its domestic repercussions. My father remained in work, though at a scrape-through wage, and my sister Ethel was in a 'good job' as bookkeeper to a greengrocer who counted actress Evelyn 'Boo' Laye and a number of seafront hotels among his customers.

My younger sister, Eva, couldn't get a job, however, and Allen West sacked my brother, now 21 and his apprenticeship completed, because there was no senior vacancy available.

By this time most of my mother's two legacies had evaporated. She wore a worried look and I embraced the impression that money was in short supply again. In reality we were no worse off than many in our neighbourhood and better off than quite a number. But in my childish mind I was convinced of impending penury. It fostered a sense of insecurity which surfaced periodically throughout my life, triggering sudden panic fears of financial catastrophe.

Despite the hard times my mother maintained a dogged determination. She was convinced, I think, that she had been destined for a higher social level in life and that only an unfortunate administrative error by the Recording Angel had miscast her into a working class environment. Now she looked to her offspring to succeed where she had lost out, an attitude she encouraged in various overt and subliminal ways. It had one other effect, certainly as far as I was concerned; an aversion to uniformity and imposed authority.

Cobden Road was the hub around which our lives revolved; a close-knit community with its own code of working class morality and mutual trust based on a shared struggle against adversity.

There was no drug culture. That was the preserve of China Town opium dens and the dilettante rich. The opiates at our level were alcohol – the 'demon' of the day, tobacco, the Hollywood dream machine and Saturday football – still the poor people's game, not yet highjacked by the money men and turned into a Stock Market commodity. These opiates had the advantage of being cheap and less addictive. There was no need to rob a building society or bash a grannie to finance the habit. In our street the one family of petty thieves were treated as outcasts for breaking the code.

This conformity within the law was driven not by altruism but by an implicit fear. There was fear of unemployment and destitution epitomised in our neighbourhood by the brooding presence, at the Race Hill end of Elm Grove, of the workhouse, known familiarly as 'Up the Top'. There was fear, as unprotected tenants, of failure to raise the 13s 1d for the weekly visit of the rent man. There was fear of authority as personified by PC Plod, pounding his beat at regular intervals, to whom my mother sometimes threatened to hand me over. There was fear even of the school attendance officer if you were absent for more than a few days. Finally there was the authority of the church, preaching the ultimate threat of eternal damnation.

Within this dichotomy of shared fear and communal camaraderie, Cobden Road, a long to-ing and fro-ing street of ninety-eight houses, went about its daily business, its motley denizens as varied as it architectural styles.

In one corner, at the Elm Grove end, was Stevens, the drapers, on the other Gillam's pub. Next to the pub was a sweet shop, run from her front room by Mrs Bishop, a widow of uncertain age.

It seemed to be permanently open except for a brief period in the mornings when Mrs Bishop, in cloth cap and carpet slippers, shuffled off to Gillam's snug bearing a large white jug. She returned a few minutes later with her daily ration of liquid nourishment.

Mrs Bishop's was where we spent our sweet money on such items as sherbet dabs, liquorice sticks, 'arrow root' (at least that's how we pronounced it), tiger nuts and dried bean pods, commodities rarely seen today. There were also freshly made toffee apples on sticks or, if you couldn't afford one, there was the alternative toffee poker – essentially a toffee apple without the apple.

On our topside of the road were the Gilletts, whose daughter I recall setting off one snowbound Boxing Day to get married. Next door, on the other side from the Gates, were the Hillmans. Mr Hillman was periodically carted off to hospital in an advanced state of consumption. I knew when he was back home because I could hear him moaning in the night as I tried to sleep.

Further along were the three Pelham sisters, Ethel's friends, sallow skinned, dressed in perpetual black and moving around in unison like

Siamese triplets joined at the hips. I never remember them sitting. Then again I can't remember them exactly standing. They hovered, like crows on an invisible branch waiting for a morsel of carrion to arrive. In the years that followed, whenever I witnessed a performance of the witches' scene from Macbeth, a vision of the Pelhams floated into my mind. Later Amy, the middle of the three, surprised us all by marrying a retired police sergeant who had landed a management job at a large estate in Surrey.

Next to the Pelhams in Cobden Road came William Wood, chimney sweep, a lugubrious man with a muddy complexion as if the product of his calling had impregnated his skin. He arrived every spring, presaged by a flurry of activity as all removable objects were shifted to another room. Those that remained were shrouded in old sheets.

After Mr Wood's departure with his jumble of rods, brushes and bag of soot there would be a period of furious dusting and replacing of the removed objects. Summer, you knew, must be just around the corner.

Beyond Mr Wood's lived the Earl family, two of whom, Ted and Jaz, were among my playmates. A builder must have occupied their house at some point because there was a large, gated side entrance leading to a generous-sized garden. Here they kept various animals including a goat which we sometimes marched up to the Race Hill to feed off the gorse, causing a good deal of curiosity on the way.

Midway along the street was the Cobden Arms, run by Mr Sopp, which my father sometimes patronised as a change from Gillam's.

On the lower side of the street, was a second sweet shop that seemed to struggle perpetually against insolvency. Next door was another war widow, Mrs Ansell, whose son, Horace, won a scholarship to Oxford, an accomplishment so rare in our neighbourhood that I decided he must be a genius. Between there and Mrs Bishop's were the children of various families with whom I hung around: the Ledwards and the Andersons, the Thomsons and, directly opposite our house, the Richardson brothers, Reg and Ronald.

One day the Richardsons' mother, a large handsome woman, staggered home from her crack-of-dawn office cleaning job and collapsed into bed. She died the next day from pneumonia. It hit the sons badly, particularly Ronald, who later joined the Royal Navy. What became of them all?

On the same side of the road lived Arthur Boiling, window cleaner, killed when a wartime German bomb fell on him while he was up his ladder outside a pub at the bottom of Franklin Road.

There was also Mrs Belchamber's laundry into which, on certain days, white-aproned washerwomen and ironers would converge like swarming bees.

At the distant end of the street were the Bakers, whose diabetic daughter occasionally fell into a coma and had to be rushed into hospital and Christopher Gaston, a huge policeman whose twin was also in the Brighton Force.

Between them was a low whitewashed, walled-eyed building that had served as a soup kitchen during the Great War. It spooked me, especially as it was now used exclusively by a gentleman of Indian or Eurasian extraction. Did he keep his harem hidden there? There was a more mundane explanation. He used it for the exotically designed packets of Indian tea that he hawked from door to door. My mother was one of his customers, impressed less by the tea than by his impeccable manners, impeccable English and impeccable wardrobe which included a selection of plus fours. We accepted him as a charming curiosity. We had never heard of either racism or racial discrimination. Like most families we had a cat to combat the mice thriving behind the lathe and plaster walls and skirting boards. He was a massive black tom, so we called him Nigger and thought nothing of it.

Public slipper baths stood right at the end of the road. They were in constant use though we never patronised them ourselves, the assumption being that we 'might catch something'. We preferred our narrow boat bath.

This then was our street. Art Deco, modernism and pastel shades hadn't yet reached us. We had to be content with workhouse brown, County Council green and the primary colours. Sunblinds were the exception with their varie-coloured stripes. They were necessary because of the vogue for varnished and grained front doors; dignified but suffering the disadvantage that the varnish blistered if not shielded by the blinds from the summer sun.

Winter brought a shivering contrast. We huddled round the fire trying to keep warm, our backs often freezing in the draughts which crept in through the doors and the sash windows. Chilblains were a common affliction.

Displayed in the front window in our house as in many others, was an aspidistra, that emblem of working class respectability immortalised by Gracie Fields. Lace curtains shielded our privacy while slatted Venetian or calico pull-down blinds were lowered at night or when there was a funeral in the street.

Behind the lace curtains life followed a set pattern. Monday was washday and that meant a hastily prepared dinner of bubble and squeak, effectively a fry-up of the leftovers from Sunday lunch.

Washday itself was so labour-intensive that it could be undertaken only once a week. Everything went into the copper along with soap, starch and Reckitt's blue to enhance whiteness and dirt resistance. After much boiling it was hauled out with a wooden dolly stick onto the reverse side of the copper lid and transferred to the mangle.

Drying was a long process, especially in winter, as was the ironing, with old-style flat irons heated on the cooker gas rings and used in rotation.

Shirts were expected to last a week so had detachable collars. But the effect of the starch was to fuse the buttonholes. Prising them apart to insert collar studs and cufflinks was a frustrating operation

During the rest of the week my mother was always capable of rustling up some kind of meat for our main meal. There were bullocks' hearts, sheeps' hearts, sweetbreads and chitterlings (pigs' intestines), pigs' trotters and brawn made from unidentifiable bits of pig solidified in gelatine.

There were also wild rabbits and perhaps a backyard broiler hen, its laying days over. Brought up in country ways, my mother could skin a rabbit and pluck a chicken – and disembowel both – at a speed worthy of a mention in the 'Guinness Book of Records'.

My sister Ethel's occasional visits to Amy Pelham and her ex-policeman husband in the depths of Surrey, produced further variations to the family fare – a rare pheasant, maybe or a brace or two of rooks. My mother, adept at plucking chickens, wasn't going to be defeated by the plumage of a few rooks and so we discovered the acquired taste of rook pie.

Vegetables went with the seasons, a surprising proportion coming from our long narrow back garden, again thanks to my father's farming background. Despite its poor soil he managed to grow potatoes, cabbages, firm-hearted cos lettuces, various types of beans, black-skinned Chinese radishes and even Jerusalem artichokes. We also had an apple tree – on which my father grafted a mistletoe pip that flourished successfully – a pear tree, a hazelnut tree and a loganberry bush. That garden was his oasis from an alien town life where he could sit and dream of his bucolic youth.

Bread was delivered to the door by horse-drawn van but we had to wait while the driver anchored the cart at the end of the road and refreshed himself in Gillam's. The horse's co-operation was assured with a nosebag of corn.

Milk arrived in churns aboard Payne's pony-powered, two-wheeled trap and was brought to the doorstep by the walrus-moustached, leather-gaitered milkman in pint or half-pint pewter cans. There were also occasional appearances of an optimistic rag and bone man offering gold fish for old clothes.

In summer, milk was boiled to prevent it turning sour and two or three sticky flypapers were suspended from ceilings. Despite the absence of refrigeration and modern packaging and storage methods I can't recall any cases of food poisoning.

Perhaps they were held at bay by my mother's faith in the purgative efficacy of syrup of figs. Her homespun remedies also included vinegar and brown paper for swellings, a plug of tobacco for toothache, dock leaves for stings, camomile for rashes and bread poultices, applied boiling hot, for anything from poisonous infections to splinters, known generically as 'gatherings'. Iodine was the universal antiseptic for cuts.

If we survived these curative measures we were able to experience the joys of the ritualistic Sunday.

This was 'slaving over a hot stove day' in the unremitting life of the working class housewife. My mother often sought relief with a mid-morning sit-down when she would thrust the poker between the bars of the kitchen range and, when it was red hot, plunge it into a sizzling glass of stout to fortify herself.

Some form of roast meat was always found for Sunday dinner even in the most frugal times. This was also the day when the fishmonger came round before breakfast, pushing his handcart and crying out his offerings of fresh-caught Brighton herrings and mackerels and, in season, sprats. The muffin man followed in the afternoon, ringing his bell, a large tray loaded with his wares balanced precariously on his head.

We always transferred to the front room for tea, the fire being specially lit in winter.

Besides muffins, Sunday tea included winkles or whelks, rounded off, if we were lucky, by a homemade trifle.

On Sunday evenings, my mother, father and I would set off on an evening stroll, travelling to one or other of the town's tram termini. We invariably ended up at a favourite pub where I stood outside regaling myself with cheese biscuits and a glass of bilious-looking lemonade while my parents refreshed themselves inside. I remember very little conversation on these Sunday evening outings but they generated the first stirrings of my imagination.

Everything emphasised that Sunday was a special day. One wore one's 'Sunday best' clothes and playing in the street was strictly forbidden. The churches were full and so were the Sunday Schools. It was part of a leisurely-paced, simplistic life buoyed by a British sense of superiority. We had an Empire and still ruled much of the world.

On weekdays, Cobden Road was our playground. We rolled our hoops and whipped our tops unhindered by traffic, used our coats for goalposts and the old soup kitchen walls as our wickets. The gutter was used for playing marbles and the pavement for hopscotch, skipping and playing tabs with cigarette cards. Collecting and swapping cigarette cards was a popular hobby. There was no shortage of supply. Smoking was almost universal, cigarettes were cheap and every packet contained a card. Brighton Race days in August were one unfailing source. We stood in Elm Grove and cajoled the stream of punters into parting with their cards as they climbed the hill to the racecourse.

According to the Elm Grove School centenary booklet, school finished early on race meeting days during term time. I can't remember this but I do recall hurtling out of the building as soon as lessons ended and chasing up Elm Grove, reaching the racecourse in near exhaustion just in time to see the horses thunder past in the final race.

Race days in the holidays were a favourite attraction, free and exhilarating. They brought colourful characters to our small world, among them the flamboyant tipster Prince Monolulu in his rainbow robes and plumage with his beguiling cry of 'I gotta horse'. This was the period, too, when the race gangs were active, among them the notorious Sabini brothers, whom I would meet many years later.

Grim reality took over later when the punters trudged back past the workhouse at the top of Elm Grove. It is now Brighton General Hospital but it is still bounded by the high flint wall over the top of which, on race days, hung a long line of the workhouse inmates. Identically dressed in rough brown suits and wearing Navy blue mittens, they held outstretched caps, silently hoping for a few coppers for baccy from the passers-by.

These were the permanent residents; men who, after slaving all their lives, discovered their reward in old age was destitution. Already lining up at the workhouse entrance were the travelling tramps who had arrived from Newhaven workhouse to the east and were seeking a night's bed.

After labouring the next morning to pay for their keep they would be off again across the Sussex Downs to the next workhouse. There was a suppressed fear that one day this might be one's own fate. Ironically I did in fact join the ranks of the down and outs many years later – but then I was paid to do so.

The wide-open spaces of the Sussex Downs offered further adventures; Ditchling Beacon and the Dyke perhaps, or Newmarket Copse where we brewed tea in our billy cans over a wood fire. But my favourite destination was Falmer village, four miles away, with its flint cottages, foursquare church and iron pump beside the pond. I had a special tree that hung across the road to Woodingdean, among the branches of which I would eat my sandwich lunch while a farm cart or two and maybe a rare car passed by.

Then we would move down to the pond and wade in to catch newts and efts – or effits as we called them – which we took home in jam jars. There I transferred them to larger receptacles from which they escaped over the following days, slithering across the scullery floor, producing squealed protests from my sisters. School biology lessons didn't run to explaining that newts and efts were amphibious rather than aquatic.

Other expeditions ran according to the seasons. At Easter it was primrose and cowslip gathering – even at times the rarer oxslip – at Whitsun bluebells. We returned with bunches of the former and armfuls of the latter. They were the main source of our interior floral decoration.

Such was their abundance that there was no prohibition against collecting them, as there is today. Woods were coppiced and managed, letting in the sunlight to encourage the ground flora. Hedges were layered and manually trimmed instead of being bashed by mechanical flails or, alternatively, being grubbed up completely to turn patchwork fields into miniature prairies.

Muscular-shouldered farmhands pitchforked the wheat sheaves, or stooks as we called them, on to horse-drawn wagons. Haystacks stood like thatched cottages in the corner of a field instead of piles of black plastic bales. It was part of the timeless nature of the countryside. Insecticides, herbicides and artificial fertilisers belonged to the future and myxomatosis had not yet swept through the wild rabbit population.

Our other free pastime, since we lived at the seaside, was bathing which progressed, by clumsy experiment and mouthfuls of salt water, to swimming. The more decorous and better off changed into their swimming costumes in one of the beach huts hired out by Daltons or Hattons. The rest of us changed in the open among the deck chairs. These were the days when clinker-built rowboats and Skylark motorboats took trippers for a 'jolly ride out'.

We swam from various beaches, including those opposite the

Riviera-sounding Hotel Metropole and Grand Hotel – later to be partly demolished by an IRA bomb which nearly killed a British Prime Minister. We watched the rich and famous entering and leaving or taking tea on the balcony. This was the opulent end of Brighton, far removed from the working class back streets. It seemed a world away. Oh to one day penetrate their portals.

Some things had to be paid for, including rare excursions on to the Palace Pier to sample the delights of the Palace of Fun; its primitive pin-ball machines and glass-encased automatons, gruesome theatres in which heads were severed, apparitions jack-boxed through trap doors and cabinets opened on to further horrors. What the Butler Saw machines voyeuristically revealed flickering images of Edwardian ladies cavorting in their underwear; far less titillating in fact than the lingerie section of the modern mail order catalogue.

Other pennies went on comics like 'Wizard', 'Eagle', 'Rainbow with Tiger Tim' and 'Film Fun', featuring Charlie Chaplin, Chester Conklin, Laurel and Hardy and Buster Keaton, whom I came to interview many years later. My favourite comic, however, was 'Magnet', recounting the continuing exploits of Harry Wharton and the odious Owl of the Reform, Billy Bunter, at Greyfriars School.

Another financial outlay was the entrance fee to the Arcadia Cinema in Lewes Road, which ended its life as a cycle shop. The front entrance and plush seats were beyond our resources, however. We queued on Saturday afternoons at the rear ticket office, paid our 4d and sat on wooden forms. At the same time my future wife was clutching her four pennies for the Coronation Cinema, some two miles away at the foot of North Road.

They were undoubtedly Brighton's two down-market cinemas. Anywhere less resembling a pastoral idyll in the one case or a world of pomp and circumstance in the other would be hard to imagine. We had a more prosaic and obvious name for them, 'The Scratch'. But they fuelled our dreams of a better future. It was still the age of the silent screen, with the dialogue translated on to caption slides. The films featured the same characters as 'Film Fun', pre-eminent among them Charlie Chaplin in those classics, 'The Gold Rush' and 'The Kid'.

My favourite was the serial, which always seemed to be a 'cowboys-and-Indians' saga starring my particular cowboy hero Tom Mix. There he was, astride his faithful 'wonder horse' Tony as it reared up on hind legs, on the edge of a precipice with a few hundred bloodthirsty Red Indians, inevitably cast as the villains in those politically incorrect days, coming up fast in the rear.

How would he extract himself from this latest ambush? We waited in nail-biting silence. Then the slide would flash up: 'To be Continued Next Week'.

So we were blackmailed into scraping together another 4d to learn the sequel the following Saturday.

I thought I had discovered the perfect short cut on one occasion. I joined the crowd of begging youngsters who, in summer and at low tide, stood on the sand beneath the Palace Pier and scrabbled for coins thrown to them by holidaymakers lining the rails above. In no time at all I had collected enough for two visits to the Arcadia. But when, triumphantly, I told my socially conscious mother, I got the roasting of my life. I never stood under the Pier again nor begged for anything ever again – except, that is, for the time I did so in the cause of investigative journalism.

In 1927 the talkies arrived – though much later at the Arcadia and the Coronation – and Tom Mix faded into obscurity along with a number of other stars who were unable to adapt to the new style of acting or whose voices lacked the necessary cadence. Sadly I said farewell to my hero, never dreaming that one day we would meet.

It was about this time that my mother told me about Robert Hounsome Allen and his silver watch chain. I was immensely impressed by his having been a schoolteacher. That meant he went to college. No-one I knew, except widow Ansell's son, went to college or university. It placed schoolteachers on an altogether higher social plane. My self-esteem rose a notch or two.

For a while I wore the chain in my lapel buttonhole secured, at the other end, to a watch nestling in my breast pocket. Then, coming in from morning break in the school playground one day, I realised the watch chain was dangling free with no watch at the end of it. Working class morality, I discovered, wasn't that watertight!

As a precaution my mother took charge of the chain. Later, during the Second World War, she told me she had had it made into a bracelet. But I never saw it again or discovered what became of it.

Through the story of the watch chain I learnt, for the first time, that my father, known to everyone as Jack, had been christened Owen. This conformed to a Hounsome family practice. Aunt Mary, for example, was known as Mollie. Years later I discovered that two other aunts, Francis and Anne, neither of whom I ever met, were known as Fanny and Topsy while Harriet used her second name of Hilda and Uncle Ernest Albert was known as Uncle Dick.

The recent improvement in my self-esteem dipped again soon afterwards. Durtnalls had long since abandoned Shire horses in favour of mechanisation. This ended my father's horse-driving days and he reverted instead to what was known in the family as a furniture packer. But my mother insisted that in any official inquiries, at school or elsewhere, I should give his occupation as 'furniture porter', though I never understood the social distinction. It suggested that being a furniture packer carried a degree of shame.

Soon afterwards I began accompanying my father on some of his furniture removing sorties during school holidays. It was soon clear that he had been selected to move the more affluent of Durtnalls' clients and that he was the man in charge. He dictated the order in which rooms were cleared and items packed in the pantechnicon. Had my mother shown more guile she could have insisted, quite justifiably, on his being referred to as furniture removal foreman, a far more prestigious title which Durtnalls might well have bestowed on him had it not meant a possible wage rise.

I recall these furniture removal trips with affection. They took me into parts of Sussex I had never seen before and, in one case, to the Isle of Wight, where I met my father's eldest sister, Kate, for the first and last time. Bouncing along at the back end of the lorry on these excursions, my father and I clutching the tailboard, engendered a joyous sense of freedom and wanderlust.

The first excursion must have been very early on because the pantechnicon was towed by Durtnalls' last remaining traction engine. On the homeward journey it gasped to a standstill halfway up Clayton Hill. While the driver stoked up with coal to raise more steam, my father and I crossed to the wood on the other side of the road and helped ourselves to a bunch of bluebells. Such was the more measured way of life in those days.

CHAPTER 3

Religion, Politics and Education

In 1927 I was still only 7. Ethel was 24, my brother 22 and Eva nearly 18. All three had clearly discovered the opposite sex and were out hunting.

It couldn't have been easy for Ethel. I remember a few afternoons when up to half a dozen of her girlfriends would arrive for tea – held, as a special treat, in the front room. They were a vivacious, well-groomed coterie and all unmarried. I realised later that they too were victims of the Great War, members of a generation of young women who had been robbed of potential husbands. I think they found in me a suitable subject for their frustrated maternal instincts. Some of them, including my sister, did marry, though often some years later.

My brother Reg was a keen dancer but he and his unemployed mates rarely paid for their pleasure. They found ways of sneaking in through the back entrances, although in winter it incurred first hiding their overcoats in secret places, to be recovered afterwards.

Eva was extremely pretty and a terrible flirt, causing my mother moments of apprehension. I remember her looking out of the bedroom window at night waiting for Eva's latest boyfriend to bring her home. The later the hour, the more agitated she became. Once Eva and the boyfriend had returned to the house, my mother would march downstairs and interrupt any doorstep canoodling, convinced that she was thereby thwarting an early pregnancy. It left Eva angry and embarrassed. Among her occasional boyfriends was Dickie Richards, the Sussex reserve wicket-keeper, and Dickie Gillam, whose parents ran the pub on the corner of the street. He had a withered arm and, as I discovered later, was studying to be an art teacher.

The prospect of unplanned pregnancies inhibited courtship right up to the Second World War. For the parents it meant social disgrace, for the daughters the threat of being cast out into a social wilderness. For us boys it spelt perpetual sexual frustration.

So I grew up in this confused world of the mid-Twenties; one of four children but in many respects an only child, accustomed to hard times and resigned to living in a social stratum from which escape seemed unobtainable.

But attitudes were changing. A new generation was searching for a new social order, a way out of the restrictive past. Many looked eastwards to Communist Russia, not yet discredited. Was this the answer? In Britain, 1929 brought the flapper vote, with the voting age for women reduced from 30 to 21, giving the franchise to six million more female voters. It was no co-incidence surely, that that year's General Election resulted in a second minority Labour Government.

It had little chance due to its own inexperience, the ripple effect of the Stock Market crash and the massed opposition of influential vested interests. But it reiterated the clamour for change. One early sign was the arrival of the Council house. By 1929 half a million had been built and erstwhile slum dwellers began to experience a more civilised home life.

The south suffered far less unemployment than the industrial north and domestically there were early signs of more prosperous times. In 1928, after two years out of work, my brother, thanks presumably to my father, joined Durtnalls, putting his engineering training to use maintaining their lorries. My sister Eva also began her association with Hadlows, a printing firm in Brighton Lanes, which led eventually to her marriage. The family was at work again.

One sign of better times was the removal of the old kitchen range and its replacement with a low-level, tile-surrounded grate, known as the Devonshire. When I called at the house in the 1990s it was still there. Electricity replaced gaslights, in the home and in the street, providing a brighter aura at night. The gas lighter, with his long pole, became redundant.

Picture rails were introduced along with brighter patterned wallpaper. Modernism and Art Deco were on the march. Girls flaunted their flapper image and men strutted around in Oxford bags.

One unlikely feature in our home was a collection of Victoriana; items that would be regarded as valuable collectibles and antiques today but which, in the Modernist mood of the times, had little value. The front room housed a vast mahogany overmantle with bevelled mirrors, an inlaid whatnot with a collection of porcelain souvenirs and a glass display cabinet with an array of brilliantly-plumaged birds of paradise. In the living room, the mantelpiece and wall above were decorated with a flower encrusted candelabra and mirror along with a shepherd and matching shepherdess, all genuine Dresden china.

Another item was a mahogany draw-leaf table into which two leaves could be inserted at Christmas, almost filling the living room. A set of red leather-bound encyclopaedias with beautiful full-colour illustrations and the collected poems of Tennyson and Longfellow were my special preserve. In the one I would lose myself in the mysteries of the Universe and in the others the chivalrous world of Sir Lancelot and the Lady of Shallot and the far-off land of Hiawatha and Minihaha.

All these treasures were the trophies of my father's livelihood, given to him, or so he said, by grateful clients. They contrasted sharply with our more homespun furniture and floor coverings.

At Christmastime a mythical Santa Claus started treating me with greater generosity including the gift of prized annuals, the most prestigious being 'Boys' Own' which I was still reading a year later. This was when my mother was at her happiest, beaming across the double leaf mahogany table at the large gathering of family and friends. Turkey and pork, jellies and trifles, Christmas pudding and mince pies would follow each other.

Through her domestic service training my mother was always meticulous in laying out cutlery in the correct order as if we were about to indulge in a full-scale banquet. Table manners were strictly imposed. Good manners in general were a high priority on her list of accomplishments. To this day I automatically hold doors open for distantly approaching females.

Ethel was party games organiser-in-chief in the evening, although the men soon tired of these and retired to gamble round the mahogany table. Defying the need for sleep, I joined in and so at the age of 9 mastered the intricacies of pontoon, nap and brag.

I now began meeting some of my uncles and aunts. One was my father's sister Alice, a rotund, merry little lady with a dewlap chin that wobbled when she laughed. She lived in Arundel in an almshouse with fuchsias by the door, courtesy of the Duke of Norfolk, her previous employer.

We also paid a couple of visits to my father's youngest sister, Hilda, in Petersfield. The youngest of her children was Winnie, about the same age as myself, who played a crucial role years later.

On my mother's side there were a couple of visits to East Grinstead on the top deck of a Southdown omnibus – a great adventure – to visit her sister Caroline (known as Carrie) and meetings with Aunt Marnie, the surviving triplet.

Marnie met her husband, Percy Musselwhite, while in service with Major Wheatley in Poole (when we moved there in 1962 his son, Sir Mervyn Wheatley, was about to retire as Conservative MP). Percy was a member of an old Poole family of maritime engineers and yacht designers. The wedding of Marnie and Percy in 1912 was a grand affair judging by the group wedding picture which included my mother, brother and two sisters.

They moved to Southampton when Percy joined the famous yacht builders, Camper Nicholson, as a marine engineer. Their only child, Freda, was born little more than two months after me. When Aunt Marnie and Freda stayed with us in 1928 I returned to Southampton with them, my first experience away from the family. Over the years Freda and I remained good friends.

Uncle Percy took me to the docks to see some of the great trans-Atlantic liners. The Cunard and White Star companies were serious rivals, not yet having amalgamated. By good fortune both their flagships were in port, Cunard's Aquitania and White Star's Majestic. I had never seen such colossal vessels. Uncle Percy organised a conducted tour of the Majestic and its opulence and grandeur overawed me. This, I thought, must be how the Grand Hotel at Brighton looked inside.

My mother's youngest sister, Ethel, lived in Harting and worked at

Telegraph House when Bertrand Russell ran his 'free-thinking' school there. She married Arthur 'Punch' Glue, a formidable village cricketer and had a daughter and two sons, Dennis and Roy, who were my playmates when I stayed with them. They still had oil lamps and an earth closet and drew water from a well, cold as ice and as smooth as liquid silk.

Living with them was the eldest of my mother's siblings, Uncle Jim. He had worked on the railway but lost a leg in a shunting accident in Portsmouth sidings. Now he occupied a large shed in Aunt Ethel's garden where he pursued his new career repairing clocks and watches. I remember him as a kindly man thumping around philosophically on his wooden leg.

Grandmother Woods clearly had her fair share of misfortunes; her husband attacked by poachers, two of her triplets dying in infancy and Uncle Jim losing his leg. Another son, William, was wounded fighting with the 21st Lancers at Khartoum and died at the early age of 43.

So we eddied and drifted through the second half of the 1920s. Unemployment remained high in the north and the Welsh coalfields. In the south there was more work about, even if poorly paid. It was labour intensive work, still the pick and shovel, sledge hammer and navvying kind. Trench digging, pipe laying, tar spraying and tram track replacement absorbed whole gangs of men.

Single working women were spreading more widely into office work but advocates of birth control were prosecuted for distributing 'obscene' literature.

In Brighton work began on the Undercliff Walk from Black Rock to Saltdean. Some of the unemployed Welsh miners were drafted in to help. Having been deprived of digging black coal in the bowels of the earth, they now found themselves dangling in mid-air hacking chalk from the white cliffs.

On a personal level I was introduced to those two insolubles, religion and politics.

I was eight years old when I was suddenly whisked off to Sunday School. My sister Ethel was probably the instigator, being the only churchgoer in the family. But instead of being consigned to her own church, St Wilfred's C of E in Elm Grove, I was shunted off to the Congregational mission hall in Bentham Road further up Elm Grove, in the care of a friend who was a Sunday School teacher there. That's where I first met my future wife.

My political education began when Eva, wearying of my mother's anxieties, announced that she would marry her next boyfriend. Soon afterwards, a colleague at Hadlows printing works asked if she would partner her brother at a Labour Party dance. Albert William 'Bill' Lewis was a remarkable man; Labour Party activist, Trade Union stalwart, the epitome of self-educated old style Socialist idealist. Meeting him subsequently formalised my growing political awareness into mainstream radicalism.

Another blip hit the family fortunes when Ethel slipped while clambering across seashore rocks with a friend to reach a ship which had run aground at Portobello on the eastern outskirts of Brighton. She was off work for three months with a badly fractured ankle. The Rev Pemberton, Vicar of St Wilfred's, became a regular visitor. The church was a grey, single-story corrugated iron building that he was anxious to see replaced by a grander, permanent edifice. His single-minded efforts to raise the necessary funds included circulating buff envelopes among his flock which he expected to be filled with regular generous donations.

My mother always disapproved of the scale of Ethel's contributions and, when Pemberton persisted in producing his envelopes during these visits, disapproval turned to anger. She felt that in our straightened circumstances the church should help us rather than take some of what little we had.

Eventually the new church was built. But it was a waste of money. With the post-war deterioration in congregation numbers it was declared redundant, closed down and converted into housing.

Sometimes after dinner during Ethel's incapacity I helped my mother push her in a wheelchair to the Royal Sussex County Hospital some two miles away, for treatment (there was no ambulance service). I still managed to have a meal and return in time for afternoon school.

Memories of Elm Grove School have grown hazy. I have no

recollection of being unhappy there so it must have been a positive experience. Bunking off was out of the question – there was the menace of a visit from the school attendance officer. Reigning over the school was the headmistress, Miss Parkes, a diminutive lady with a cottage loaf hairstyle. I remember only a few of the teachers. All were, of course, unmarried, the penalty of marriage being career termination. Apart from Miss Bailey, I recall a youthful Miss Girling who bravely invited the entire class to her home in Lewes one Saturday morning, followed by a ramble over the downs. A Miss Greenway figured in another of those frozen frames, standing beside a map of the world splattered with an impressive array of red outposts of the British Empire.

In geography and history lessons no-one questioned the established view that it was our birthright to be there and that the natives were the grateful beneficiaries of our superior wisdom (our exploitation of their natural resources was never mentioned).

All teaching was conducted on a whole-form basis. We sat side by side in tandem wooden desks equipped with inkwells and blotting pads. We were taught the three 'Rs' by rote and learned the alphabet, phonetically at first, repeating every character in its shortened form. We read and were read to assiduously, learning the basic spelling rules on the way. The time's tables were drummed into us on a daily basis until we could answer any random multiplication demanded of us from two-times-two to twelve-times-twelve. The constant repetition took on an almost poetic measure.

The school stood over the entrance to a tunnel and a diversion was to spot the two-carriage trains chuntering between Brighton Station and Kemp Town on the eastern outskirts. The line has long since closed and the tunnel entrance blocked off to provide a school nature trail.

In 1928 I graduated to the senior school but within a year was back in the juniors when the age limit had been raised to 11; a disorientating experience due to one of those periodic educational reorganisations beloved of politicians. My new headmaster was Owen Hughes, undoubtedly one of those men who influenced my life. I remember him descending on our classroom and reading poetry to us, his starched white collar catching the light as he raised head and arms heavenwards as if in direct communication with the Almighty. Clutched in one hand was an open poetry book to which he would occasionally refer.

I was transfixed by his soaring rhythmic rendering in what I now recognise was a lilting Welsh intonation. It sent me hurrying home to read again the collected poems of Tennyson and Longfellow. Through Owen Hughes's poetry reading I began to discover the beauty of words.

CHAPTER 4

A Bright New World

In late 1929 my sisters let slip a family secret; my father had been 'in Haywards Heath'. Today Haywards Heath is recognised as a salubrious mid-Sussex commuter town but in my youth it was noted for one particular association – Haywards Heath lunatic asylum. If you were an inmate of a lunatic asylum you were automatically a lunatic. The term covered every shade of mental diagnosis from depression, through Downs Syndrome to dementia and clinical madness. It also covered, as in my father's case, alcoholism.

His drinking became so heavy that one night, before I was born, he imagined pink elephants were climbing up the bedroom wall and tried to climb after them. He was carted off to Haywards Heath and it took my mother a week to get him out. He took the warning to heart and, although he continued to drink, I never saw him drunk in my time. So he couldn't have been a true alcoholic.

The lunatic asylum would now be classified as a psychiatric hospital, most of the patients treated in other ways and my father directed to a drying-out clinic.

It was a worrying, even shameful, episode but my brother and sisters appeared to accept it with complaisance. Influenced by the anti-drink indoctrination of the Bentham Road evangelists, however, I was shocked by the sudden revelation; my father guilty of a major disgrace in addition to his unmentionable job. It was nonsense of course and many years later I recognised the adverse circumstances that drove him to this low point and the strength of character required to lift himself up again.

At the time it left me with a dented self-esteem alongside the sense of financial insecurity. An immediate reaction came early in 1930 when the lengthy grammar school selection process began. Those expected to be chosen in our class occupied, with smug confidence, two right-hand rows of desks and included, to my envy, Jaz Earl. I sat among the anonymous also-rans.

There were three eliminating examinations, each requiring a mile and a half march to other school premises. I had no expectations other than being there to make up the numbers. I should have had more faith in the spirit of Robert Hounsome Allen. I was 10 years old, at the start of another quinquennial cycle and that meant another turning point.

To my surprise I passed the first test and, a week or two later, joined a smaller snake marching back to York Place school premises for the next hurdle. I passed that too. Even then I had no great expectations and just as well, since the crucial final stage was a disaster.

By chance I occupied a remote rear corner desk and the introductory words of the invigilating teacher were largely inaudible. We were handed a printed card and instructed to read the text. It took me about thirty seconds after which I put it aside and awaited the anticipated maths and English papers. Instead I was ushered into another room to be cross-examined by a semi-circle of grey-haired suits about the contents of the barely read card. I stared back at them, petrified. Then they switched their third degree to the subject of Southampton Docks, a subject about which, thanks to my visits to Aunt Marnie, I did know something. But I was sure more erudite answers were expected than those that came to mind. I stammered a few unconvincing replies and mercifully escaped.

I knew straight away that I had flunked it; my first 'very nearly' miss. My mother was disappointed. She had relished the possibility of one of her children going to grammar school and the street cred it would command.

My failure to qualify proved, in the end, to be another defining moment. I had resigned myself to an inevitable pathway to the factory gates or, at best, a job as a Post Office telegraph boy when a letter arrived advising that I had been allotted a place at Brighton Intermediate School.

The Intermediate was one of a limited number of experimental schools which had been set up in various parts of the country two years earlier. Their purpose was to provide a 'half-way house' education for those marginal children who had missed out on grammar school. For me and for many others, including my future wife, it opened the way to a new world.

The next four years brought other changes in the family's fortunes. It was as if we had been trapped within a domestic chrysalis. Now we were metamorphosing into creatures capable of future flight.

In August, 1930, Eva and Bill Lewis were married at St Luke's Church, Queen's Park, Brighton. Bill had established his political credentials ten years earlier. The Trade Union history of Brighton records that, as a 16-year-old apprentice at Southern Railways' Brighton Loco Works, he addressed a strike meeting. Five years later, in 1925, his apprenticeship completed, he opposed the sacking of older craftsmen and their replacement by cheaper recruits. He was sacked but later rejoined Southern Railways at their Lancing Carriage Works eight miles west of Brighton. He and Eva followed the common practice of starting married life renting rooms in private houses, one being the home of a certain Mr Sargent.

By 1931, Lancing Carriage Works had been slimmed down and many of the employees sacked. Bill Lewis was offered the chance to transfer to Eastleigh in Hampshire but turned it down. With Eva now pregnant, it was decided they should move back into the family home in Cobden Road. Their only child, John Evan Lewis, was born on 31 October; a difficult birth with the baby almost strangled by the umbilical cord.

In April, 1931, my brother Reg had wed his long-time girlfriend, Gertrude 'Jean' Wright, also at St Luke's, Queen's Park. She, too, had had a tough childhood, one of eleven brothers and sisters whose parents had both died prematurely. Eleven months later their only child, Barbara Yvonne, was born in March, 1932.

Reg had already deserted Durtnall's vehicle workshops, preferring to drive the lorries instead of maintaining them. His job involved running a package service to Durtnall's London depot, returning the same day with another consignment. I accompanied him on some of his trips during school holidays, starting out around 5.00 am. or 6.00 am. and arriving back in time for tea. The high point was the pull-in at Sam's Half Way House, a greasy spoon café on the outskirts of Gatwick where I was treated to scalding tea and a bun while gossip was swapped with other drivers. After the war Sam's café was swallowed up by Gatwick Airport.

All roads were single carriageways, running straight through towns and villages. Traffic was sparse and there was a sense of adventure as we lumbered through the countryside. In summer we saw the dawn come up. In winter we drove through sleeping ghost villages and caught frightened rabbits in our headlights.

The lorry was a Leviathan of its day; a pantechnicon with a large trailer crudely attached by a hook and eye system and dependent on a primitive steel-cable braking system applied by turning a wheel in the cab. Operating it was the driver's mate's responsibility but, being in love and a late-night romancer, he was soon slumped asleep and had to be nudged awake at trailer-braking moments.

The London run spanned a tough twelve hours and wages were less than generous. But then my brother had a quick brain and made a few extras on the side I'm sure.

In September, 1930, I had joined one hundred and thirty newcomers at the Intermediate School. It was at York Place, in the same building where we had taken the selection tests. The girls' school occupied an adjoining building. The two had previously been used by the grammar schools, now relocated to the outskirts of the town.

Elementary school education ended at 14 but the Intermediate extended this by an extra year to provide a four-year course. The first two years were devoted to general studies but for the last two years there was a division into specialised 'commercial' and 'technical' streams. Selection for one or the other was based on aptitude and personal choice.

The curriculum throughout the four years included French, hitherto limited to grammar and public schools. Those of us who opted for the 'commercial' stream developed this further and were also introduced to typewriting, Pitmans shorthand, double-entry bookkeeping and the esoteric world of the Stock Exchange.

The concept was to provide a practical rather than an academic education. It proved invaluable when I set out on my chosen career. But an overriding benefit was the atmosphere created and the standards set by the dedicated staff. The teachers, almost all graduates – unusual below grammar school level – wore academic gowns and mortarboards. We were divided into houses and introduced to a wider perspective through class parliaments, Christmas plays, a school magazine, the prefect system and public school type morning assembly.

We felt we were part of something special, that there was life beyond the factory gates. The names of the staff are engraved on my memory: headmaster John F.W.Cooper and the teachers – Hill, Ireland, Scharer, Ross, Wilcox, Bowles, Jerman, Bowers and Coxhead the art master. Their Christian names are unremembered; they were always addressed as 'Sir'.

Mr Bowles first ignited my passion for English, broadening my vocabulary and, through endless 'parsing' sessions, leading me through the intricacies of grammar.

There were plenty of out-of-school diversions. There was swimming of course and clambering over the rocks at Black Rock, where Brighton Marina now sprawls, harvesting winkles and prodding sea anemones in the rock pools. There was a brief period of fishing with a second hand rod off the Palace Pier landing stage where Richard Attenborough later plunged to his death in Brighton Rock.

These excursions were facilitated by the acquisition of a second hand bicycle. I could also reach the farther end of Marine Drive where Jack Sheppard's concert party performed its twice-daily routine of sketches and solo acts at his box-shaped open air theatre. Audiences sat in deck chairs on a grassed enclosure but viewing was equally possible from the pavement outside so that's where most of the audience, myself included, congregated. A resting member of the cast circulated occasionally, optimistically shaking a collecting box.

Jack Sheppard's was a whimsical survivor from Edwardian days. He arrived in Brighton in 1904 with his male-voice quartet, The Highwaymen, performing four times daily on the beach. By 1912 he was running four concert parties, one of them on the West Pier where, later, a young comedian joined the cast after serving in the war. His name was Thomas Henry Sargent, nephew of the Mr Sargent from whom my sister Eva and her husband had once rented rooms. Thomas Sargent of course, became better known as perennial Cheeky Chappie Max Miller. Another performer was Tom Walls, famous for owning a Derby winner and for his partnership with Ralph Lynn in the pre-war Aldwych farces.

By the 1930s Jack Sheppard was reduced to just the one concert party. The format was invariable. White-haired now, pince-nez clamped to his nose and red carnation in his buttonhole, he would introduce the show with a few flourishing remarks. Then pianist Walter Waller would rattle off the opening bars and on would dance the rest of the company, resplendent in boaters and striped blazers, the men in white trousers, the women in white skirts.

Jack Sheppard's Entertainers survived anachronistically until the outbreak of war in 1939. Back in journalism in Brighton after the war, I searched out Jack and found him, aged 74 and as buoyant as ever, running a boarding house, along with 82-year-old Walter Waller, in Rugby Place, Kemp Town. It had a period look; aspidistras on the front steps, old-fashioned furniture inside and faded photographs of old-time musical comedy, music hall and beach entertainers; a time warp. It was Jack Sheppard's concert party that helped kindle my growing interest in show business and the theatre.

At the Intermediate I participated in football and cricket and competed in athletics (I briefly held the high jump record). I was also a committed supporter of Brighton and Hove Albion Football Club and Sussex County cricket team.

Both sports were almost unrecognisable measured by modern standards. Governed by the maximum wage rule, professional footballers, certainly in the lower divisions, earned only marginally more than artisans. But they were our heroes: outside left 'Tug' Wilson, nippy little Scot Bobby Farrell, muscular centre-half Frank Brett and Sid Webb in goal. Another was Potter Smith, an educated inside right who was suddenly transferred to Crystal Palace pursued by rumours that the daughter of one of the Albion directors was pregnant.

There were no soccer hooligans. Unmolested, we caught the tram to the Seven Dials and tramped the two miles to the Goldstone Ground in Hove. Inside, policemen were outnumbered by St John Ambulance volunteers, trading free entrance in exchange for handling any heart attacks.

As the only youngster in Cobden Road to attend the Intermediate School I gradually drifted apart from my former playmates and became a bit of a loner. But I didn't find it irksome. When Sussex were playing at Hove, I spent the day sprawled on the boundary line; except for the lunch interval, when I would stand in the tunnel under the main stand collecting players' autographs. Cricket was then a different, gentler game. The amateur Gentlemen (identified as 'Mr' on the scorecard) and the humbler players (the pros) had separate dressing rooms and emerged from segregated entrances. Sledging hadn't been invented and appeals for dismissal were genuinely made.

The players sprang from local village teams. You could tell this from their drawn-out Sussex burr; men like the Langridge brothers – James who played for England, and John, a fine slip fielder who became an umpire, Jim Parks senior and his brother Harry, the great Maurice Tate and 'Tich' Cornford, the diminutive wicket keeper.

I continued to attend Bentham Road Sunday School. One incentive was participation in the free weekly gym session. Somehow, without any visible signs of financial support, the mission had acquired a vaulting horse, springboard, parallel bars, climbing ropes and tumbling mats. Sessions were supervised by Fred Homeyard, a diminutive, moustached bundle of energy, who doubled as poultry farmer and mission superintendent, and George 'Doc' Barnard, window cleaner and Fred's deputy. They were totally dedicated to saving souls and keeping us children on the straight and narrow.

Once a year we put on a public display for admiring parents and mission regulars. Some of us also went camping, under 'Doc' Barnard's supervision, on the floor of a disused chalk pit at Saddlescombe, a tiny hamlet lying under the towering brow of the Devil's Dyke. The hamlet had a corrugated mission hut that had some kind of fraternal link with

Bentham Road.

We relished the hardy camp life, foreswore the easy options and cooked breakfast over fires made from wood we had laboriously collected. After breakfast we clambered down to wash in the ice cold spring water gurgling out from the foot of the Dyke.

It was at Bentham Road Mission that I first saw Sylvia. Her father, Charles Heise, must have been at a loss as to what to do when his wife died. He was still only 22.

An immediate solution was provided by the next door neighbours in Stanley Street, the Brumans. They offered to take charge of his baby daughter – a decision which no doubt saved her from being taken into care. Charles Bruman worked a permanent night shift at the GPO sorting office. He and his wife had one child, a daughter May, who had been born partially paralysed on one side but who was still mobile. Sylvia became her substitute daughter and, as 'Auntie May', she remained a close friend right through to the time when our own children were born. Sylvia also benefited scholastically from the attention of Mr Bruman's sister who became her teacher at St Mary's C of E School.

Charles kept in close touch with his daughter as he moved around from one lodging to another and various aunts also maintained contact. But he wanted a more permanent arrangement and the chance came unexpectedly. He was living with the Bliss family on the new Queen's Park council estate when the father, Alfred, died following a traffic accident. His widow, Jess, was left with four young sons and in financial straits.

The solution seemed obvious – Charles would bring in his daughter and the two families would unite. There is no evidence that the relationship between him and Jess was ever anything other than platonic but it endured.

Sylvia had been happy with the Brumans. She was doing well at school and had her own neighbourhood friends. She was told that she was visiting Firle Road for a holiday. When she realised that the move was permanent and that life in Stanley Street was at an end, she was shocked. 'I wanted to run away,' she told me years later, 'but I didn't know where to run to.'

This is no reflection on her father or Jess Bliss. They were acting from the best of motives and child psychology wasn't readily available in the 1930s. In time Sylvia settled down and became like a sister to the Bliss boys. Our cordial relationship with them and their mother endured to the end.

Sylvia moved to Firle Road in 1931 when she was 10 years old. It meant moving school, a disruption to her education that, in turn, probably ruined her grammar school chances. She, too, was directed instead to the Intermediate School. As with me, she found a new world opening up and responded particularly to English lessons.

The move to Firle Road led her to Bentham Road Sunday School, already attended by the Bliss boys, and I began to notice this round-faced, fair-haired girl with a fringe.

In 1932, as Sylvia started at the Intermediate Girls' School, I entered the commercial stream in the third year at the boys' school. I now came under the influence of the senior English master, A.E.Smith, an inspiring teacher and one of my heroes. He demonstrated, as Owen Hughes had a few years earlier, the beauty of words and cultivated my talent for stringing them together. I learned to appreciate Shakespeare and was introduced to 'Lorna Doone', 'The Cloister and the Hearth' and the works of Dickens, Bernard Shaw and Hilaire Belloc.

Through Brighton Lending Library I discovered J.B.Priestley (I read and re-read 'The Good Companions'), P.C.Wren (the Beau Geste series), Warwick Deeping ('My Son, My Son') and Anatole France, whose aphorisms I laboriously copied into an exercise book. Others were Francis Brett Young, Rider Haggard, Edgar Wallace, 'Sapper', G.K.Chesterton, Aldous Huxley, Hemingway and Steinbeck. Later came Vera Brittain's influential 'Testament of Youth' and, when Victor Gollancz started his Left Book Club (sixpence for each slim publications with its blood-red covers), I became an early member.

One of my prized possessions is an autographed copy of 'Reading with Understanding' (a textbook of 'selected passages with comprehension tests and exercises' by A.E.Smith, Brighton Intermediate School). After I left the Intermediate he was appointed the first headmaster of the new Patcham Senior Mixed School in Brighton and later became Principal of a teacher training college.

In the third year I teamed up with Don Beattie, a classmate who shared my love of English. He was one of the five children of a couple who ran a fish and chip shop in Elm Grove where we bought evening meals – a penn'orth of chips and tu'penny piece of fish or a faggot and portion of pease pudding. Don's father shuffled around as the result of severe war wounds. A cultured accent and courteous manner suggested a more affluent past.

Don and I visited the library and museum and roamed the South Downs together. We were both selected for the school football team, he on the right wing and I – being left-footed – on the opposite wing. He was a better footballer than me, swifter for one thing while I was too one-footed.

He also played for Brighton Boys (a distinction previously achieved by my brother, I was told, in 1919) and for the South of England team. Another member of the side was centre-half Len Wheeler who went on to play twice for England Boys. That season we were the Manchester United of the Brighton and Hove Schools First Division, winning every match, usually by a large margin and carrying off the championship.

At home, there was better news for my brother-in-law, Bill Lewis. He landed a job as temporary fitter at Southwick Power Station, then part of the Brighton Corporation-owned electricity undertaking, to repair water pipes inside a faulty turbine boiler. The pipes proved to be undamaged and the fault relatively minor. He and his fellow fitter kept this to themselves, however, completing the task in what appeared to be record time. As a reward the management gave them permanent jobs.

My mother had given up taking in holidaymakers, with one exception. Emily Ellis, a housekeeper in London, was a long-standing visitor. In 1932 she surprised us by arriving with a son none of us had previously known about; and she was unmarried, a combination which, in the 1930s, carried a degree of social stigma.

The son, Leslie, lived in various households during his childhood and had a succession of mundane jobs after leaving school. Soon after his 15th birthday, however, he realised his ambition and joined the

Royal Navy as a boy seaman. It was the start of a remarkable career at odds with his background.

He was 21 when he appeared in Cobden Road and had just completed two and a half years on the East Indies Station. He was immediately attracted to my sister Ethel even though she was ten years older than him. They were to enjoy a happy marriage that lasted sixty years and produced three sons. When my sister died in 1995 at the age of 92, her husband followed just twenty days later.

By early 1933 I was beginning to have doubts about the restrictive nature of the teachings of Bentham Road Mission and the literal acceptance of the biblical version of the Creation as opposed to evolutionary theory. Rationality battled with unquestioning faith.

Through my contact with Bill Lewis and animated discussions with schoolfriends, I became increasingly interested in politics and the quest for a fairer society and I wanted to explore the wider world.

That summer the weekly gym was abandoned in favour of forming a Boys' Brigade company. To me it meant donning a uniform and accepting regimentation, however lightly imposed. My refusal to join was greeted with surprise but it gave me the excuse gradually to sever links with the Mission. But I remain grateful to it for providing me with a moral template and for some boyhood good times.

In September, 1933, I moved into the fourth year at the Intermediate. Don Beattie and I were appointed Prefects, one of the privileges being the use of a different entrance from the rest of the school; a walkway parallel to the girls' entrance. Occasionally I glimpsed Sylvia and we exchanged shy smiles.

A highlight of the fourth year was a day trip on the SS Paris from the Palace Pier to Dieppe – tame compared with modern school expeditions but a pioneering step for us. We practised our faltering French and bought souvenirs for our parents. Mine, impractically, was a French loaf. As the school magazine recorded: '...a yard-long loaf of bread which, despite the anxious care of its owner, was most appropriately divided into three parts soon after it had left its native Gaul'. But we enjoyed it.

The legal school leaving age was still 14 so that fourth year pupils who were 15 were free to leave early if they found a job. With money tight and jobs scarce some took advantage of this including Don Beattie. He had been Senior Prefect, a position in which I succeeded him for the last few months. I couldn't leave even had I wanted to. Due to my October birthday and the arbitrary cut-off date for the 11-Plus, I was still only 14.

I already knew I wanted to be a journalist. English lessons were those I looked forward to most. I took essays home with me to finish and contributed to the school magazine, which we printed ourselves in school. I read the local *Evening Argus* and the official Labour Party mouthpiece, the *Daily Herald*, at home and other newspapers at the Public Library.

For a working class lad with continuing self doubts, the ambition appeared out of reach. But when I mentioned it to my mother she bravely marched off to see A.E.Smith. When we met the following day he said: 'So you want to be a journalist,' adding prophetically: 'You realise, don't you, that you'll never be rich? But you'll have an interesting life.'

He wrote to a former pupil who was a reporter on the *Evening Argus*. His name was Bob Black. He asked me to meet him at the prestigious Savoy Cinema, a place I admired but seldom entered. I arrived a quarter of an hour early wearing my freshly ironed Co-op suit and with my hair slicked down. My formal education was officially over but I was still a couple of months short of my 15th birthday.

Bob was easily identifiable. He wore a green bird's eye suit with an emerald tie and matching handkerchief spilling from the breast pocket, horn-rimmed spectacles, brown patterned shoes, a curly-brimmed brown trilby and a designer tic in one cheek. The only item missing was a tab marked Press in the hatband. He was the archetypal reporter of 'Hold the Front Page' films.

I was even more impressed when we moved into the cinema restaurant where linen-covered, waitress-attended tables ringed a maple wood dance floor on which a few couples were languidly circulating.

Tea and cream puffs arrived followed by an elegantly dressed girl with a deep sun tan and even deeper cleavage. Next moment she and

Bob joined the dancers, gliding effortlessly off to the rhythm of a slow foxtrot. At that moment any remaining doubts about my choice of career evaporated. If this was journalism, I wanted to be part of it.

Back at the table, Bob Black guided me through a job application letter to the Editor. It began: 'Sir, Young and ambitious, I am keen to seek a career in journalism.....' My contribution was largely to the effect that I could touch type and had reached 80 words a minute in shorthand with a few details about my school career. But the construction and phraseology were pure Bob Black; fraudulent maybe but I wasn't going to argue and I remain grateful to Bob for his help.

The reply was of the stock 'No vacancies at the moment but keeping your letter on file' variety. I wrote to the editor several times over the following weeks – all my own work this time – and called at the editorial offices. No replies came and, resignedly, I found work at a coal agent's office in Grand Parade. It occupied a single large room and was run by a man-about-town type who looked in once a day. Otherwise I was left on my own. It was winter and there was a depressing absence of customers. To keep warm I took up skipping in the curtained-off rear of the office.

Eventually a customer did arrive – a dapper little man accompanied by his wife to order some coal. He sported a butterfly-shaped moustache that appeared to be painted on. He asked my advice on which type of coal best suited his domestic needs. My half-hour training course hadn't explained the difference between anthracite and kitchen nuts and he wasn't fooled.

'You don't know much about coal do you?' he challenged. 'No,' I replied. The couple disappeared. I had lost my first order.

It couldn't go on. The place must have been leaking money and closure was inevitable. I had worked for surely the smallest coal merchant in the south of England. Over thirty years later I would represent the largest.

Unemployment remained high in the industrial north but in the south a more confident younger generation of married couples was seeking independence and privacy. To meet the demand, property developers improved production techniques to cut costs and banks and building societies reduced the deposit on new houses to ten per cent or less. Private estates appeared with houses at affordable prices. Suburbia was on the march and a new middle class was emerging.

With Bill Lewis now in a permanent job at Southwick Power Station, he and Eva scraped together the £25 deposit on a new house within easy reach of his work. The purchase price was £529. Because of his job, Bill's household electricity was supplied at a subsidised rate so he and Eva elected to have the first all-electric home in Southwick. It had panel electric wall fires, an early form of fitted kitchen and the first interior bathroom I had ever seen.

Leslie Ellis, now stationed at the Royal Navy Barracks at Chatham on a gunnery course, continued to court Ethel. But in 1933, soon after competing in the winning Royal Naval tug-of-war team (110 stone division) at the Royal Tournament, he was posted to HMS Sandhurst in Malta.

From there in 1934, having been promoted to Leading Seaman, he wrote asking her to marry him – in Malta. Off she went accompanied by her wedding dress. She never wore it. The boat ran into storms and arrived in Valetta on the morning of the wedding – December 1st, 1934. There was no time to change. Leslie was 22 and Ethel twenty-five days short of her 32nd birthday. The rest of the family celebrated, by proxy, with a cake in Cobden Road.

With my brother Reg and his family already living away from home, the house suddenly felt empty. I was alone with my parents, only then realising how much I missed my siblings.

CHAPTER 5

Entering Journalism and
Buying a Ha'porth of Snuff

I seemed to be the only one going nowhere. I should have known better. I had to wait until my 15th birthday and for the start of another five-yearly cycle to actuate further changes. Eight weeks later, the day after sister Ethel's wedding in Malta, a letter arrived from John Chillman inviting me to an interview.

Panic; what should I wear? My one Co-op suit had a tired look and appearances were important. My brother came to the rescue, producing a magnificent black overcoat complete with vermilion satin lining, a survivor from his pre-marital dancing days. It gave me an extra edge especially when, at the interview, I was asked to stand up for inspection.

I hoped John Chillman was impressed and waited apprehensively for a week. Then the letter arrived. I was to start as a probationary junior on Friday, 14 December, 1934. It was a newsworthy day in the story of Brighton. A man named Tony Mancini was surprisingly acquitted at Lewes Assizes of the murder of sometime minor actress Violette Kaye (aka Mrs Violet Saunders) in the second of the notorious and simultaneous Brighton Trunk Crimes that had been hitting the national headlines for many weeks.

The papers didn't record that it was also the day I joined the *Evening Argus*. But for me it was the day I climbed out of the basement. I was on my way.

The *Evening Argus* and its associated newspapers were based at the top right hand side of fashionable North Street, in a neo-Gothic Victorian building, complete with bow-fronted balconies. A pigeon loft still perched on the rear of the building where it nudged against the rear of the Regent Cinema and Ballroom.

It was pointed out to me and to all other juniors in their turn, by Cecil 'Diddle' Kerman, the *Argus* sports sub-editor (later sports editor). He had joined the company as a 14-year-old messenger boy in 1908 when public telephones were a rarity and he lugged carrier pigeons around in baskets to carry back local football results and reports tied to their legs.

The thundering rotary presses on which the papers were printed were located about three-quarters of a mile away in Robert Street, where silence descended for only a brief period in the morning hours and on Sundays.

The *Argus* itself ran to six editions a day – seven on Saturdays when the high-selling Classified Football edition was added. The *Sussex Daily News* was more dignified and liked to be known as the *Times of Sussex*. There were also three weekly papers – the Brighton and Hove Gazette, the *Southern Weekly News* and the *Crowborough News*, a heavily editionised version of the *Southern Weekly*. These last two were directed towards a rural readership.

The weeklies had their own sub-editing staff but, with only limited help from the reporters, they depended on extensively lifting and re-editing stories from the *Argus* and *Sussex Daily News*. The country weeklies also relied on reports from local correspondents – parish council clerks, Women's Institute secretaries, grocery store owners and so on. They had a habit of putting the story in the last paragraph and producing schoolboy howlers which were assiduously recorded by Freddie Miles who ran the *Southern Weekly*. One lady, reporting the annual parish meeting of her village, wrote that following the business agenda 'the rest of the evening was spent in social intercourse'.

District reporters and offices were spread across the county. The offices received adverts, sold papers and were equipped with Bush machines for printing local and late news, horse racing and football results in the *Argus* Stop Press – 'Bush fudging' to use the vernacular.

In the 1930s the only other news outlets were cinema newsreels and BBC 'wireless' bulletins, limited in frequency and content. Newspapers had a virtual monopoly in disseminating up-to-the-minute local, national and international news and an increasingly literate and politically conscious readership boosted circulation figures to record levels.

They were vintage years for newspaper journalism and prosperous times for the proprietors, including the Southern Publishing Company, the family business which owned the *Evening Argus* group. The Chairman and Managing Director on my arrival was J.Henson Infield. When I mentioned his name my mother recalled serving him tea when he visited the family for whom she worked as a parlourmaid in Haywards Heath.

My self-belief took another knock when a man named Russell, who was my English teacher at nightschool – every teenager with any ambition attended nightschool – advanced the bogus theory that our station in life was pre-ordained by our ancestry; once a peasant, always a peasant. It was an unforgivable elitist gospel to preach to impressionable teenagers who were attending nightschool for the precise purpose of escaping from the constraints of such a philosophy.

My confidence was slowly restored through the help of willing colleagues and contact with the first class journalists then based in Brighton. There was no formal training. It was up to you to learn from others who were prepared to teach you.

Editorial secretary George Oliver, an avuncular, bulbous nosed, snuff-taking Pickwickian with impeccable shorthand was one guiding hand. Another was Ada Guy, tall, willowy, doe-eyed, protective and on the shelf (or so it was thought). She ran the telephone room and later succeeded George Oliver. Her secondary job was maintaining the 'morgue', cupboards accommodating buff envelopes bulging with press cuttings recording the exploits of the famous and the infamous of Sussex, ready for resurrection when they died.

Thirdly, there was John Corbyn, my predecessor, who continued working in the office but was now given minor reporting jobs – an easing-in process to full-time journalism. We got on well and I was grateful to him for introducing me to newspaper language and customs.

Our duties included running copy to the composing room, making tea and filling pastepots with a repellent glutinous mixture in which floated fragments of old newspapers. Duplicates of the reporters' stories were speared on vicious spikes. A daily task was to retrieve the copies for storage as a precaution against future queries or possible libel claims.

The editorial office was equipped with heavy, old-fashioned typewriters but there were never enough to go round. So written copy was acceptable – unavoidable in the case of court and council reporting. In the interests of speed, a range of word abbreviations, largely involving the elimination of all vowels, had been evolved. There were technicalities and esoteric terms to be learned such as fonts and type sizes. Times Roman and Gill Sans were favourites of the day while type sizes were expressed in Caxtonian terms – Pica (12pt), brevier (8pt), minion (7pt), nonpareil (6pt) and even Pearl (5pt).

I learned about story lengths from fillers and sticks to page leads, about galley proofs and flongs, crossheads and bust headlines. I was on a steep learning curve, that's for sure.

The second half of my morning was spent walking backwards and forwards to the Town Hall – the best part of half a mile – to collect copy from the reporters sitting in the two Magistrates' Courts. There was a compelling urgency to get that day's news into the *Argus* to compete with the three national evening papers. *The Star, Evening News* and *Evening Standard* (the only one now surviving) had local Bush fudging facilities and distribution offices and, although printed in London, could be on the streets of Brighton in an hour and a half.

The regular No.1 Court reporter in my early years was Pat Maguire, a kindly man with glasses perched on the tip of his nose, who had worked on general news until, as it was explained to me, 'his legs had gone'. From Pat, in the Magistrates' Court and, periodically, in the Quarter Sessions, I learned court reporting. I absorbed especially the colour and atmosphere of the Quarter Sessions, with robed Recorder and wigged and gowned barristers. One young counsel was Geoffrey Lawrence, a man with a mellifluous voice and beguiling manner, who obtained some spectacular successes. 'Watch that young man,' Pat told me, 'one day he'll be a judge.' I was to recall his words many years later.

Reporting methods were not the only knowledge I gathered at Court. It was also responsible for much of my sex education. One case was considered too indelicate for my sensibilities and the chairman of the Bench surreptitiously sent word that perhaps I ought to leave.

My daily trips to the Magistrates' Court included one other duty. I had to call at a tobacconist in Duke Street and purchase a ha'p'orth of snuff, a pinch of which Pat transferred to the back of his hand immediately I arrived and sniffed up his nostrils. The use of snuff was prevalent in the composing room, originating no doubt from the need to combat the pervading smell and taste of oil and molten alloy vapours and the practice had spread to some of the veteran journalists.

Magistrates' and Crown Courts – replacing the old Quarter Sessions – are now concentrated in fewer locations (many of those quaint old rural courts especially have disappeared) but sittings have greatly increased in length and frequency, such has been the spread of lawlessness.

In the mid-Thirties the volume of crime was so manageable that on a normal day the magistrates could reckon on being home in time for lunch. The occasional exceptions were summonses arising from illegal gambling and drinking club raids, the rare murder and equally rare drink-driving charge.

In the afternoons I came under the authority of Ada Guy in the telephone room. She had two regular assistants – fanciable Audrey Sheppard, a blonde with a mesmeric bosom, and anaemic-looking Miss Poulter whose temporary absence every month puzzled my gynaecologically ignorant mind.

My job was to help man the antiquated switchboard, with its tangle of plugs and keys and two old fashioned telephones which looked as though they had been designed by Emmet or Heath Robinson. They were the direct link with the district offices and were used to transmit racing and football results and brief news items for Bush fudging in the country editions of the *Argus*. They were also the channel for receiving urgent news from the district reporters.

Sports news came by direct phone from the Exchange Telegraph Company and national news from the Press Association in the form of Morse tapes delivered by a stream of telegraph boys.

Afternoon duty was obligatory on Saturdays during the football season. As Ada Guy took down the results from Exchange Telegraph, one copy would be rushed to the *Argus* sub-editors while we passed them on to the district offices. At the same time John Corbyn and I up-dated the League tables, a skill at which we became surprisingly proficient. Getting the Classified Edition out to newsagents and the street sellers was top priority.

Our day ended in cutting out the editorial columns from the *Evening Argus* and pasting them on to galley proof paper for the chief sub-editor of the *Sussex Daily News*. Then we were free to go, nine hours after we had started. I worked a five and a half day week. My starting wage was 12s 6d (62p), 10s of which I handed to my mother every Friday as my contribution towards the family income. I usually had to ask for a sub towards the end of the following week but 2s 6d (half-a-crown) went a long way. A pint of beer cost fourpence (about 1p) for example and a packet of five Woodbines only twopence (less than a modern penny).

Over the following weeks I got to know the rest of the editorial staff. I had arrived during a time of transition. Five years earlier, John Chillman, an outsider from the *Worthing Herald* and former editor of the *Welwyn Times*, had become group editor in place of the long serving traditionalist Henry Bone. He began introducing a new generation of modern thinking journalists and the *Argus* became a recognised jumping off ground for Fleet Street. Bob Black was a typical example. He was chief crime reporter and made his name on the Brighton trunk crimes.

Other young reporters included Victor Gorringe, destined to succeed John Chillman as group editor when the approaching war was over, and Les Cluett who later played a significant part in my life.

Alongside these were the veteran survivors of the old regime. One was chief reporter, Teddy Poland, a tall, balding man with pebble glasses and a generous figure who trailed a superfluous walking stick behind him. He was the one who attended banquets and receptions where white tie and tails were de rigueur, giving him the appearance, when he arrived back at the office, of an overweight penguin.

Mr Clothier, a thin-lipped acerbic man, produced voluminous 'Church Notes' for the *Sussex Daily News* once a week and doubled as a sub-editor. We reporters dreaded our copy falling into his emasculating hands.

Mr Brooks was a complete contrast, a deferential man who wore a fedora hat and wing collar and carried a furled umbrella even in high summer. He smiled a lot, revealing double the normal array of porcelain teeth. He was apt to acknowledge any mistakes with the comment "I am a silly-billy" long before impressionist Mike Yarwood attributed the remark to Dennis Healey. One of the older brigade whose style I admircd and whose advice I appreciated was Pat Walker, later a wartime sub-editor on the *Daily Sketch*. Nearly seventy years later I met his daughter, Pat Brightwell, through the Friends Re-united website and shared some pleasant memories with her.

Some of the district reporters also belonged to the old brigade, among them Mr Graveney who covered a large area around Shoreham and produced an endless stream of copy. Without an office like other district reporters had, he had come to the practical arrangement with the Shoreham Station staff of turning part of one of the waiting rooms into his own private fiefdom.

The *Sussex Daily News* chief sub-editor, Sidney Evans, was another veteran. He had joined the company thirty-eight years earlier as rural reporter in West Sussex, cycling everywhere and often using pigeons to send his reports to head office. White-haired and white moustached now, Sidney worked a ten-hour day and followed an unwavering routine. He would bustle in, remove his jacket, produce an ancient crescent-shaped biscuit tin containing neatly cut sandwiches and don a green eyeshade. One half expected him to overturn a section of the subs' table to reveal a hidden roulette wheel.

Then he cleared his in-tray of the mountain of reporters' copy and the *Argus* editorial columns we had cut out. There was also a batch of galley proof stories that had failed to make it into that morning's *Sussex Daily News*. 'I don't know,' he would invariable sigh, as if the end of world was nigh, 'another six (or however many) columns of overset.' He always advanced this as an argument for larger papers without regard for the economics involved. But Sidney was basically a kind man who later took a paternalistic interest in Sylvia and gave her some of his treasured books when she left.

The two regular *Argus* subs were in a different category. Chief sub, Jimmy Hyslop, a bustling, bullet-headed man in his 50s, was a product of the Sheffield Telegraph. His sidekick, 'Diddle' Kerman, wore thin horn-rimmed glasses and permanent worry lines. Both were shirt-sleeved to indicate the arduous nature of their job.

The members of the weeklies' sub-editing staff were a class apart, probably minor public school, with a dilettante stance. They included Dick Grierson, the heir to a baronetcy, and Frank Usher.

Provincial journalism was male dominated; the entire editorial staff included only two women. The talents of Barbara Graham, very much middle class, were directed almost entirely to the exploits of the County set and her *Sussex Daily News* feature 'Mainly About Women'. Vivienne Marles, a grammar school product and a pioneer in helping to break the male mould, deputised for Barbara and covered general news although she was patronisingly shielded from the rougher end of the trade.

Barbara later married 'Jock' Miller which was regarded by many as an unpromising match – the bubbly hunt ball society scene reporter and the cautious, some would say taciturn, Scot. But it endured. 'Jock' migrated from the weekly Sussex Express to the Argus group and subsequently became editor of the *Sussex Daily News* and assistant editor of the *Argus*.

There were two photographers – Ernie Hawkins and his assistant Charles White. They were supplemented later, on a freelance basis, by Johnnie Neville, otherwise known, confusingly, as John Silversides, an amateur ice hockey player whose mother was a palmist on the Palace Pier.

I had to wait until I was 16 in October, 1935, before getting my indentures which would tie me to the company until I was 21. The impressive looking document laid down my wages during that period and specified my continuing attendance at night school. We should have read the contents more closely but I doubt whether my parents, whose signatures were required, would have understood its legalistic terminology. I was so anxious to secure my career that I would have signed had it been written in Chinese Mandarin. I was now also considered eligible for much-prized membership of the National Union of Journalists. Nearly seventy years later I was still an active member.

My sister Ethel returned from Malta in 1935, preceding her husband, Leslie, who was brought back to attend a gunner's mate course. It led to his promotion to Petty Officer and a posting to HMS Woolwich at Chatham. Ethel departed again to join him.

Around the end of 1935 I was allowed to write my first pieces for publication. I still have them. We had no film critic but every week the *Argus* printed what could only be described as fulsome reviews of the week's screen offerings. Information was obtained from lavish, full colour synopses provided by the film companies. They would be collectors' items today but we threw them away when finished with.

My first efforts praised the merits of 'Tarzan and His Mate' at the Regal and 'Cleopatra' with Claudette Colbert at the Prince's. Each piece ran to about 16 lines of brevier. But they meant as much to me as a front page lead. I was a professional journalist at last!

On leaving school I automatically became a member of the Intermediate Old Boys' Association which had been given an abandoned ex-caretaker's house as social club premises. I was recruited on to the executive committee and became a friend of Geoff Moore, the secretary, and George Hood, one of those people who can reproduce a tune on a piano after a single hearing. He was adept at producing Gang Show type revues, in which I also participated.

Geoff Moore had joined a jobbing printers and owned an Adana printing machine which he kept in his bedroom. We started an Old Boys' magazine, the Bison Gazette, the first edition of which appeared in October, 1936, to coincide with my 17th birthday. We had a back-up committee which included my old pal Don Beattie and Frank Loder, who was two years younger than me and who was to play a significant role in my future. Geoff's stock of type was so limited that one double page had to be printed off and the type dismantled before the next pages could be set. But we persevered.

About this time my brother had saved the deposit for a new £625 bungalow near Eva's house at Southwick.

It coincided with the arrival of a new junior, Percy Roberts, at the *Argus*. He was 16, the same age as myself, but he was a product of the boys only Brighton, Hove and Sussex Grammar School, which took mostly fee-paying boarders and day pupils plus a proportion of scholarship boys. It was considered a cut above the Council-run grammar schools. It freed John Corbyn to move to full-time reporting while I began part-time reporting of minor events.

It was small stuff to start with. It was customary to report on everyone whose death was advertised in the obituary columns. Since it was the practice to keep the body in the front room or bedroom until the funeral, I was frequently ushered in to pay homage to the deceased. My count of dead bodies rose rapidly.

I also had to report on local property auctions and, while attending these, spent the whole time in rigid immobility, terrified that the slightest movement would result in my inadvertently purchasing a house I had no means of paying for. Apart from this there were flower shows, annual meetings, local football matches and amateur dramatic performances. I used my old bicycle to attend some of these early events which meant I could sign my Expenses Sheets with a clear conscience. A relic from the past, they still bore, above the signature, the legend: 'My bicycle is in good working order'.

At the end of 1936 the editorial department and composing room moved to Robert Street, to link up with the printing works. The premises had been extended until they stretched along almost the whole of one side of the road. At the same time a new rotary press was installed enabling the *Argus* to be increased from eight to twelve pages.

Percy Roberts and I could now retrieve copies of the *Argus* hot off the presses for cutting up. It meant we could leave earlier but, as a penalty, when pasting the columns on to backing paper, our hands became black from the still-wet ink. I blame this for originating a mild form of eczema from which I was to suffer intermittently over the years.

I was now old enough, when time and money allowed, to patronise the Golden Fleece (since renamed the Market Inn) at the entrance to The Lanes in Market Street. The saloon bar had been unofficially commandeered by the Press as its off-duty watering hole. Here I could mix with, not only my own colleagues, but also the locally based staffers and freelancers who represented the national newspapers. Among them was Lindon Laing, who became News Editor of the *Daily Express* and would have progressed further had he not, while travelling home to Brighton one day, stuck his head out of the carriage window just as the train passed under a bridge. He died instantly.

Others were his brother Bruce Laing, Laurence Wilkinson, who became a foreign correspondent and died prematurely from some tropical illness, Lionel Crane, who went on to report from Hollywood, Sydney Bull of the *Daily Mail* and Leonard Knowles, who later levered my own move to Fleet Street.

So I learned my craft – in the office, the magistrates' court, the council chamber and, most of all, in the saloon bar of the Golden Fleece. At that time it was presided over by a Swiss national named (at least, phonetically) Brum Boller, a pot-bellied, wax-moustached, bonhomie character who cheerfully accepted our sometimes wayward excesses.

Today's young journalists learn their trade in more formal ways. 'A' levels, including English, are almost obligatory. Entry is normally by way of specialist university or college courses or block release schemes under the aegis of the National Council for Training Journalists, with 'on-the-job' familiarisation weeks on local newspapers, usually ending with proficiency exams. It is as it should be. There are pitfalls to ensnare the unwary journalist that never existed in my day: privacy laws, race relations acts, sexual discrimination regulations, spin doctors, the Press Complaints Commission, more complex libel laws and an all-pervasive political correctness. On the other hand the competition from television imposes, on the nationals at least, an incessant demand for a more intrusive and ruthless type of journalism. The pre-war parameters were more accommodating. It is hard to believe that the mutual agreement in 1936 to withhold news of the developing romance between the then Prince of Wales and the married American Wallis Simpson would be acceptable in today's tightrope climate.

Around the end of 1936 a new sports reporter arrived. Victor Champion ended up in Brighton after a career in the Army and was running a magazine dealing with sport and local controversies. He quickly established his ground rules, objecting to any alterations to his copy while at the same time lapsing into a strangulated syntax, a conjunction which caused 'Diddle' Kerman's worry lines to etch even deeper.

But writing under the name of Crusader, he certainly stirred up interest. His vitriolic attacks on the directors and management of Brighton and Hove Albion for their alleged lack of ambition and inept team selections and his furious reporting of poor play bolstered circulation and generated a massive readership response.

It also led to frequent clashes with the Albion hierarchy and near physical confrontations with Charlie Webb, the beleaguered manager and former Albion player, despite the team usually finishing in a respectable position in the League table. I was familiar with this because I accompanied Victor to home and to one or two away matches in the 1936/37 season in order to phone his running report back to the office.

In a wider context the pattern of life was beginning to unravel in the backwash of national and international upheavals. Nationally, there was an expanding home-owning middle class, congregated largely in the more affluent south, while millions of Britons, mainly in the north, were living in poverty. To them the decade became known as the 'Threadbare Thirties'.

Resentment of the apparent absence of a political will to alleviate the situation found expression in the 1936 Jarrow hunger march after the Jarrow shipyard closed, rendering two thirds of the town's male population unemployed. Two hundred of them marched the three hundred miles to London to present a petition to Parliament pleading for a contract to build warships. All the marchers got, according to a report at the time, were 'tea and cakes and a brief debate', a dismissive attitude which was to be remembered by a new generation of voters nearly ten years later.

Political unrest was more ominous. By 1936 Sir Oswald Moseley's British Union of Fascists had grown sufficiently for him to lead seven thousand of his followers into clashes in the Jewish East End. I attended one of its rallies, out of curiosity, at Brighton Aquarium. Witnessing an arrogant Moseley striding down the hall flanked by his blank-eyed, black-shirted acolytes and giving the Nazi salute to the applause of his supporters certainly frightened me. The manner in which Moseley's flawed genius could so easily seduce the minds of these people reflected the gathering political tensions of the time and explained how Hitler was able to mesmerise the citizens of a bankrupt Germany.

The point was emphasised that same year when many were deluded by the friendly facade created by the Nazi hosts at the Olympic Games in Berlin, some competitors and visitors being induced to give the Party salute. Sadly, the warped philosophy of the Nazi doctrine survives and even flourishes today in Britain and other European countries, its adherents even denying the overwhelming evidence of the Holocaust.

Back in 1936 war fears were temporarily deflected by the unique experience for Britain of life under three different monarchs in a single year. George V died and Edward VIII decided to abdicate in favour of marriage to Mrs Simpson, bringing a reluctant George VI to the throne. But already Germany was re-occupying the confiscated Rhineland and backing the General Franco-led rebellion against the Republican government of Spain.

CHAPTER 6

Fully Fledged Reporter – At £1 a Week

Brighton at the time was a pulsating town, alive with colourful characters. One of its most celebrated citizens, the bon vivant sportsman, hotel owner and host to the literati, Sir Harry Preston, was prominent during the early Thirties and, though he died in 1936, his spirit survived. Others ranged from the resident theatricals to wealthy Socialist councillors like Sir Herbert Carden and on to the bowler-hatted chimney sweep Harry Cowley who fearlessly fought for the rights of the underdog by unconventional methods which exasperated the Establishment. Queen Mary descended on The Lanes in search of antiques and the Sabini Boys were on the racecourse in search of protection money. It was heady stuff for a working class lad.

More juniors arrived in 1937: Sydney Curtis, Mike Dell and Frank Loder, my former colleague on the Bison Gazette editorial board. Now at last I was promoted to full-time reporting. I was 17 and my wage had risen to about £1 a week. Among other functions I was required to cover were the annual dinners of various firms and associations. Evening dress, boiled shirtfront, wing collar and black bow tie were obligatory. I felt terrible having to ask my mother for help but, uncomplaining, she took me off to the Co-op and picked up the bill. The evening dress alone cost four guineas. Thank goodness for Co-op dockets and dividends.

I came to hate the annual dinner season, sitting at the end of remote sprig tables, talking perfunctorily to strangers and listening to speakers massaging their egos. To be fair some speeches were newsworthy. The one advantage was that you got a free meal.

If it wasn't an annual dinner there were always other engagements, from hard news stories to amateur dramatics and parish council meetings out in the sticks. At night the pressure was always on to get the story back for the next day's *Sussex Daily News*. I remember the induction of a vicar in a remote village and trying to write the story while bouncing around on the back seat of the bus back to the office. To be honest I was driven not by fear of missing the paper's deadline but of missing the last tram home. That's how I learned to knock out a story in double quick time.

It was the norm to be allocated three assignments a day. The time between was your own but you were left in no doubt that, as a journalist, you were always on duty. I remember in November, 1937 – I was just 18 – arriving home for lunch and overhearing my mother and a neighbour gossiping about the sudden death of young Constance Knight, who had lived nearby. The name stuck. She had been taken to hospital the previous day but was quickly discharged after a small office fire started in a waste paper basket. It rated only a down-page filler in that day's *Argus*. But Constance had collapsed during the night and died back in hospital. True to that 'always on duty' tag, I rushed back to the office – we had no home telephone – wrote the story and got a top-of-the-page double column show. Then I returned home to enjoy the rest of my half-day off.

I now travelled everywhere by bus or tram. The exception was for assignments attended by one of the photographers. Because of their heavy equipment, they were the only staffers with cars. They used large plate cameras with cumbersome slides and wooden tripods – essential for any group picture because of the slow exposure times. Flash bulbs hadn't been perfected and lighting was provided by magnesium powder sprinkled on a tray.

Hitching a lift with a photographer had reciprocal benefits. The reporter got a free return ride and in exchange carried the tripod and later held the magnesium tray, Statue Of Liberty style, as high as possible above the subject to be photographed. This was advisable because sometimes a too-generous supply of powder resulted in a blinding explosion that scared us rigid.

Snatch pictures and telescopic close-ups now possible with miniature cameras and long focus lenses were impossible with the old style plate cameras but an ingenious photographer could overcome the disadvantages. When police investigating the Brighton trunk crimes began digging in the communal gardens at the rear of Regency houses in Park Crescent a high boundary wall blocked the view of photographers.

Ernie Hawkins, who wasn't above flogging the occasional news picture to the nationals, found the answer. He climbed to the open top deck of one of the trams that trundled past the wall and then enlisted Bruce Laing to lie across the tracks bringing the tram to a halt. Ernie's picture got national exposure.

The company's print workers were non-unionised – a consequence of the General Strike – but office membership of the National Union of Journalists was solid. About this time the local branch discovered that, under our indentures, Percy Roberts and I were being paid below the Union minimum wage for juniors. The Branch sought authority for industrial action but the older members turned it down. I was bitter at the time but have since realised that they feared for their livelihoods. Most of them lived in rented accommodation, there was very little employee protection and where would an elderly journalist find another job if sacked? So nothing happened.

In fact we were no better or worse off than juniors on any other provincial newspaper or in any other commercial undertaking come to that. It was part of the prevailing workplace climate of the times.

Percy and I could not foresee, of course, that he would later become successively director, managing director and finally chairman of Daily Mirror Newspapers (in the days before rapscallion Robert Maxwell) and that he would be chief management negotiator with the print unions when they were at their most militant. Equally unforeseeable was that, at the same time, I would be the one of the Mirror Group's accredited freelance correspondents.

By now I often reported the proceedings of Brighton Magistrates' second court which dealt with less serious cases. I followed the custom of carving my initials on the Press table, joining the profusion of others left by my predecessors. Occasionally the court converted half-way through proceedings into a domestic court to hear affiliation order applications by unmarried mothers. This was often their only way of obtaining financial support from the fathers. As likely as not they denied paternity or pleaded near destitution. Sometimes the proceedings would descend into angry claim and counter-claim between the two parties, mercifully separated by the width of the court, sometimes with the woman's mother and bawling infant contributing to the chaos. The magistrates had not only to adjudicate but, if they found in favour of the woman, to also decide on the payment to be levied against the reluctant father.

It couldn't be reported but we had to sit through it while waiting for normal proceedings to resume. In this way I learned the financial penalties of illicit sex.

Sex was never mentioned at home. I suspect my mother regarded it as an unfortunate obligation that came with a wedding ring. She belonged to that age when, among the lower orders at least, men married for sex and women for security.

For a period I was consigned to cover Hove Magistrates' Court, one half day a week usually being sufficient to dispense with the town's catalogue of crime. For the most part the misdemeanours were minor key but there were exceptions.

One of my reports began: 'Sobbing bitterly and twisting his blue felt hat in his hands, a man who gave his name as James Kelly told Hove Magistrates this morning that he was responsible for the condition of a woman who had been charged with attempted suicide.'

There are two interesting points here: use of the word 'pregnant' was forbidden, only 'a certain condition' was permissible; and committing suicide was still a criminal offence (the only example where you had to fail before you could be charged!).

It was a distressing case. The defendant was a 35-year-old Austrian domestic servant with only six months left on her work permit. She had swallowed two hundred aspirins. Mercifully the magistrates dismissed the case under the Probation of Offenders Act after being told of offers to help her. My own reaction was that sex seemed to be an ever more hazardous pastime.

Hove had its own police force and while waiting for the court to begin I chatted with the Chief Constable, William C Hillier. Over twenty-five years later I met his son in very different circumstances.

Occasionally I covered Steyning Petty Sessional Court proceedings when Mr Graveney, the local reporter, was otherwise engaged. They were enjoyable outings; the leisurely chug to Steyning via the now-vanished Brighton to Horsham railway branch line, the reporting of fairly minor offences and the sandwich lunch in the local hostelry before the journey back.

During the summer of 1937 I stood in for Victor Champion to report one or two Sussex County and Second XI home cricket matches. On Saturday afternoons I also produced colour pieces on the local club cricket scene. Wednesday mornings were allocated to writing a page round-up of the week's sporting events for the Brighton and Hove Gazette.

Sport wasn't my only interest. The theatre, whether legitimate or vaudeville, also interested me and, when the chance occurred, I volunteered to write critiques for the Brighton and Hove Gazette. My first venture was on 'Bees on the Boat Deck', a long-forgotten comedy by J.B.Priestley, at the Theatre Royal.

The Royal was frequently used – still is I believe – as a try-out for plays prior to their London run. The legendary licensee, J. Baxter Summerville, and the still-remembered house manager, Jack Keats, commanded respect among the cognoscenti. Long serving Bill Tupper held the official title of assistant manager but was more familiar in his commissionaire's uniform bawling out the numbers allotted to waiting cars after the show. He was an institution.

In July, 1937, when I was still only 17, I arranged, through Jack Keats, my first celebrity interview. French comedy actress, Yvonne Arnaud, was appearing in a play called Laughter in Court. She tolerated my gauche questions as she sipped her coffee and nibbled her biscuits in her dressing room before the show and with some grace complimented me afterwards. The play included a court room scene and Jack Keats afterwards asked me if I would like to sit on the stage jury. It was my first and last appearance on the professional stage and gave me a nice tailpiece to the interview.

My search for showbusiness copy also took me to the Rex Leslie-Smith Repertory Company at the West Pier Theatre, where young actors and actresses learned their trade. Among them was a budding 19-year-old named Jon Pertwee.

Brighton was a magnet for showbusiness people because they could catch the midnight train home after appearing on the London stage. Film stars were drummed into making personal appearances when their films were in town. One special occasion was interviewing Tom Mix whose Wild West serials I had once saved up to watch at the Arcadia. Now, in the twilight of his career, rejected by the 'talkies', he was touring the variety theatres of England accompanied by his 'wonder horse' Tony, though not the same one (now 24, he was living in retirement back in Hollywood). Equally significantly, we met in the Metropole Hotel. I had made it at last.

Tom Mix appeared at the Hippodrome at the height of its popularity. It regularly staged pre-London runs of the Crazy Gang, top variety acts from Max Miller and Tommy Trinder to Harry Lauder and G.H.Elliott, the (politically incorrect) coon singers and big bands, such as Harry Roy, Ambrose and Billy Cotton.

Ambrose's lead girl soloist was Evelyn Dall, a blonde American belter with whom, it was rumoured, he had rather more than a professional relationship. I preferred to praise his second string, a newcomer who had been taken on somewhat reluctantly and had yet to fully establish herself. I thought I was being prescient in recognising her potential. But years later, when reading her autobiography, I discovered that many others had shared my view. She went on to fully justify our judgment. Her name was Vera Lynn. Sylvia and I related to her because her song 'Yours' was at the height of its popularity when we were courting during the war. We finally met her after the war.

During the 1937/38 football season Vic Champion's feud with the Albion board became so vituperative that he was either banned by the directors or was voluntarily taken off by John Chillman. For a time I deputised for him, just a season after first phoning in his copy. As I explained in a wartime letter to Sylvia: 'Believe me, it called for plenty of diplomacy.'

I was 18 and getting about £1 10s a week. Ethel had by now returned home and on 2 October, 1937, gave birth to her first son, Christopher. I still maintained my links with the Old Boys' Association and Geoff Moore and I, working mostly on Sundays, managed to produce another five issues of the Bison Gazette, including a special number in May, 1937, to mark the Coronation of George VI.

But international events were increasingly intrusive. In Spain German planes, operating on the side of the Franco rebels, pulverised the Basque city of Guernica causing colossal loss of life and horrifying the world. We realised this was how it would be in any future war. Civilians would be in the front line for the first time. Apprehension was heightened by the arrival of the first Jewish refugees from German persecution while Edward VIII and his wife, now the Duke and Duchess of Windsor, caused a flutter of alarm in political dovecotes by visiting Hitler on what appeared to be cordial terms. Was it political naivety or part of some deep plot?

Against this backdrop our dilettante weekly papers' staff began preaching peace. Leading the movement was Alan Rye who wrote a play 'Men That Come After', set in ancient Greece and staged under the name of the Pax Players, with Francis of Assisi proclaiming 'Peace, Peace, Peace'. We juniors were pressed into playing minor roles while Percy Roberts was cast as an assistant stage manager. I was a proverbial spear-carrier. It was my first and last appearance on the amateur stage.

Despite the threat of war a new ambitious company had taken over the Greyhound Racing Stadium in Hove. It was spending a lot of money on advertising and wanted better editorial coverage than the perfunctory publicity the stadium had received previously. John Chillman appeared to think there was only one man for the job. So I became the new Greyhound Racing Correspondent. I had never, at that point, seen a greyhound, although I had once or twice, as a schoolboy, witnessed Sunday morning whippet racing on the Race Hill. One explanation of course was that, as Greyhound Racing Correspondents go, I came pretty cheap.

The new owners had invested heavily in the stadium, up-grading facilities and the standard of racing. The main stand had been refurbished for members to enjoy a six-course dinner while watching racing through picture windows. It also had a long bar and Tote betting facilities.

Better class greyhounds were introduced for graded races supplemented by frequent open races with generous prizes. With the country's third longest track, the Stadium claimed to be the best venue outside London and Manchester. Greyhound racing was at its most popular and people were desperate for escapism. The opening meeting was held on 21 March, 1938, and the punters flocked in.

For me it was another steep learning curve; racing regulations and terminology, greyhound identification methods, time and distance calculations and betting terms had to be learned in double quick time. I was generously schooled by racing manager, Bob Curtis, and his secretary, Peggy Briault.

I was also expected to act as tipster. I'm not sure how confident the punters would have been had they known they were following the selections of an 18-year-old who had never previously seen a greyhound!

The opening preview, complete with the full card and selections, took up three columns. The first meeting report occupied another two columns. Subsequent meetings normally commanded a double column page lead. Re-reading a wartime letter to Sylvia, I see that I added three thousand to the Stadium's estimated attendance figures and several hundred copies to the *Argus* circulation.

Writing up the meetings didn't leave much time for worrying about split infinitives. I had to type, in duplicate, the full finishing order in each race with brief commentary, finishing distances, winner's time, trainer's name, Tote dividends and starting prices all in the seventeen minutes between races. The accompanying report might run to a column on open race evenings when celebrities presented the trophies. The meetings finished as late as 10.15 pm so that getting the four miles back to the office by bus in time to catch the last tram home afterwards was cutting it fine.

The only practical solution was to have my own portable typewriter. I felt guilty having to turn to my mother for help once again. She bought the typewriter and I never missed the last tram.

I had to report on the legally permitted one hundred and eight meetings a year on one hundred and four days. The rest of my time was spent back on general reporting and Teddy Poland made sure I was fully occupied.

The demands of journalism severed my links with the Old Boys' Association. Geoff Moore, too, had taken a new printer's job in Watford. We had produced five editions of the magazine. Now it was time to hand over to others. I had to wait another five years before I saw Geoff again.

A.E.Smith left for his new post of headmaster and I lost contact with George Hood. That spring of 1938 was the last I saw also of Don Beattie. He made the news when he rescued the office cat from a fire at the premises where he worked. In 1939 I heard that he had joined the *Brighton and Hove Herald*, as a probationary journalist. Regrettably I was too busy to contact him and after that came the war.

Old friendships disintegrated and life moved on. Both my brothers-in-law made significant advances. Bill Lewis, firmly established as a shop steward at the power station, had been elected to Southwick Urban District Council in 1937 on the Labour Party ticket, resuming a political, trade union and civic career which was to span the next thirty years or more.

Leslie Ellis was selected for a Warrant Officer's gunnery course at Chatham after which he was promoted to Warrant Gunnery Officer. Ethel and their young son Christopher joined him in Gillingham.

It left my parents and me as the only occupants of 37 Cobden Road. My father was 66 and still working full-time. With only the old age pension to rely on he felt he had no option. My contribution to the family finances was marginal. I was earning £2 a week, little more than half what my father was getting as an unmentionable furniture packer.

It was a strange dichotomy. Much of my time was spent mingling among wealthy people and putting on my evening dress. Then I would go home to a tin bath in the backyard, a father still working when he should have retired and a mother worried about how she would cope. Sometimes I was able to take her with me on cinema or theatre visits but that was about it. I liked to dream of the day I would buy them a cottage back in the country where they belonged. Then the war intervened, other priorities followed, time ran out and the dream died.

Greyhound racing continued its popularity through the summer and among the visiting celebrities I met were Hollywood film stars Bebe Daniels and her husband Ben Lyon. They had recently settled in England where they remained right through the war, re-establishing themselves as radio entertainers. I was to be associated with them another twenty years later.

Local celebrities among the Stadium patrons included Tommy Farr, the recently retired heavyweight boxing champion who went the distance with Joe Louis. He and his family had moved to Hove and his life story was being ghosted for the News of the World. It was a few years before I discovered who was helping him with the articles.

There was no copy deadline on Saturdays so, on hot summer nights, Peggy Briault and I were invited to a beach hut on Hove seafront rented by her assistant, a superior girl with a hyphen and an accent and wealthy boyfriend to match. Together the four of us swam in the moonlight and afterwards consumed hot sausages and coffee while the moon laid a silver path across the sea; halcyon times in a dying peace.

In September Hitler annexed Sudetenland, showing contempt for the guarantee given by Britain and France to Czechoslovakia. Instead Prime Minister Neville Chamberlain flew to Munich to meet Hitler. Back at Heston airfield he waved his famous piece of paper to the waiting crowd. It was an agreement, he said, which meant 'Peace in our time'.

We wanted desperately to believe him but our instincts told us otherwise. The following March Hitler ignored the piece of paper, grabbed the rest of Czechoslovakia and began threatening Poland. Britain and France had signed a solidarity pact with Poland. This time there could be no backsliding. Appeasement had become a dirty word.

Another junior had just joined the staff. Ken Webb was the son of Charlie Webb, the Brighton and Hove Albion manager. He was older than me and as far as I knew had no journalistic experience. Perhaps his arrival implied some kind of truce with his father. He was a genial character with the distinction of being married and having a baby son. Ergo, he must have had sex, which put him on an altogether higher level of human experience.

In April, 1939, the first conscripts were called up for two years' military service. We young reporters talked about the coming war and the inevitability of call-up. We questioned whether we should join one of the voluntary armed services or wait to be called up. Percy Roberts joined the Sussex Yeomanry TA unit and Ken Webb went straight away into the RAF for aircrew training. The rest of us waited to be conscripted, thereby buying a little more time in Civvy Street

I still hoped war could be avoided. My indentures would run out in a year's time and I would become a senior reporter. Overnight my wages would leap from £2 to £5 8s 6d – a fortune in my terms; another 'very nearly' case.

In August, Nazi Germany and Communist Russia confounded everyone by signing a non-aggression pact, a political ploy to enable them to carve up Poland and give Hitler time to develop his strategic plans.

The fighting services were mobilised, including the Royal Navy, with Leslie Ellis being posted to HMS Woolston. It was a worrying time for Ethel, now pregnant with their second son, David.

Other war plans were activated. ARP personnel were mobilised, blackout orders approved and arrangements made to evacuate children and hospital patients from London. On September 1st German troops marched into Poland and two days later, on Sunday, September 3rd, Britain declared war.

I had special reason to remember the date. We reporters took our turn on Sunday duty. My turn came that Sunday. It was also the day the Brighton Town Council agenda arrived. We were expected to search it for stories for the next day's *Sussex Daily News*.

There were plenty of them and I conscientiously wrote up all of them. None was published. Next morning's paper was devoted almost entirely to national and international war news. It was an historic edition and I did contribute two war stories.

One covered the moment the large crowd waiting on the concourse at Brighton station – myself among them – heard Chamberlain's 11.15 am 'We are at war' broadcast. Shortly afterwards that first false air raid warning wailed across Britain. Everyone on the concourse froze, not knowing quite what to do. Then a woman screamed hysterically and we dived for shelter down the subterranean steps leading to Trafalgar Street. It was a foretaste of the hazards ahead.

The other story covered the arrival of trainloads of London evacuee children at the station and local preparations for the coming hostilities.

Six weeks later I celebrated my 20th birthday and the start of another five-yearly cycle. The next twist in my life was already being decided. I had received a card advising me that I had been registered under the National Service (Armed Forces) Act, 1939, listing various penalties if it was misused and ordering me to produce it if requested by a constable. In anticipation of my call-up I handed over my Greyhound Racing responsibilities to Vic Champion.

Meanwhile life continued in an anti-climactic atmosphere. Once war had been declared and the first flurry of mobilisation completed, nothing happened. Hitler was bombing Warsaw into near oblivion, executing Jews and massacring civilians. But it all seemed far away. The Western Front was a theatre of masterly inactivity. The mass bombing raids of British cities had not materialised and ten RAF Blenheim's flew over Germany and, in a gentlemanly act, dropped anti-war leaflets. It gave rise to what became known as 'the phoney war'.

The British and French High Commands, still caught in a First World War trench warfare mentality, had learned little from Germany's new blitzkrieg tactics and were lulled into a false sense of superiority. In any event, how could the Germans get past the Maginot Line, the labyrinthine underground defence system laboriously constructed by the French along its entire border after the Great War?

Only at sea were there reverses. In less than a month more than 185,000 tons of Allied shipping were lost and two British warships sunk – another sign of Britain's lack of preparedness.

On 8 January, 1940, I reported at the Rechabite Chambers in Queen's Road, for interview and medical examination. An Army major asked me if I had any service preferment. I said RAF aircrew, please.

Not much chance of that he said. The RAF was so short of planes that qualified pilots were being used to clean the latrines. The Army it had to be. A medical officer ordered me to strip, breath in, cough and bend down and passed me A1 fit for service.

Then came the shock news that Ken Webb had been killed on an RAF training flight when his plane crashed. He had not even seen any action. Of the young *Argus* reporters who joined the Services he was the only one who was married and a parent and he was the only one not to survive.

The news was a terrible blow to his wife with her young child and to Charlie Webb and his wife and daughter. Ken's wife emigrated to Australia after the war but her son, who also had a son named Ken, returned to Brighton for the Albion's centenary in the year 2000.

Ken Webb's death was a sombre prologue to my own call up. It soon came. By some obscure logic, I had been assigned to the Royal Artillery. I was to report for duty at Fort Gomer, Gosport, on 15 February, 1940.

Ernie Hawkins took a picture of fifteen of us boarding the train at Brighton station. It appeared in next day's *Sussex Daily News* above the caption 'Sons of Sussex Called to the Colours'. One chap must have mistakenly thought he was off to a holiday camp. He had his ice skates draped round his neck.

CHAPTER 7

We're In the Army Now

I never truly reconciled myself to the hierarchical structure of Army life and when the war was over I walked away without a backward glance. I have been able to flesh out my fragmented memories only because of the discovery in my loft of half-forgotten picture postcards, photos, course notes, documents and above all my love letters to Sylvia which have miraculously survived. I have also found help from war books and military archives.

The first ten weeks of basic training established my attitude; all that endless blanco-ing and polishing of buttons, boning boot caps with polish, spit and the handle of a toothbrush until they looked like black glass. We marched pointlessly backwards and forwards – 'Quick march, mark time, about turn, forward march', 'Salute, one, two, three', 'Slope arms, one, two, three'. 'One, two, three' became the mantra of one's sleep.

There were the daily kit inspections – blankets and equipment neatly arranged with geometric precision on one's bed. The slightest deviation earned a reprimand or the whole shebang would be tipped over with orders to start again. Sometimes the MO would appear which meant dropping one's trousers and coughing again. What happened to dignity?

It was all about brainwashing, removing one's free thinking brain and inserting a cypher programmed to march unquestioningly into action however suicidal. By chance it was a hazard I somehow avoided. Or perhaps the responsibility belongs to my guardian angle. The fact is I had a lucky war, often purposeless but lucky.

Yet, despite my laissez-faire approach, I managed to drift through three different armies, two different service arms and six different units.

I was required to sign the Official Secrets Act and ended up smuggling women out through Russian-occupied Germany.

It all began with that train journey from Brighton station. Our destination, Fort Gomer in Gosport, had a derring-do, Beau Geste ring about it. The Western Front remained quiet and speculation persisted that the war would be over by the end of the year. With the optimism of youth we regarded it as a brief adventure.

Then came the reality. Fort Gomer turned out to be a ramshackle Napoleonic period piece which had been abandoned and deserted since the First World War. Hastily rehabilitated, it was ill equipped to cope with the Arctic winter of 1940.

Outside latrines frequently froze up, the washhouse was an ablutionary nightmare and off-duty facilities primitive. Thirty of us were consigned to a Spartan barrack room which would be our home for the next ten weeks. Keeping it clean and the central stove permanently stoked was our joint responsibility. We took it in turns to act as room orderly. Our individual space comprised a bed made of low-lying planks cushioned by a straw palliasse and a single locker. There were blankets but no sheets.

Life began at some God-forsaken hour in the morning. A bugler sounded Reveille supplemented by the rousing shouts of a malevolent NCO. In shorts and singlets we stumbled round the fort perimeter followed by a stampede to wash and shave in the inadequate washhouse. We assembled our bed space in the required order and dressed for breakfast parade. I always ended up among the stragglers. The rest of the morning was spent mostly one-two-three-ing on the parade ground, the boredom occasionally relieved by a route march to Lee-on-Solent.

Afternoons were devoted to the field gun and how to aim and fire it. One drawback was that, although we were being trained to use the Army's latest field gun, the much heralded 25-pounder, we didn't actually have one! We had to make do with First World War 18-pounders which added to our confusion.

Our gunnery sergeant, a sinewy timeserver with parchment skin, a spinal column atrophied in the ramrod position and the appearance of having spent too many years guarding the Khyber Pass, was determined we should master the manhandling art. After our first attempt we had managed to traverse the gun about one foot. His patience finally ran out. 'Push with your shoulders,' he pleaded. 'Only a woman,' he explained, thereby adding to the sum total of our knowledge of the female coital response, 'pushes with her arse.'

Other diversions were rifle practice on the firing range, Sunday church parade and Dervish-yelling bayonet practice.

Meanwhile the British and French governments continued to dither over the conduct of the war. Plans to send a military force to Norway were postponed and, when we finally landed, the Germans were already there.

At Fort Gomer we were more concerned with surviving on 10s a week. I linked up with Leslie Port, who came from Hove and had the same magical gift as George Hood for extemporising on the piano, and a chap whose name escapes me but who had been a News of the World darts champion.

On free evenings we descended on any pub with a piano and a dartboard, bought half a pint of ale each and charmed the rest of our evening's alcoholic intake from the hostelry's civilian patrons. Leslie would play the piano, guaranteeing a constant supply of pints for himself, while the News of the World darts champ, with me as his ineffectual partner, saw off all challengers, each victory rewarded good naturedly with another pint. We rolled back to camp well oiled at a combined personal cost 6d.

20 March, 1940, and still nothing was happening on the Western Front. Ronald Cartland, an MP and an officer serving in France, wrote home: 'We've settled in again to a comparatively peaceful war existence. The "season" is with us. I give "smart" lunch parties and dine out twice a week with our Batteries.'★

It typified the general complacency. On my first leave home I found the same lack of urgency. Sister Ethel had given birth to her second son, David. It was the fourth and last family birth at Cobden Road. Her husband, Leslie, was on active service with the Royal Navy, though

★*Second World War* by Martin Gilbert, published by Phoenix Press.

there were no precise details of his movements.

Bill Lewis was busy on Southwick Urban Council and over the coming years was to serve as Chairman three times and as Chairman, in turn, of every Council committee. My sister Eva was working in the Ministry of Fuel office and helping to run a Services canteen in the evenings. She was also coping with two East End evacuee sisters whom she had taken in. They were to become lifelong friends.

My brother Reg, then 35, continued driving his lorry to London but my father, approaching his 68th birthday in June, was at last about to retire. My mother renewed her worries about money.

The *Argus* office seemed much the same except for the absence of us young reporters. Frank Loder was still there, having volunteered for the Royal Navy but been turned down because of poor eyesight. Others were too old or physically excused service including Les Cluett who suffered from asthma.

I needed some therapeutic relief from the mind–numbing discipline of basic training. I volunteered to write some publicity material. So, having taken the precaution of changing into civilian clothes – itself a military offence – I found myself at Stanmer Park (today, in part, the campus of Sussex University), to report on an Army unit camping out on exercise. Fifth-column security scares hadn't yet caused alarm and publicity was thought to be a useful aid to recruitment.

Details obtained, I was invited back to the Officers' Mess – a large marquee – for drinks. So there I was, a nobody rookie, knocking back G and Ts and swapping pleasantries with a brigadier and other commissioned ranks; a moment to relish.

Suddenly, our basic training was over. Most of the intake at Fort Gomer dispersed to active service units. This was around the beginning of May, 1940. Many, I suspect, were despatched to France just in time for the impending debacle. Instead I had my first piece of luck.

I was one of a small group considered bright enough for further training as 'Specialists' to assist the gunnery officers responsible for laying the guns on target or those directing gunfire from forward observation posts.

For a month we learned how to calculate gun bearings, plan a creeping barrage and much more. I was introduced to the theodolite and the slide rule. Much depended on trigonometry, at which I happened to have been quite good at school. Over sixty years later I still remember the formula for laying the guns onto the target by using map grid co-ordinates: the log of the Diff E's over the log of the Diff N's equals the log of the tan of the angle. As things turned out I never put my 'Specialist' training to direct use but it did influence my future in the Army.

We were now at another Napoleonic period relic at Gosport – Fort Brockhurst, a distinct improvement on Fort Gomer. While we were there the phoney war came to a shattering end. Hitler launched his meticulously planned blitzkrieg on the Western Front on the morning of 10 May, 1940. Forget the Maginot Line; the Germans simply drove round the unguarded northern flank through Holland, Belgium and Luxembourg. By teatime they were across the River Meuse and pressing on towards Brussels. There were to be no more smart lunch parties for Ronald Cartland, MP.

The onslaught dramatically exposed the lack of preparedness by Government and Generals and the vulnerability of the under-equipped BEF.

An indecisive Chamberlain attempted to form a National Government but the Labour leaders refused to serve under him. He was forced to step down in favour of Winston Churchill, the man who had, for so long, warned of the dangers ahead. The nation found new hope in this pugnacious, cigar-smoking new leader and in the broadening of the Government to include such Labour heavies as Clement Attlee, Ernest Bevin and Herbert Morrison. On 13 May Churchill made his uplifting 'Blood, toil, tears and sweat' speech to the Commons and the German advance continued to roll forward at a frightening speed.

Allied resistance was a shambles. On 20 May, the Germans began driving a wedge between the British and French forces along the River Somme. Famous First World War towns were captured – Tournai, Douai and Arras and now Amiens, taking in the military cemetery where Robert Hounsome Allen was buried. The following day the enemy reached the mouth of the Somme and the bulk of the British

Expeditionary Force and large numbers of French and Belgium troops were trapped with their backs to the sea.

The German troops, exhausted and overstretched, halted temporarily while Hitler turned his attention to pursuing the fleeing French Army. It was a tactical mistake which gave the BEF vital breathing space. Churchill appealed to the owners of all seagoing craft to mount a cross- Channel rescue mission.

The evacuation began at midnight on 26 May. What followed became one of the greatest military escapes of all time and brought everlasting fame to the obscure French port of Dunkirk. By 2 June, 338,226 servicemen were back in Britain thanks to the heroic efforts of the 'little ships' as they became known. It was twenty-four days since the German blitzkrieg had begun.

Churchill rallied morale with his stirring 'We shall fight them on the landing grounds…in the fields….in the streets…in the hills' speech. But the German tactics had by now depressingly exposed the ineptitude and archaic thinking of the British High Command. Bad news continued. King Haakon of Norway and his government fled to England and the last British troops in the country followed, leaving the Germans in full occupation. In France another 46,000 British and French troops surrendered at Valery-en-Caux.

The general confusion extended to Fort Brockhurst. We dug trenches, filled sandbags and gathered what information we could through brief access to the radio and random newspapers. I felt isolated and detached.

Over the next week or so detachments were stood-to, stood down and stood-to again. Some departed – for Western France it was rumoured. By a hair's breadth I avoided joining them; another near miss. My pay book contained the entry: '12/6/40 – Trained and Qualified as a Specialist'. It was also Sylvia's 19th birthday.

Two days later the Germans entered Paris and the French caved in. It was a miracle that Germany did not immediately invade Britain. For all Churchill's defiant speeches there seemed little to thwart an attack. Maybe Germany's resources were overstretched or perhaps Hitler believed an isolated Britain would itself sue for peace.

The British Army was in a bad way, numerically, logistically and organisationally. I had evidence of this when I was one of a detachment – Leslie Port was another – sent north to join our first regiment. It was the last I saw of Fort Gomer, since demolished to make way for housing, and of Fort Brockhurst now, however, owned by English Heritage as a showpiece.

We initially fetched up in Newcastle-on-Tyne where, for one depressing night, I slept in a prison-like Victorian barracks. It was a huge relief when we were told next morning that there had been a mistake. We packed again and headed for Haydon Bridge, a Northumbrian village dissected by the fast-running South Tyne River, half-way between Newcastle and Carlisle. There we joined 52nd Field Regiment RA,* the former Manchester TA regiment, now part of 42nd Division. It had formed part of the British Expeditionary Force but, only a month after landing in France, was retreating back to the Dunkirk beaches. It arrived back in England having lost all its guns and vehicles and a number of men.

My spirits were lifted when we newcomers were directed to Langley Castle to sleep. My billet was a stone-floored chamber complete with tapestries and other historic artefacts.

I could live with this. Once again it was all a mistake. Next morning I was moved to a room above the village fish and chip shop.

That day, on parade, came the order that determined the future course of my army career: 'One step forward all those who can type and know shorthand.' Les Port and I and a few others obeyed. It was a reflex action. But there were two immediate benefits. I was moved from the fish and chip shop and excused guard duties.

Les Port went to the Quartermaster's stores – a lucky stroke since the elderly RQMS vanished and Les was promoted to the rank himself – others went to battery offices while I ended up at Regimental headquarters.

*I am indebted to the Royal Artillery Museum at Woolwich for providing me with a summary of the Regiment's wartime diary, thereby refreshing my memory and filling in long forgotten details of my time with the Regiment.

I was now dogsbody to the Commanding Officer, a gentlemanly Regular Lieutenant-Colonel, the Second-in-Command, an Adjutant and Orderly Officer – all ex-TA, the Regimental Sergeant Major and an office staff comprising two sergeants and a gunner named Lewis. Further down the line was an assortment of drivers, Don Rs (despatch riders), cooks and batmen, a mixture of old sweats, Territorial Army volunteers and conscripts.

I was cast into a whirlpool of military procedures and terminology, King's Regulations and Daily Orders, so monumentally dull and old-fashioned that I couldn't take it seriously. Instead I sought sanity in humour and became the self-elected office wag. It didn't do my promotion prospects any good but I was tolerated. Even the RSM acquiesced but he had other things on his mind. A chunky, Bruce Bairnsfather character, he looked as if he had been in uniform since the First World War. He had been due to retire in late 1939 and he wasn't going to let a little matter like another war deflect him. He was busy working his ticket by pretending to be increasingly deaf. He accentuated his supposed affliction by waggling his little finger in his left ear and saying 'Pardon, sir' whenever addressed by an officer. A few months later his ploy succeeded and he disappeared into Civvy Street. I tried to take advantage of a volunteer scheme for transferring to the RAF for aircrew service but my application was consistently blocked. Shorthand-typists were too rare a commodity.

Instead I found relief in drafting Daily Orders (Pts I and II) which were despatched to every battery and troop in the Regiment bearing news of promotions, disciplinary actions, exercise plans, new regulations and all sorts of minor matters. It was left largely to me and I assiduously included every available morsel in the most convoluted phraseology possible. I aimed to produce the longest Daily Orders in the entire British Army. But I also took the precaution of becoming an expert on military regulations.

Haydon Bridge had a rugged grey-stone charm in complete contrast to the softer, sun-drenched villages of Sussex. But the people were warm, welcoming us into their homes and tolerating the disruption to village life. The only strain was trying to interpret the Mancunian accent prevalent in the regiment and the Northumbrian dialect in the village. Then, on 18 July, RHQ moved the few miles to Hexham.

I wrote home regularly because I knew my mother was anxious for my welfare. War news was sombre, Germany tightening its grip on France and occupying the Channel Islands. But one bright spot, which few people knew about, was Britain's success in breaking parts of the German Enigma code, enabling vital enemy messages to be interpreted. Another was that, although America remained neutral, it did begin supplying quantities of arms and equipment. Britain also sank the bulk of the French fleet at anchor to prevent it falling into German hands. But at home the British Army, including the 52nd Field, remained ill-equipped. It wasn't until mid-August that the regiment received sixteen new guns – all 75mms – together with a few vehicles, trailers and motor-cycles.

We were now able to embark on our first two Divisional exercises. They were something of a novelty as far as I was concerned. But in the following months they became so frequent that I grew to hate convoying round unfamiliar towns and countryside, fighting imaginary Germans. We staggered under the weight of full combat kit, ate tasteless iron rations or unspeakable field kitchen meals, dug earth closets, slept in cowsheds or draughty tents and became increasingly cold and filthy. At regimental headquarters we worked in a mobile office truck with heavy, extending canvas sides and sent a stream of messages down field telephones or via the Don Rs.

On 4 September, 1940, I took my first leave since joining the 52nd. Typically – I always seemed to miss the big occasion – the Regiment was 'Stood-To' three days later and all leave was cancelled. Codeword 'Cromwell' had been received.

Hitler had finalised 'Operation Sea Lion', his plan for invading Britain, timed for mid-September. There was one stipulation – Germany must first achieve dominance in the skies above Britain.

On 13 August 1,485 German aircraft crossed the Channel in a massed raid. There had been scattered attacks before but nothing on this scale. The Battle of Britain had begun. The outnumbered pilots of Fighter Command shot down forty-five enemy planes for the loss of only thirteen aircraft and seven pilots. From then on the dog fights over the Channel and Hell Fire Corner and above the airfields of southern Britain became a spectacular daily sight. On 16 August alone eight airfields were attacked. Our available stock of fighters was down to seven hundred. But Germany also suffered punishing losses totalling three hundred and sixty-seven in six days. On 20 August Churchill made his famous 'Never in the field of human conflict has so much been owed by so many to so few' speech.

On 3 September four spies were captured coming ashore on the south coast and claimed the invasion was imminent. Air reconnaissance photos also confirmed a build-up of landing barges along the occupied Channel ports and German air raids intensified on ports along the south coast.

On 6 September a 'Yellow' invasion stand-by alarm was issued with the warning 'Probable attack in three days'. Next day it was upgraded to 'Cromwell' – invasion imminent.

On leave I was unaware of the unfolding drama. The Regiment was ordered south and on 11 September landed up at Hampstead Park at Newbury in Berkshire. My first warning of the crisis was a telegram ordering me to report back to Newbury the same day.

I was late arriving due to German bombs on the railway lines out of Paddington station, delaying services. I hadn't a clue where to find Regimental HQ and finished up at the local police station. They gave me a bed for the night in one of their cells. I caught up with the Regiment the following morning.

For a week the state of emergency continued. By then RAF Fighter Command was near breaking point. But its successes forced Hitler to postpone the invasion. Relief came when Bomber Command began raiding Berlin in reprisal for a raid on the East End. An enraged Hitler, who had once boasted that Berlin was invulnerable, made massed retaliatory night attacks on London. Goering was convinced that where the daylight attacks had failed the new strategy would succeed but it was another miscalculation. The London Blitz had begun and the Battle of Britain, at the point when it was almost lost, was now won.

It was due in particular to one man, the now often-forgotten C-in-C of Fighter Command, Air Marshal Hugh (later Sir Hugh and then Lord) Dowding. Yet he was shabbily treated. He had been due to retire in July, 1940, though still only 58. Termination of his service was reconsidered several times only to be cancelled at the last moment. Not until August 12th – a day of heavy attack by the German air force – was his retirement finally cancelled.★

Following the Battle, Dowding became embroiled in high-ranking disputes over tactics for counteracting German bombing raids. His views were subsequently justified but at the time he was out-manoeuvred. On 25 November, 1940, Sir Hugh, now a KCB but known affectionately as 'Stuffy', was shunted off to make a propaganda tour of the United States. He was never promoted to the ultimate rank of Marshal of the Royal Air Force.

Less well-known is that Lord Dowding and his wife were eminent spiritualists, and it was at this level that I met them, nineteen years after the Battle of Britain, when writing a series of articles on the subject. I was struck by their modest charm and established an immediate rapport with Lord Dowding who displayed no bitterness over his wartime treatment.

I celebrated my 21st birthday on 8 October, 1940. I doubt if I was alone in feeling depressed and wondering when the war would end. The Army hadn't yet grasped the morale-boosting value of putting the troops 'in the picture'. If you wanted to know anything about moving, exercises, promotions or new officers you consulted the Don Rs who spent their lives motor-cycling round divisional, brigade, regimental and battery headquarters and had their own jungle telegraph system. Most of the time their information proved to be accurate. It took Montgomery in North Africa and Mountbatten in South East Asia to understand the importance both of personal contact with the men at the front and of treating them as intelligent beings.

By November, 1940, Hitler had abandoned his invasion plans. We moved to Yoxford in Suffolk and, on a calm Christmas Day, attended church parade which was followed by dinner served, in accordance

★With acknowledgements to *The Battle of Britain – A Nation Alone* by Arthur Ward

with tradition, by the officers which I thought jolly decent of them.

Travelling back from another leave soon afterwards I met, by chance, Don Beattie's older brother standing next to me in the train corridor. He stunned me with the news that Don had been killed at Dunkirk. I felt physically sick and deflated. The stupidity of it all enraged me. Twenty-five years earlier Robert Hounsome Allen had died in France on the threshold of his career, a pawn in the politicians' and generals' chess games. Now, so soon afterwards, it had happened again to my best schoolfriend; another lost talent. His image lives with me still: his loping walk, his lop-sided grin, his style as he swept up the right wing on the football field. Losses like this make one hope for an afterlife.

CHAPTER 8

Changing Units and Falling in Love

For eighteen months after leaving Yoxford the Regiment moved around East Anglia, poised to repulse any lingering possibility of a German invasion. I still didn't fancy our chances. We remained so ill-equipped that at one point I was given a bayonet welded to a steel tube to help defend a strategic crossroads.

It was almost laughable that in the midst of all this backs-to-the-wall lark Hitler's deputy, Rudolf Hess, flew to Britain on his own initiative and parachuted over Scotland in a deluded attempt to engineer some kind of peace pact. His reward was to spend the rest of his long life in gaol.

Another move took the unit to Le Cateau Barracks at Colchester where, following an unremembered series of training courses, I was re-graded Unit Clerk, Group C, Class III (b) tradesman. The entry in my AB64 is dated 1 June, 1941. The immediate advantage was that, with the Lance-Bombadier stripe I then sported, my pay rose to roughly the level of a non-tradesman sergeant.

The war was now spreading across North Africa, Western Europe and the Middle East. Britain invaded Iraq and, with Free French forces, entered Syria and the Lebanon. But it looked as if we were destined to remain in the backwaters of East Anglia for the duration. We lived sometimes under canvas, sometimes in requisitioned buildings, made friends with the locals, played darts in their pubs and ogled the women at their village dances. My speciality was helping to organise whist drives in parish halls – a chance to contribute something positive. Marooned in our billets we played blind brag out of boredom. Occasionally lorries were detailed to carry us to the nearest town. Passion wagons we called them, optimistically, but the passion was hard to come by.

My brother Reg, now in his late 30s, had joined the Home Guard. Out on a weekend exercise he was accidentally shot by a Canadian soldier. It must have been a very small pellet because his wife and my sister Eva were able to dig it out of his back with a pair of tweezers. Odd that he, a civilian, should suffer a war wound while I, a member of His Majesty's fighting services, got through six war years without a scratch!

In June, 1941, a fatal month later than planned, Germany invaded Russia. Hitler dreamed of succeeding where Napoleon had failed and initially his troops surged forward at breakneck speed, inflicting heavy casualties. But by mid-July the advance had slowed. Moscow held and so did Leningrad. Winter brought snow, temperatures dropped to 35 degrees below zero and sentries who fell asleep froze to death. Nearly 80,000 cases of frostbite were reported, 14,000 of them so severe that amputations were necessary.

Then, on Sunday, 7 December, 1941, what had been essentially a European war exploded into global conflict. Japanese aircraft swooped on Pearl Harbour, America's main Pacific anchorage and air base, and created havoc.

Hitler commented: 'Now it is impossible for us to lose the war.' But with America drawn into the conflict and the Soviet Army preparing to launch its massive counter-attacks, it was certain that Germany could no longer win.

Britain declared war on Japan and a deluded Hitler declared war on America. A combined Anglo-American General Staff was set up to control operations against both enemies.

Initially the Japanese also made spectacular gains, invading the Philippines, seizing American garrisons on the China mainland and landing troops on the Malayan Peninsular, leading to the capture of Singapore. The British battleships Prince of Wales and Repulse were sunk.

I felt detached as if great events were passing me by. On a week's leave in February, 1942, I found the people of Brighton stoically working long hours, taking their turn on fire watching, running service canteens and voluntary aid organisations, dodging the occasional hit-

and-run air raid and still finding time to relax . One new element was the arrival of the first American servicemen who set about earning their reputation of 'overpaid, over-sexed and over here'. The women loved it, though the lower paid and more drably dressed British squaddies were less enthusiastic.

The local newspapers struggled with newsprint rationing and reduced advertising. When our leaves coincided we journalists headed for the Golden Fleece or Sussex Hotel and swapped stories. One was that John Chillman, whose wife had died leaving him with four young children, had wed Ada Guy.

Then, in the summer of 1942, I unexpectedly parted company with 52nd Field Regiment and was posted to No.20 Air Liaison Section based at Bottisham RAF Station near Cambridge. I was told I was one of only four in the Regiment with the suitable qualifications although, typically, no-one told me what they were. I was selected because it was thought to be an overseas posting and I was the only unmarried candidate. It proved to be another slice of luck.

At the same time a letter from my mother announced that Ethel and her two sons were moving to a rented house in Southwick, the urbanised former village six miles east of Brighton where my brother and other sister already lived. My parents were going with them. I could understand my mother's decision. She and my father had only his old age pension and were living in a rented house with no security of tenure. But I felt it was a bad move. With Ethel's husband serving as a regular in the Royal Navy there was no knowing where her future might lie. If she departed where would that leave my parents? There was the psychological effect, too, of moving away from their established environment, neighbours and friends.

I discovered later that my mother had also sacrificed those antiques acquired by my father, all sold to a door-to-door salesman for small change. No-one wanted antiques in those modernistic, utilitarian war days and my mother could not have foreseen the prices they would eventually fetch.

The move meant that I was now officially homeless. My brother or sisters, I knew, would put me up when the war ended but it could be only temporary. Finding a place of my own, with no capital and a post-war accommodation shortage, wouldn't be easy. The old uncertainty returned. Adrift and aimless, I needed something or someone to cling to, an anchorage, a raison d'etre.

Nos.4, 168 and 268 Squadrons were already at Bottisham when I arrived. They were the core of 35 Recce Wing to which No.20 Air Liaison Section was attached. Two other squadrons drafted in for brief spells later were Nos. 2 and 170. The rest of the Section arrived over the next few days, headed by the CO. Major Packe, a pipe-smoking First World War pilot, belonged to the old them-and-us school. I was still in my anti-authoritarian mode. We were to have a mixed relationship over the next twenty months.

Two other lesser officers came and went at regular intervals. Apart from myself, there was another office type named Bill Tilley, three batmen and four drivers and Don Rs.

I was the only one with a stripe which automatically put me in charge of the Other Ranks. They were all late call-ups, only six months or a bit in uniform, so that, although I had the longest service, I was their junior by several years. Finally, they were all Royal Army Service Corps personnel and I was the only Gunner. As far as Major Packe was concerned I was an NCO thrust upon him, and a journalist no less – disreputable beggars.

Bill and I got along harmoniously from the start. He had been something in the Stock Exchange before being called up and was also unmarried. He had a wry sense of humour and was more receptive to Army ways.

No.35 Wing, together with the Liaison Section, was part of what was still Army Co-operation Command. It had been formed in December, 1940, 'to organise, experiment and train in all forms of land-air co-operation'. I knew about Lysander aircraft being used for air observation duties by the Royal Artillery and supposed that this was the kind of service in which I would be involved. Major Packe never enlightened me.

There was better news on the broader war front. The Russians counter-attacked at Leningrad and America in the Pacific while Malta, on the brink of surrender, received fresh supplies from a convoy that had battled its way through the Mediterranean. Essentially, it enabled fresh naval attacks to be made on German supplies to its troops in North Africa.

In our smaller world, the last half of 1942 was a period of acclimatisation for the pilots of 35 Wing. American Tomahawk IIs were used as training aircraft. They had an unfortunate characteristic of having collapsing undercarriages and we would make bets when they came in. Would they pancake or nose dive?

On a week's leave that August I stayed for the first time at my sister's new home in Southwick. It was clearly up-market from Cobden Road. For one thing it had a bathroom. It emphasised that I was now truly adrift; no capital, no home to call my own and a dubious future. The search for permanency, a safe anchorage became more urgent.

As usual, I headed for the *Argus* office for a news up–date and joined Frank Loder, now a seasoned reporter, at the Golden Fleece. We were exchanging farewells in Old Steine afterwards when a girl hurried across the road. Frank waved. 'An old friend of mine. We met at night school,' he explained.

I recognised her straight away. The Sunday School fringe and Intermediate School hair slide had been replaced by blonde waves, the flat shoes by high heels. She had filled out and displayed the sort of legs to weaken a man's resolve. You couldn't have wished for a more attractive anchorage. So Sylvia Heise came back into my life; and I nearly let her go. After reminiscing on our past contacts she went on her way, back to work in the Town Hall. The date was 19 August, 1942.

In Brighton at lunchtime the following day I waited for the bus back west to Southwick and there she was on the opposite side of the road waiting for her own lunchtime bus home – but going east. I wasn't going to lose her a second time. I dashed across the road. Would she meet me that night? Years later she told me she had caught one bus but, having just seen me, got off at the next stop and walked back.

We went dancing that night and met again the next night and the next night…by the end of the week we were in love. Our meetings are the only recollection I have of that leave.

Back at Bottisham I wrote my first love letter to her. It began tentatively 'Dear S' and ended 'To my intelligent blonde, Yours Ever' though I did add a PS: 'You're lovely'. The phraseology became more amorous in subsequent letters.

Through my letters I helped her to sustain her own self-confidence, although she was remarkably buoyant given her mother's early death and the frustration she had suffered, simply by being a working class girl, in realising her own journalistic ambitions.

Her ability was recognised by the *Brighton and Hove Herald* in a report on the Intermediate Girls' School magazine of December, 1938: 'The outstanding contribution is a composition by Sylvia Heise (then an ex-pupil of course) in the form of a diary of a young lady who visited Brighthelmston (the original name of Brighton) in 1780'. It continued: 'So admirably has this young lady caught the right manner that one could easily be misled into believing that she was quoting from a genuine diary'.

At 16, she had applied for a trainee reporter's job on a Sussex country weekly. She recounted the interview later: 'Today when there are women editors on national newspapers it is unthinkable that a female would be denied a job as a journalist on the grounds of her sex. But I'll never forget my amazement when this editor told me "we don't take ladies". To make matters worse he had a patronising smirk on his face as if the idea of a female reporter was a huge joke…what's more he had cigarette ash all over his waistcoat….'

Other weekly papers reacted to her applications with discouraging 'no vacancies…will file your letter' replies.

In desperation and without any formal training she began sending stories to such unlikely trade journals as Farmer and Stockbreeder, The Drapers' Record and The Ironmonger – and getting them published. By the time we met she had moved to Brighton Borough Treasurer's Department, which enabled her to contribute to NALGO local and national journals.

She used her initiative on another occasion when, on her way to work, she saw workmen arriving to deal with a landslide which had caused a house to collapse. She called at the *Argus* office with the story and John Chillman promptly despatched a reporter and photographer to the scene. It made the front page lead.

Sylvia spotted another opportunity. She wrote to Tommy Farr asking for an interview just when he had contracted to write his life story for the News of the World. Impressed, he took her on as his part-time secretary – at 10s (50p) a week – to help with the research and correspondence.

Tommy's life story was subsequently published in a series of articles in late 1942. He asked Sylvia to become his full-time secretary. She had to refuse because she had already registered for call-up but she remained a good friend of Tommy and his family.

That's how it was when we met in August, 1942. It was a pivotal year for Sylvia. Her life, like mine, seemed to follow a ten-year cyclical pattern, running three years behind my own like two strands of a helical spiral.

Our relationship progressed rapidly, our letters swapping news, philosophising about the present and discussing our hopes for the future.

One letter typifies the blanks in my wartime memories: 'There's a newcomer to the staff, a naturalised German Jew shorthand typist and boy is he funny. He has already added a large number of stories to my stock....' His name was Henry Blumenthal. Looking through our wedding souvenirs for 1943, I found a congratulatory telegram from him. But 60 years on I had only a vague memory of his appearance and none at all of his stories.

I was soon writing 'when we are married' letters to Sylvia and with some temerity suggested she spend a weekend in Bottisham. Some cigarettes accompanied her affirmation.

The war, now truly global, was beginning to swing the Allies' way. Montgomery was appointed commander of the 8th Army in the Western Desert and preparations were finalised for Operation Torch, the invasion of North Africa through Morocco and Algiers. The launching of the Second Front was also under serious discussion. The disastrous Dieppe raid by British, Canadian and some American and

Free French troops demonstrated how difficult it would be. Valuable lessons were learnt but it cost the lives of one thousand men with another two thousand wounded.

Despite setbacks in Russia, Germany remained a formidable force and was developing its much-rumoured 'secret weapons', the V1 (the buzz bomb or doodlebug as it became known) and the two-ton V2 rocket at Peenemunde, a remote island on the Baltic coast.

With 35 Wing non-operational, life was easy going at Bottisham and mostly free from regimentation. We visited Cambridge, attended village hops, patronised the civilian canteen in Bottisham and suffered indifferent ENSA shows. Sylvia and I were getting through a number of books from 'Gone With The Wind' and A.J.Cronin's 'The Citadel' to Steinbeck's 'The Moon Is Down'.

The Brighton and Hove Gazette, World's Press News and The Journalist, official newspaper of the National Union of Journalists, were also getting through to me. The latter was spotted by an RAF chap I had dealings with. He turned out to be a fellow journalist from the Leeds Mercury and editor with the Bucks Free Press. Later I met an ex-reporter from the *Leicester Evening Mail*. All of us were office wallahs down among the lower ranks. What was it with ex-journalists?

Many of the World's Press News stories I was reading were now being sub-edited by the late Gordon Wood, another youngster who had been trying to break into journalism in Brighton. But a wonky arm, the result of a schoolboy accident, minimised his chances. Eventually he was taken on as a copyholder and reader. Through this he met another ground-breaking young trainee, Vera Ranger. Gordon progressed to the World's Press News, then to a London freelance agency and finally to the *Evening News* where he rose to Production Editor in the 1960s, later transferring to the *Evening Standard* when the two papers amalgamated. Vera and Gordon beat Sylvia and me in getting engaged but we were married a year before them. We remained good friends thereafter although they beat us in offspring output with six to our three!

Towards the end of 1942, 35 Wing became operational. Nos.168 and 268 Squadrons were equipped with the American Mustang designed as a fighter but outstanding as a ground attack and aerial photography aircraft. It was highly manoeuvrable and very fast at low-level wave hopping, a dual ability which made it ideal for the role of 35 Wing.

The Mustangs were fitted with high speed 8-inch cameras in the side of the fuselage and capable of taking long sequences of oblique photos at high speed. No.4 Squadron was equipped with the five-blade propellered Spitfire XIs, unarmed and dependent on their speed to get them out of trouble. They were fitted with 36inch lens cameras in the belly of the fuselage to take large-scale vertical pictures. Mosquito XVIs were brought in later.

The Wing's role and our part in it were never formally explained to us. Admittedly there was a lot of secret stuff going on but Major Packe's problem was the same inability to communicate with his men as the majority of his officer generation. Bill and I picked up the details as we went along.

Then a letter from a former colleague at 52nd Field Regiment put things into perspective. He had just completed embarkation leave and the Regiment was awaiting sailing orders.

As I wrote to Sylvia: 'So I've missed going over the briny again – this time by about two months!' Should I consider myself lucky or was my guardian angel protecting my interests again?

The Regiment embarked on 28 September, 1942, making various stops down the West Coast of Africa before landing at the southern end of the Suez Canal. After Christmas in Egypt it moved on to Palestine, Baghdad and finally to Syria.* But the rough part was still to come.

I was more concerned with arranging Sylvia's weekend in Bottisham. A contingent of WAAFs had mopped up most of the civilian accommodation but I eventually found a B&B vacancy at The Gables, a chocolate-box thatched cottage owned by a Mrs Sarll.

There were conditions of course. The moral climate, a lecture from her father, and night time Army restrictions ensured a platonic visit. 'Such a nice girl to have about the house,' was Mrs Sarll's verdict.

---

*I am grateful to the Royal Artillery Museum at Woolwich for supplying me with a copy of the Regiment's War Diary containing these details.

Bottisham provided a suitably romantic setting. We strolled past thatched cottages, country gardens and a real-life watermill to a bridge I'd discovered across a chuckling stream where we stood and caressed and dreamed our dreams.

The frustration of inaction in the Section erupted the day after Sylvia's return. Some of the lads had a huge argument over some trivial subject which led to some aggressive clinches if not actual blows. A wooden form, a couple of beds and a bucket went flying ending with two of the protagonists seeking solace in the NAAFI while the others collapsed exhausted on their beds. By bedtime they were the best of friends again. While the officers had their cosy mess and ready-made social life we other ranks were left to fend for ourselves. Sometimes it led to friction.

I suggested we join evening classes which I discovered were available at the school in Bottisham and one or two of us enrolled, improbably, for a woodwork course. With future marriage in mind I opted to make a footstool.

In October, 1942, my mother and I sent each other 10s (50p) for our birthdays. I worried that she was now 62 and my father 70 – fairly advanced by contemporary life expectations. I had seen too little of them over the previous eight years and I wondered if the opportunity would ever occur for me to draw closer to them. Curse this war.

For the people of Britain the morale-boosting news they had waited for since Dunkirk came on 23 October. Montgomery launched the battle that would imprint the name of El Alamein and Montgomery himself in the history books.

It took the enemy by surprise. But according to a letter to Sylvia the next day it was no surprise to me. 'I was told last Tuesday that the offensive would open this weekend', I wrote. 'Good security! Incidentally my source of information originated from Fleet Street'. What was that about? Another blank in my memory.

By 28 October, the Germans were in full retreat, leaving behind 2,300 killed and nearly 28,000 captured. It was another major turning point of the war.

Nearer home, Brighton had had another air raid and the condition of

Sylvia's father, who had been admitted to hospital, caused some anxiety (fortunately he quickly recovered). Sylvia and I were now discussing marriage plans. Would £100 cover my contribution? I reckoned it would take me till the following autumn to accumulate that much.

I was on leave when Operation Torch was launched in French North Africa aimed at linking up with Montgomery's Desert Rats to drive the Germans out of Africa. It inspired another of Churchill's speeches. 'This is not the end,' he warned. 'It is not even the beginning of the end but it is perhaps the end of the beginning.'

Back at Bottisham there had been suggestions that I might get at least another stripe, which would mean a little extra money. But the CO ('the old man' as I referred to Major Packe) had been told that under Section establishment the rank could go only to a member of the Royal Army Service Corps. There was no chance of my being transferred to the RASC. The Royal Artillery was too short of men. The Major was, therefore, putting Bill Tilley forward instead on the grounds, or so he said, that 'someone might as well have the cash' and that he was doing his best in a difficult situation. As I wrote to Sylvia: 'I know far more about the job than Bill because I have been at it longer…' It would also mean Bill would be in charge of the section. Apart from the injustice I was annoyed that the news came from Bill himself rather than the CO – all a bit too cosy to my mind – but there was little I could do against an implacable military mind-set. Bill was clearly embarrassed and offered to go halves with the extra money he would receive. I refused of course.

It was ironic that 35 Wing and the Section were at this point on standby to move to the long-established RAF Station at Odiham in Hampshire and it was left to me to organise the mountain of extra work involved. We also had to rush to finish our woodwork efforts at Bottisham evening school. My footstool cost a modest 4s (20p) to cover the materials. I parcelled it up with a lot of surplus books and other items and sent it by rail to Sylvia; just in time to learn that the move had been postponed. The footstall still survived, somewhat battered, over 60 years later.

Odiham was a big improvement on Bottisham. Eight of us were

allocated peacetime married quarters: three rooms, a kitchen, a bathroom and hot water on tap. This was living. Odiham village had an ancient pub, shops, a café offering steak dinners on Mondays and Fridays and a Services' canteen run by village women. There was a rumour that our mail was now liable to censorship, disconcerting for someone writing to his beloved, but Odiham was an operational aerodrome with Spitfires around and frequent sorties taking off.

Sylvia was becoming increasingly concerned about being called up. I was equally concerned. I couldn't visualise her in the Land Army or any of the services. And how would we keep our romance going? Something had to be done — like bringing the wedding forward. Then she would be exempt.

We dared to think about the future peace, especially when December brought publication of the Beveridge Report, 'a charter for social security from the cradle to the grave'. The upsurge of national optimism infiltrated our billet at Odiham. We began speculating when the war would end, ranging from 'by Christmas' to a more reasonable three years. The argument became heated and I escaped to the NAAFI for a half-pound block of Cadbury's chocolate for Sylvia. I queued for half-an-hour but the last bar was sold to the man in front of me. Next day we had to leave our cosy married quarters and move into a vast barrack room shared by RAF lads. The new-found euphoria evaporated but worse was to follow.

The Major cancelled my planned weekend leave because the officers would be away for a briefing. I would have to remain behind 'to look after things'. If Bill was going to be promoted now was a chance for him to take charge. As I wrote to Sylvia: 'The Major's such a cantankerous old so-and-so it's impossible to convince him on the point.'

As a result I missed the opportunity of meeting Ron Bliss for the first time since the days we had camped together at Saddlescombe chalkpit. He was now an RAF wireless operator/air gunner and off to India. His older brother, Ken, had survived the siege of Tobruk and another brother, Denis, was training as a pilot in Southern Rhodesia. Now the youngest of the four brothers, Gordon, was awaiting conscription into the Royal Artillery. It was a worrying time for their mother, Jess – Sylvia's adoptive 'auntie' – but all four sons survived the war.

My delayed leave gave Sylvia and me a few more hours together. But when I returned to Odiham on the Monday morning Bill Tilley was sitting self-consciously at his desk with three stripes on his sleeves; a fait accompli.

It proved to be my last chance to make Sergeant. I had the sympathy of the rest of the boys in the Section. 'Everyone concerned knows how the position has arisen and it's all very awkward and embarrassing to both Bill and me,' I explained to Sylvia. But I suspected that Major Packe was happy with the excuse to deny me promotion. We came from different ends of the spectrum. But I claimed the moral victory. He had first discussed the promotion with Bill on one of my leaves and carried it out on another. It was his prerogative but he had had neither the courage nor the courtesy to do so in my presence. It gave me the edge and he knew it.

Bill Tilley and I remained buddies despite everything. The more I knew him, the more sympathetic I felt towards him. He seemed a bit of a loner and sometimes spent his leave at a London hotel. One day there was a general discussion about our post-war plans and how to make money. It was then that Bill started reminiscing about past booms and crashes on the Stock Market and revealed that he himself had been caught up in the infamous Hatry Crash in 1929.

Clarence Hatry, a fraudster born in 1888, successfully hoodwinked investors in the feverish days of the 1920s to build up an industrial and commercial empire. He was hailed as a financial genius but it was a house of cards that sensationally collapsed in 1929. Many investors who thought they were comfortably off were impoverished. Among them was Bill himself. He went flat broke he told us, losing all his money, his job, his car and the girl he was engaged to. 'I don't think Bill has ever quite got over the latter', I wrote to Sylvia. 'I feel really sorry for him. It made me think how knocked over I would be if I lost you'.

Clarence Hatry was sentenced to 14 years' penal servitude but was released in 1939. He died in 1965. I never knew what happened to Bill.

But his involvement in the Hatry Crash meant that he must have been over ten years older than me.

Henry Blumenthal must have left by now to be replaced by Private Fish (his Christian name escapes me). He was even older than Bill, another pipe smoker with a kind of wizened appearance. He had terrible problems with his bile duct, an affliction which induced painful post-prandial oohs and ahs and eventually landed him in hospital for corrective treatment. He had been a rural area bank manager. Despite this he shared my sense of humour and irreverent attitude.

We formed an unlikely collection – the journalist, the Stock Exchange trader and the bank manager serving under a First World War pilot.

Things were hotting up at Odiham. There was no mention of operational activities in my letters to Sylvia, probably out of respect for the censoring officer, so I'm unsure when 35 Wing began taking aerial photographs over enemy territory. I started collecting surplus prints, the first taken, probably, during early 1943. At the same time the Mustangs were continuing low-level strafing attacks on trains, marshalling yards and other targets. I have transcripts of two *Daily Mirror* stories published in February, 1943. One described attacks carried out by Mosquitos, Whirlwinds and Mustangs over France.

It reported: 'The Mustangs accounted for 15 trains, ten barges, four trawlers, many road vehicles, a parade of troops and a barracks apparently housing SS Guards'. At least some of this stirs recollections as does a further item (which I remember clearly) that one pilot, flying about 20ft above the waves – a typical Mustang tactic – hit a flight of seagulls, showering the cockpit with feathers and damaging the fuselage.

The photographic output steadily increased with sorties setting out at dawn and I steadily increased my secret collection including mosaics I made of enemy airfields – not an easy task using oblique photos.

The Mustangs always flew in pairs and one was often caught on the photos taken by the other. The officers briefed and de-briefed the pilots and made preliminary appraisals of the prints. In the office we maintained the war maps and sortie records. We also sorted the prints into sequence – and each sortie could produce dozens of them – for onward transmission to the Air Photo Interpretation Section (APIS) at West Drayton for in-depth study. At last, after nearly three years in the Army, I felt I was making some small contribution to the war effort.

I had another important undertaking however. I departed on leave on 15 January, 1943, and two days later Sylvia and I became engaged. First I had to observe the formalities of the day and, red-faced, asked her father for her hand in marriage. He said 'Yes' with Sylvia giggling in the background.

I had also told my mother. 'You can rest assured that you are accepted,' I told Sylvia. 'She recognises you as "an intelligent girl" but she does say we both seem rather fond of spending our money and getting engaged might be an incentive to make us both a bit more careful.'

We got engaged in North Street, Brighton, with a second-hand ring that Sylvia had spotted in a jeweller's shop. It cost £7 – all I could afford. Nearly sixty years later Sylvia still had the ring, though four of the five diamonds had disappeared.

CHAPTER 9

Getting Married

A congratulatory telegram from the lads in the Section impressed Sylvia. I was popular at the time. A few weeks earlier, as the result of an appeal to Vic Champion and the Mayor of Brighton, we had received a generous supply of books, games and cigarettes.

Our engagement coincided with the Casablanca meeting between Churchill and Roosevelt to agree the future course of the war. Succumbing to my journalistic instincts I wrote to Sylvia: 'I would like to have been at Casablanca. What a story to write around'.

By now Germany was suffering huge losses in the battle of Stalingrad and Allied planes were mounting devastating attacks on enemy territory. The German people, struggling against shortages and air raids, were showing signs of dissent and some of the generals were beginning to plot Hitler's assassination.

At Odiham our long working day reflected the increasing tempo of 35 Wing operations. One clue, in a letter to Sylvia, was the throwaway line that 'it was our boys who got the SS Johnnies' – a reference to a Press report on low-level strafing attack by our pilots.

Sometimes more personal considerations took precedence over the war. A week before their wedding date a WAAF in the office heard that her RAF boyfriend was being posted overseas. But she was determined to go ahead with the marriage because, she confided in me, she intended to get pregnant for the purpose of obtaining her discharge from the service. It looked like being an arduous and ardent honeymoon.

Then came another diversion. Some anonymous higher authority decided that I should attend a three-week specialist course at the Royal Artillery School at Larkhill on Salisbury Plain. It confirmed my specialised Gunner role in the Section and it was beyond Major Packe's remit.

'I'm beginning to feel life's worthwhile,' I told Sylvia. It was encouraging also to know that she was now sending news items to the *Argus* and getting them published.

On a snatched weekend leave before my course at Larkhill we decided on a September wedding or maybe earlier if we could manage it. I also received the latest news on my two brothers-in-law. They were having rather more success than me.

As a member of AEU district and national committees, Bill Lewis had been a signatory to an agreement, drawn up in Edinburgh, allowing women into engineering for the duration of the war. He was still shop steward at Southwick Power Station and in 1942 was appointed a magistrate at Steyning, the court whose proceedings I had occasionally reported before the war. He continued on the Bench for over 30 years, including six as Chairman. Other public service appointments followed later.

My other brother-in-law, Leslie Ellis, was having a rugged war. He obviously impressed as a Warrant Gunnery Officer because he was selected for a course at Roedean, the exclusive girls' school east of Brighton. Its pupils had been evacuated for the duration and it was now a Naval Officers' training centre. When it ended he was promoted to Lieutenant and posted to HMS Ameer, an escort carrier.

My next letter to Sylvia was written at West Camp, Larkhill, which I reached after a tortuous journey of missed rail connections and a lorry lift which dumped me a mile from my billet in full service kit. But a roast dinner in the Camp canteen restored my spirits.

The purpose of Course 206, Air Co-operation Wing, was to train specialist operators in a new use of oblique aerial photographs to enable RA gunners to engage targets unobservable from the ground. It could also be used by Survey Regiments to fix battery positions and assist territorial identification for advancing infantrymen. This new application went under the name of Merton Gridded Obliques after the Army major who had developed it.

It was based on a special grid which could be superimposed on oblique prints similar to the grid on Ordnance Survey maps. But the vertical lines had to be fan-shaped to compensate for the inbuilt perspective of oblique photos and the horizontal lines had to be curved to match the curved horizon. The resultant distorted grid could then be used in the same way as a conventional map grid. Oblique photographs could cover far more territory than the former vertical pictures and give greater clarity. A camera fitted into the side of the fuselage was also more suited to the new generation of high-speed planes like the Mustang.

The planes had to fly at precise altitudes and various technical calculations had to be made if the photos were to be of use to the gunners. That was my job if called upon. Terms like Apex Angles, Plumb Points, Orienting Points, Tetley Fan, Angles of Depression, Tilt Graticules and Collimating Crosses pepper my voluminous course notes – expressions which must have been comprehensible to me at the time.

I was determined to do well. After the earlier promotion injustice I had a point to prove. My fellow students included a Sergeant Major, a Sergeant, two Canadians (one a Sergeant) and a member of the Polish Army. We were given a guided tour of the local countryside as part of the course and made expeditions to Salisbury and Amesbury.

While walking round Salisbury I met by pure chance, among all the hundreds of soldiers thronging the city, my former Old Boys' magazine collaborator, Geoff Moore, now a full-blown Corporal. We spent a pub-crawling evening and never met again. I learned some years later that he had married a Dutch girl; another severed link with the past. Meanwhile, another casualty of the war was the Intermediate School which reverted to a standard catchment area school; the end of a brave experiment.

Sylvia was growing more concerned about being called up. She thought it might come in May. Why not, I suggested to Sylvia, get married in April? It was cutting things fine but I reckoned we could manage it. It was quickly settled and I could concentrate on last-minute swotting for the end-of-course exam.

It proved its worth. I quote from my course report when it arrived at Odiham: 'L/Bdr Hounsome showed an extremely keen and enthusiastic interest in the work. Worked hard and obtained good consistent results. Very conscientious worker. With periodic practice consider him capable of carrying out the work under active service conditions'.

As I told Sylvia: 'The old man hauled me in and congratulated me. I told him I'd feel more gratified if I got some financial benefit from it. He's sent a letter to Records trying to get me another 9d a day. I don't hold out great hopes but there's no harm in trying.'

I didn't get the 9d needless to say but it allowed me to fantasise about the day when I would be called upon to convert photographs taken by our Mustangs into Merton Gridded Obliques for some gunnery regiment. The rest of the Section, including the CO, would be sidelined while I took charge.

It never happened of course. I believe gridded obliques were used by the infantry but I have no knowledge of their being used by the gunners, certainly not in Normandy.

There was a sequel, however. I kept my course notes and accompanying photos and charts. Years later an RA officer acquaintance to whom I lent them passed them on, through a misunderstanding, to the Royal Artillery Badley Library at Larkhill. They, in turn, forwarded them to the Royal Artillery Firepower Museum at Woolwich. No-one in the present computer-oriented generation, seemed to have heard of Merton Gridded Obliques. Now my original notes and photos are held at the Woolwich museum – my own miniscule contribution to British military history!★ I took the precaution, however, of retaining photocopies.

After Larkhill I grabbed a couple of weekend leaves to finalise wedding plans and at 11.30 am on Easter Saturday, 24 April, 1943, Sylvia and I were married at St Luke's Church, Queen's Park, Brighton, where my sister Eva and brother Reg had been married before me.

Wartime restrictions and shortage of cash dictated the wedding arrangements. Sylvia's cousin and my brother's daughter were the bridesmaids and their dresses could be made but with no extra clothing

★Museum Archive Catalogue MD/3298; Accessioned under No.2003.06.24

coupons. Sylvia was forced to follow the example of various girl friends and borrow a wedding dress that had already graced a few altars.

As for me, couponless and with my one and only civilian suit now threadbare, I made do with a Royal Artillery patrol blues forage cap to go with my battle dress. My best man had to be Frank Loder.

We squeezed forty-two people into Auntie Jess's Council house for the reception. But this was wartime. One of several of Sylvia's girlfriends among the guests was Kate Hemsley, who worked with her in the Borough Treasurer's Department.

Kate was descended from the Suttons, an old Brighton family of blacksmiths and wheelwrights. She herself had an uneasy childhood, her parents having divorced when she was a baby.

She met Frank Loder at our wedding. Then she joined the WRENS but nine years later they met again and married. But tragedy was to strike when their lovely daughter and only child was thrown from her horse while out riding. She died instantly. She had been preparing for her own wedding at the time. Sometimes words are inadequate.

Frank and Kate remained good friends through the years and it was Kate who was instrumental in my breaking one of my big stories.

On the recommendation of Bill Tilley I tried to book a week's honeymoon at the Strand Palace Hotel in London. It was full and we had to wait another fourteen years before staying there. We managed instead to take over a cancelled booking at the associated Regent Palace in Piccadilly Circus.

That first night, just as we headed for the bedroom, the air raid warning sounded. We didn't make a dash for the shelter. We reckoned that if we were going to die there was no better way to go. We were still alive the following morning.

As with most of our generation, embarking on copulation was rather like driving into unknown territory without a road map; you eventually reached your destination by trial and error and much fumbling. Things improved later.

We rubbernecked around London, took in the theatres, had a couple of expensive lunches and visited Madame Tussaud's, where Sylvia almost fainted in the Chamber of Horrors.

I still have the receipt for our stay at the Regent Palace Hotel. The bill – five days' accommodation, breakfast and evening meals – totalled £5 16s. I paid cash ('Cheques are not accepted') but left no tip ('Visitors are asked not to offer tips to the employees who are adequately paid by the management'); not a bad deal.

The war continued to flow in the Allies' favour. The invasion of Sicily was imminent and plans were well advanced for the invasion of Northern France eleven months later.

As part of the preparations the old Army Co-operation Command was replaced by the Tactical Air Force, absorbing 35 Wing and our own Section. The *Daily Express* called it 'the most significant re-organisation of Britain's air strength since the formation of the RAF out of the Royal Flying Corps and the Royal Naval Air Service on 1 April, 1918.....At first, Army Co-operation pilots flew in slow, vulnerable Lysanders – the planes with the "butterfly" wings. Then they changed to Tomahawks and finally to Mustangs – with a speed of 400 (sic) plus, one of the world's fastest planes. Instead of keeping an eye on the British coast to warn of invasion, they turned to hazardous operational sorties over Northern Europe, plotting and photographing enemy movements, joining in Fighter Command's destruction of locomotives and communications'.

That was certainly what we were about. The reorganisation brought other changes. We were attached to the 1st Canadian Army and wore their insignia. No explanation was offered to us lower ranks but it may be that even then we had been allocated to the Courseulles-St Aubin sector of Normandy where five Canadian brigades were destined to land as part of British 1st Corps.

One result was that we were equipped with Canadian Chevrolet vehicles and – much to the delight of the Don Rs – with Harley Davidson motor cycles. It was probably at this time also that we changed our name from No.20 AL Section to No.431 (my AB64 gives 25 November, 1943, as the date).

Marriage having saved Sylvia from call-up it now opened up the possibility of her changing her job and realising, at last, her ambition to become a journalist. On my next leave I asked John Chillman if there was a chance of a job for her. Call-up was certainly biting into the editorial workforce. An interview followed at which she obviously impressed him – especially with the contributions she had been sending to the *Argus*.

Allowing for the notice she had to give to the Brighton Borough Treasurer she joined the *Argus* on 30 August, 1943, as editorial assistant/reporter. At the age of 22, she was finally on her way.

Three days later – the third anniversary of the outbreak of war – Allied troops, among them my old 52nd Field Regiment, invaded Italy. Benito Mussolini had already been forced to resign but he won a brief reprieve when German troops rescued him in a brilliant coup. Hitler now had to shore up the Italian resistance while preparing for the coming Allied invasion of Northern Europe. Germany itself was being bombed almost at will and was also being forced into further retreats on the Eastern Front.

Operations at Odiham were interrupted by a field exercise to test communication efficiency under mobile and ALS (Advance Landing Strip) conditions. There was also a visit to a remote area of north-east Yorkshire where the Pioneer Corps had laid an experimental steel mesh ALS for our planes to test. The purpose of the exercise was not confided to us but events showed that it was a dress rehearsal for Normandy.

I managed another leave but snatched weekends had ended under the pressure of operations and I was seeing less of Sylvia than before we were married. She was making her mark in her new job, however. She was already full-time reporting and, among other things, writing the Diary gossip feature in the *Argus*.

By late 1943 Germany's position was becoming desperate. Goebbels wrote: 'We are in danger of slowly bleeding to death in the East'. Hitler was pinning hopes on the V1 doodlebug, details of which were slowly being gathered in Britain through intelligence reports and aerial photography.

APIS and in particular a certain WAAF officer, Constance Babbington-Smith, finally established the V1's profile and ramp and catapult launching method and photo reconnaissance sweeps identified identical launch sites in the Pas de Calais area of France. They were called ski sites from the concrete storage bunkers, curved at one end to give the appearance of a ski on its side. Most of the ramps were pointing towards London.

The general public were kept ignorant about the imminent danger. The only clue was almost daily newspaper and radio announcements that 'our aircraft attacked military targets in the Pas de Calais'. The attacks were code-named 'No-Ball'. A specialised task of No.4 Squadron's Spitfires was to follow the bombers in and take vertical photos of the damage. We Other Ranks weren't informed but we soon worked things out. I have a few of the photos that show the bombed sites looking like over-ripe Gruyere cheese. Many were destroyed but many survived due to their heavy reinforcement.

From October, 1943, we spent time at Sawbridgeworth in Hertfordshire and North Weald, north of London. According to Wing-Commander C.G.Jefford, MBE, RAF, in his book 'RAF Squadrons' (Airlife Publishing Ltd), 168 Squadron was at Sawbridgeworth from 12-30 November, 1943, and at North Weald from then until 4 February, 1944. On the other hand he has 268 Squadron at North Weald from 17 January to 1 March, 1944, while 4 Squadron is listed at North Weald from 14-30 November, 1943, and then at Sawbridgeworth until 4 April, 1944.

Given that he spent some twenty years researching his book I must respect W/Com Jefford's conclusions. My own recollection is that all three squadrons stayed together.

The Army now had another surprise. Having once denied me a transfer to the RASC so that I would be eligible for promotion, someone somewhere suddenly decided, without consultation, that I should be transferred after all. It would deprive me of my gunnery role and my special Merton Gridded Oblique training would be dustbinned. It didn't make sense. Who were these faceless bureaucrats so preoccupied with the life of an unremarkable one striper? Was there some conspiracy? It was spooky so I decided to give them an identity; Cedric and Jeremy seemed appropriate.

My transfer date to the RASC was 25 November, 1943. Sylvia was surprised that New Year's Eve when I turned up with a different cap badge. It was to be my last home leave for some 14 months; Cedric and Jeremy still had a few more surprises for me.

It was clear that 1944 would be the turning point of the war and in mid-January we were persuaded to make a short will, using the appropriate pages in our AB64s. I still have mine, witnessed by Pte A.C.Sheldon, one of our Don Rs. I couldn't see much point in legally willing all my worldly goods to Sylvia. All they amounted to were next week's pay packet.

In Italy the Allies began their assault on Monte Cassino, the massif which barred the way to Rome, while on the Eastern Front the Russians finally broke out of Stalingrad and rolled back into Poland. In Britain tension was mounting, with the southern coastal belt converted to one vast invasion transit camp in preparation for D-Day.

As part of the build-up 35 Wing moved to Gatwick in March, 1944. It was still a comparatively small airfield and we could see the main railway line, the end of the old Gatwick racecourse and, later, farm workers haymaking using old style pitchfork methods. This, one reflected, was what the war was all about. I wondered if Sam's Half Way Cafe was still there but I never had the chance to find out.

Surplus aerial photographs in my possession show that from July, 1943, if not before, our Mustang squadrons had been photographing the Normandy beaches and underwater obstructions. Other sequences took in rivers, canals, railway lines, marshalling yards and key urban areas – some so low that signs on the sides of buildings were legible.

The Mustangs wave-hopped across the Channel to keep under the radar and to take advantage of their low-level speed. When the pilots began meeting with heavier flak (the tell-tale puffs of smoke can be seen on some of the prints) they developed the technique of climbing steeply at the last moment then going into a dive and levelling out to make their run. No doubt as part of the well-documented deception plan, some of the runs were as far east as Cap Gris Nez. The Mustangs were also going on strafing runs, attacking any form of transport they could find, all designed to disrupt German communication and transport systems.

For the first time we were now beginning to lose pilots too regularly to be ignored. You could sense the growing tension as they waited outside their tents for orders to scramble. We never quite knew what happened to those who didn't come back, except for one who parachuted over the French coast, was picked up by the Maquis and smuggled back to England within forty-eight hours.

Brighton was only twenty-five miles away but unauthorised visits were now too hazardous. A ten-mile coastal strip was closed to visitors, with police and Red Caps at railway stations, bus terminals and entry roads. But Sylvia continued to do well and on 22 April, 1944 – two days before our first wedding anniversary – the Brighton Gazette published her first women's page. In keeping with the times she called it 'The Feminine Front'. It was the first of a long series of women's pages that she was to write for various provincial newspapers over the next fifty years.

I missed being at home for both these occasions and also for another family event, the birth of my sister Ethel's third son, Peter, on 1 May, 1944. So did Ethel's husband, Leslie, now a Naval lieutenant serving in the Far East, where he was to establish his own small place in the history of the war.

On the political front the Coalition Government was looking to the post-war reconstruction years. Having already adopted the Beveridge Report it now announced plans for a national health service and what later became the 1944 Education Act.

With D-Day only a month away Bill Tilley, Private Fish and I were under enormous pressure. Low level attack and photo reconnaissance sorties were being despatched from dawn to dusk and we were working into late evening clearing up and despatching aerial photographs – dozens of them – to APIS. Afterwards we simply fell into bed. My letters to Sylvia suffered in frequency as a result.

For me it brought another personal set-back of the sort I'd become hardened to. Our office was a trailer with a drop side to which a tented extension was added. We took it in turns on night duty, which meant sleeping in the trailer with the Duty Officer in another section. It was my job on this occasion – I don't know why – to awaken the officer some time before dawn. I was dead beat but I now know that I did manage to stagger over, half asleep admittedly, shake him by the shoulder – fairly perfunctorily I have no doubt – before staggering back to bed again.

Obviously I didn't shake him robustly enough because he too went back to sleep. Later all hell broke out. It had caused some chaos in briefing pilots on the early sorties. Inevitably I was blamed. I was stunned; so much so that I half believed that perhaps I hadn't awakened him. But a scapegoat was needed. The old man, not needing any encouragement, had me up on a charge and took away my stripe.

Afterwards the officer, a lieutenant of indeterminate social class, asked me tentatively if I really had woken him up. 'I reckon,' I replied. Even today I'm certain that I did. It remains with me as one of those frozen frames.

My reaction was a combination of disillusion, contempt and a philosophical shrug of the shoulders. Why couldn't he have woken his own bloody self up anyway? Finally the whole incident turned into a small playlet with its own denouement some four months later.

For the time being, with D Day ever closer, there was little immediate action I could take. But my position was now, I felt, finally untenable. At some time I would have to get away.

Towards the end of May, Major Packe hauled us into his office and at last 'put us in the picture' – and in some detail – about the German V1, adding something we didn't know. Despite the continuous bombing, which had put two thirds of the launch sites out of action, the first attack on southern Britain was thought to be imminent. The British people were still in the dark and if it happened, and was sustained, they were in for a nasty shock.

Having imparted this highly sensitive information he then told us that we were required to sign the Official Secrets Act, warning us of the dire penalties if we breached confidentiality. What a story. My journalistic instinct caused teeth-grinding frustration.

So effective had been the Allies' decoy schemes that the Germans remained unsure where the invasion would come. Hitler and his generals held to the view that Normandy would be the feint and that the real invasion would be in the Pas de Calais. So troops were kept in reserve for that eventuality. The dilemma gave the Allied forces a precious breathing space.

Another vital factor was that the Germans reckoned the Allies would need four consecutive days of fine weather to invade and the forecast for early June was against this. It is history now that 5 June, the original date, was ruled out by weather but a window of better conditions was forecast for 6 June and Eisenhower took a gamble. It undoubtedly took the Germans by surprise. So much so that Rommel, in command in Western France, was back in Germany for his wife's birthday. Two days earlier the Americans had reached Rome and were advancing into Northern Italy. It was ironic that at that very moment the most popular tune among the British troops was the German song Lilli Marlene.

CHAPTER 10

D–Day and Beyond

The invasion was led by 1,000 RAF night bombers and 8,000 paratroops. They were followed by 1,300 American daylight bombers and an Armada of over 6,000 ships crossing the Channel with assault troops. By nightfall 155,000 troops were ashore on Utah, Omaha, Gold, Juno and Sword beaches. At the same time 35,000 French resistance guerrillas were activated. During the first day Allied aircraft flew 13,000 sorties, 750 by the RAF and 35 Recce Wing's Mustangs, Spitfires and now a few Mosquitoes were among them. It was a hectic day at Gatwick.

I still have my copies of the eve-of-invasion messages from Dwight Eisenhower, Supreme Headquarters, Allied Expeditionary Force – 'You are about to embark on the Great Crusade', from General Bernard Montgomery, C-in-C 21 Army Group – 'The time has come to deal the enemy a terrific blow in Western Europe' and, for good measure, since we were still attached to it, from Lt-General H.D.G.Crerar, GOC-in-C, lst Canadian Army – 'I have complete confidence in our ability to meet the tests which lie ahead'.

All five Normandy bridgeheads were secured on the first day – even at Omaha, where the Americans, pinned down beneath the cliffs, suffered heavy losses – but it was a precarious toehold far short of the planned advance.

The target for the first twenty-four hours was a link-up of the bridgeheads and the establishment of a continuous front line six to twelve miles inland taking in Caen and Bayeux. Caen was the focal point on the British and Commonwealth sector, the conjunction of a dozen roads, the hinge from which the Allies would swing round to Paris and the Channel ports. Its capture was imperative. But though the 3rd British Division eventually got to within four miles of the city the

21st Panzer Division halted them at the final hurdle. It was to be another fifty-five days before Caen was captured.

On Juno beach, adjoining Sword, the 3rd Canadian Division, supplemented by British troops, managed to land 2,400 troops and advance six miles inland.

Many of these same Canadians had been billeted in the Brighton area and had left behind British war brides and fiancées – among them some of Sylvia's friends – who now anxiously awaited news from Normandy. Gradually the beachheads were extended as more troops landed.

No French airfields had yet fallen however, so it was up to the Pioneer Corps to lay down metal mesh runways (ALSs) to enable planes to fly in from Britain. The first was ready on 9 June – D Day plus 3. The Normandy bridgeheads finally merged on 12 June – D Day plus 6 – forming a continuous fifty mile front some ten miles deep.

It was also the day I specially remember. It was Sylvia's 23rd birthday and it was also the day when I landed in Normandy along with the rest of the Section. It was a bit of a surprise, with only a few hours' notice and, as usual, no explanation from the CO. We took the easy route of course. No wading up bullet-sprayed beaches for me; my guardian angel wasn't going to expose me to that kind of hazard. Instead we flew over in the comparative luxury of an American Douglas Dakota, the transportation work horse of the Second World War.

We landed on one of those newly laid metal mesh airstrips and I now saw the purpose of that exercise on the Yorkshire moors back in October. Its exact location wasn't revealed to us but guided by W/Commander Jefford's book it seems almost certain that it was at Plumetot, the advance location given by the W/Commander for 4 and 268 Squadrons. It also fits in with the fact that we were within the Canadian Sector, inland from Juno beach and immediately north of Caen.

It was a very hot day and my first sight on disembarking was of a few hundred captured Germans herded inside a hastily erected wire compound patrolled by British infantrymen. Every now and again a bottle of water would pass through the wire to the thirsty Germans.

Money changed hands – they were selling it to them! War, like power, corrupts. C'est la guerre. Welcome to France, my first visit since that day trip to Dieppe as a schoolboy. That night we managed to get into the nearest French village for a drink. I remember its wide street and forlorn appearance but not its name.

That night Hitler launched his first V1 doodle bugs. Ten were fired. Four crashed almost immediately, one disappeared over the Channel and only four reached England. Only one caused any damage or casualties –six people killed in Bethnal Green.

Over the succeeding months the people of London in particular, but also those living along 'Doodlebug Alley', came to fear the sudden cut-off of the angry buzz of the V1's engine. Other areas in the south-east also suffered from malfunctioning V1s.

The subsequent loss in human lives and property was enormous. Between 13 June and early September, by which time all the ski sites in northern France had been overrun, more than 6,000 civilians and almost as many soldiers and airman had been killed and nearly 20,000 more injured. In addition 23,000 homes were destroyed and another million more damaged; and the V2 rocket was yet to come.

The day after our landing in Normandy, the Section was back in business and the squadrons were engaged largely in low level attacks.

I have few impressions of the following weeks except for constantly using an array of Chinagraph pencils to up-date forward positions and intelligence reports on our display maps. The fact is that the battle had become, for the moment, a slogging match.

The last I had seen of the pilots was of them sitting outside their tents at Gatwick, tension disguised beneath an outward veneer of casual bonhomie. I never had direct sight of them in France and never thought I would see them again. But I did meet two of them unexpectedly again in somewhat different circumstances some twelve years later.

As the battle for Caen continued one of our officers decided, presumably with the authority of Major Packe, to head for the front line area to see how things were going. He took a Jeep and his driver with him. There was, I'm still convinced, no good reason for the recce; he wasn't going to find out anything we didn't know already or make a positive contribution to the build up. A few hours later he returned, on foot and dishevelled. They had run into a German outpost, had ditched the Jeep and dived for cover. He got back but the Jeep was lost and we never again saw or heard of the driver, a passive 30-something-year-old.

The officer was the same one who had caused me to lose my stripe. In my view his recklessness was a chargeable offence. But nothing happened. There was a closing of ranks, a sweeping under the carpet. I felt slightly sick and, with one of the lads dead or captured, drew little satisfaction from another moral victory. The names of the officer and the driver are forgotten but their images remain graven on my mind.

Just about this time, on 20 July, Count von Staffenberg, acting on behalf of a group of dissident German officers, bungled an assassination attempt on Hitler. The culprits, among them Rommel, it was claimed, subsequently paid with their lives. Had they succeeded the war in Europe would have been shortened by many months, thousands of lives would have been saved and the Allies may well have reached Berlin before the Russians.

Soon afterwards, on 31 July, came the turning point in the battle in Normandy. British and Canadian forces, supported by Polish tanks and preceded by a concentrated RAF bombing raid, finally fought their way into Caen. Simultaneously the Americans under General 'Blood and Guts' Patton, having cleared the Cotentin Peninsula, overran Brittany and St Lo in Normandy and headed east along the River Loire. The two forces now converged on the little-known town of Falaise and occupied it on 17 August. The scene was set for a classic pincer movement and two days later the Falaise gap, as it became known, was snapped shut. The German troops trapped inside fought tenaciously to escape but at the end of the battle 10,000 lay dead and another 50,000 were taken prisoner. Over 20,000 managed to escape but they found their route harried by Free French parachutists who had landed at Salornay and many of them were killed also.

I visited the Falaise pocket a few days later. The fighting troops had moved on. Left behind was a nightmare landscape of carnage. Long dead Germans, leather brown and balloon-bloated, sprawled in the hedges, their families back home wondering anxiously no doubt if they had survived. There were grotesquely mangled bodies of once proud heavy horses, overturned tanks and burned out lorries, bomb craters and uprooted trees. Wounded cows moaned unmilked and in distress. Over it all, hung a pervasive stench. A shell-shocked French farm worker and his family surveyed the wreckage from their shell-pitted cottage in stunned silence. The memory lives with me still.

With the Allies now racing towards Paris and the Seine Hitler finally gave up Normandy as a lost cause. At the same time 94,000 Allied troops landed between Cannes and Toulon on the French Riviera and within twenty-four hours had pushed twenty miles inland. Two day later Hitler ordered his troops to evacuate southern France back to Dijon.

On 22 August the Free French 2nd Armoured Division led the entry into Paris and after a gap of four years the Tricolour was hoisted on the Eiffel Tower. That night Charles de Gaulle returned in triumph and proclaimed the founding of the Fourth Republic.

Meanwhile the Russians had crossed the East Prussian border and Hitler faced the defection of his satellites in the east.

Our Section was suddenly ordered to up sticks and head north-east. I have this on the authority of a piece I wrote for the *Evening Argus*. I wrote: 'Since D Day plus 80 we've rolled our way right through Normandy and are now in Belgium'. The story appeared on 7 October, 1944. We had covered some three hundred miles in six weeks.

We were tracking the Canadian Army to whom we were still attached and who were on the left flank of the advance. I travelled in our 15cwt office truck as we drove along narrow roads with periods of immobility in nose-to-tail convoys. We snatched sleep in cowsheds, lived off the land, foraged for eggs in deserted farmyards (fried eggs for breakfast, cooked on my prized Primus stove).

Meanwhile the drama of Operation Market Garden was unfolding. In our remote rear position we were only vaguely aware of it but it was an inspired concept: a lightning land dash along a narrow corridor to link up with airborne troops seventy miles to the north at Arnhem. It would have split Holland in half, opening the way to cross the Rhine and penetrate the industrial heartland of Germany.

The offensive included the largest airborne operation in history but almost from the start there were problems. After nine days the battle was lost and, of the 10,000 British Paras landed at Arnhem, barely 2,000 made it back to Allied lines. While the battle raged, I was buying picture postcards in Boulogne.

Market Garden had failed but the Allies were having continued success on the broader front. One result of the advance through France was that the V1 launch sites in the Pas de Calais were overrun.

For the British people, however, there was worse to follow – the V2, a 15-ton rocket with a one-ton warhead which could descend faster than the speed of sound from fifty miles high without warning. Most of them were launched from the Hook of Holland, an area which would have been occupied had Market Garden been successful. Instead V2 launchings continued until the end of March, 1945.

Memories of my own progress beyond Boulogne are vague. One clue is an unlikely visiting card bearing the names of M and Mme Pont-Buquet, Grand Place, Aire-sur-la Lys, Pas de Calais, with a hand-written message on the reverse introducing me to 'Mademoiselle Buquet of Bon Marche, 53 Grand Place'. What was that about?

There were more picture postcards – St Omer, the Den en Heuvel Hotel, Kesterlee ('A typical Belgium pub,' I told Sylvia) and Ghent, our final resting place which we reached at the beginning of October, 1944.

For the Section the war was becoming more like a coach tour. I remember rubbernecking round Ghent and Bruges and marvelling at the apparent affluence and lack of war damage. As I wrote for the *Evening Argus*: 'Notices thanking us for our speedy liberation confront us everywhere…The big surprise comes on looking in the shops, which are full of every commodity except for leather goods. Prices however, are astronomical'.

I bought a pair of 'spun glass' stockings – really nylons of course – for Sylvia and the first item of plastic clothing I had seen, a green raincoat.

8 October, the day after my piece appeared in the *Evening Argus*, was my 25th birthday. Another five yearly change was due – the end of the war no less.

By the time we reached Ghent the Section seemed to have run out of purpose. I was considering what to do next when the decision was made for me. Cedric and Jeremy were interfering again and suddenly I was declared surplus to requirements. My next stop was Breda in southern Holland where I joined yet another liaison section, this time attached to the 1st Polish Armoured Division. Snapshots of my new comrades suggest it must have been in November.

I must have remained 'seconded' to the 1st Canadian Army, which included Polish elements, since I later received a copy of a Christmas message from the Canadian GOC-in-C. The 1st Polish Armoured Division was resting and it never went into action during the time I was there. Because of this I never discovered the new section's full brief, although there seemed to be an ample supply on non-commissioned personnel, including a sergeant major, a sergeant and a lance-corporal.

My main activity was filling in forms, including indents for rations for the entire division. This clearly suited the oleaginous gourmand of a major who was in charge of the section and must have weighed in at 20 stone. Two acolyte lieutenants acted as his aides. They certainly weren't suffering gastronomically.

My taste buds protested at the Polish culinary offerings. Rice wrapped in a cabbage leaf, boiled and served up whole was a typical lunch. I definitely lost weight during my stay in Breda.

Communicating with the Polish troops, whose English was severely limited, was difficult. But I felt sorry for them. Many had no knowledge of the whereabouts or fate of their relatives back in Poland or where their own post-war future would lie. As a safeguard, a number were busy in the Black Market. I don't know how the system worked but the only thing they were interested in was convertible jewellery.

The one major military event of my stay in Breda was Hitler's final gamble on the Western Front – the offensive that became known as the Battle of the Bulge, launched on 16 December. Thirty divisions – around 250,000 troops – made a surprise attack through the Ardenne Forest region between the British and American forces – the same route the Germans had taken in 1940.

The advance covered sixty miles in ten days before being halted.

They were still seventy miles from Antwerp, their ultimate objective, and by 20 January they were back where they started. The offensive lasted five weeks and cost the lives of 15,500 Americans and 25,000 Germans. It was the last flourish of a defeated Army.

I have a copy of 'Spearhead' dated 23 December, 1944, giving a resume of the battle. It is typewritten on the back of a detailed analysis of the various movements of a symphony – an inexplicable combination.

The Battle of the Bulge wasn't allowed to interfere with our celebration of Christmas that year. The Dutch had undoubtedly suffered far worse than the Belgians during the German occupation. Everything had a threadbare appearance, there was little in the shops and the guilder was on the floor.

There was bitter resentment towards the Germans for their arrogance, their looting, the deportation of thousands of Jews and the ruthless treatment of members of the resistance movement. Their gratitude for the liberation was palpable.

It was epitomised by the lovely van Looveran family on whom I was billeted and with whom I built up a close friendship. The family comprised veterinary surgeon Mr J.C.E.Looveran – there didn't seem to be a Mrs van Looveran – and his four grown-up children, Louk, a student vet, Adri and two daughters, Honoree and Henrietta.

I still have several snaps of the family and two souvenirs they gave me showing the poverty levels to which they had been reduced. One souvenir – 'a present to Bob' – is a hand-made brochure containing paste-in pictures, cut from old magazines, of prominent Breda buildings, with hand-written captions. In it I find a message which points out that I write 'very fast' with my left hand and that I 'like to learn Dutch'.

As I reported to the *Evening Argus* – I seem to have become more an unofficial war correspondent for the *Argus* than an active service soldier! – '...For food, clothing, heat and other necessities they are in even worse straits than the French and Belgians but despite this they are saving and scraping to make their Christmas a happy festival'.

I managed a visit to the ENSA Garrison Theatre in Antwerp. I still have the souvenir programme for the show: a production of Bernard

Shaw's 'Arms and the Man' by the Old Vic Theatre Company. It had a cast that a West End impresario would die for: Laurence Olivier, Ralph Richardson, Sybil Thorndike, Margaret Leighton, Joyce Redman, Sidney Tafler, Nicolas Hannen and Weyman Mackay. An evening to remember.

One way and another we had a good social life at Breda, including occasional weekend visits to Brussels. What made me really popular was that I was in charge of issuing leave passes. While the Dutch guilder was pretty worthless the Belgian franc was, for some reason, quite strong. Consequently the Dutch people were desperate to lay hands on Belgian currency.

I soon worked out how our weekends could be financed in Brussels by trading in as many guilders as possible for Belgian francs. The Brussels bank handling the deal would stamp one's pass and paybook, so that only one transaction could be made. But this could be circumvented if one had three passes and a bottle of ink remover to expunge the stamp in the paybook. Then the process could be repeated in other banks. In this way we flogged our surplus Belgian francs for guilders back in Breda and ended richer on the Monday than we had been on the previous Friday.

I'm not proud of what I did but it was the corrupting influence of war. I don't know that it did any great harm; nothing on the Harry Lime scale.

One other memory of my Brussels visits was a chance meeting with Peggy Briault, last seen some five years earlier when she was the Racing Manager's secretary at Hove Greyhound Stadium. She was serving in the ATS. We had coffee together and never met again.

During another break I spent three-nights in a rest camp set up in a college in 'a large Belgian town' as I reported to the *Evening Argus*. The facilities were remarkable: morning tea in bed, served by NCOs, central heating, free cigarettes and three-course dinners served on fine china on real tablecloths. There was a swimming pool, library, games room, a cinema, an evening show, dances with supper to follow and – glory be – a mattress to sleep on. Butlins with bells on.

My stay in Breda lasted only three months. I had, on arrival in the town, slapped in a request to transfer back to the Royal Artillery; a defiant gesture or perhaps a quirky spur-of-the moment decision. I hardly expected any reaction but, without warning, by GHQ, 2nd Echelon Part II Order 450 of 13 February, 1945, it was decreed that I be transferred back to RA (Field) in the rank of Gunner. Did I detect the fertile minds of Cedric and Jeremy at work once again?

It was clear that the approach of spring would bring the final offensive against Germany. A new phase was about to begin for me also. Following my transfer back to the Royal Artillery I was posted to a transit camp at Knocke on the Belgian coast. I said goodbye to the van Looverans and to Breda with considerable sadness. To my mind the Dutch are nearer to the English in culture and outlook than any race in Continental Europe.

I imagined my stay at Knocke would be temporary. Some artillery regiment somewhere was bound to welcome an all-in-one trained specialist, expert on Merton Gridded Obliques and shorthand-typist; no battle experience it's true but one can't have everything. But the call never came. I had got lost in Cedric's filing system.

Units and detachments and single servicemen came and hurriedly left again, off to where the action was. But I stayed on and on. For me the war had ended three months early.

My transit camp duties were less than onerous. My only memories are of making my bed and cleaning up the communal dining room after breakfast – a fitting task for my talents I thought. After that time was my own for sightseeing, reading and writing to Sylvia while the rest of the British Army was busy crossing the Rhine. Later, while the Army set about stabilising a defeated Germany, I swam and sunbathed among the sand dunes of Belgium's No.1 resort. The next time Sylvia saw me I was so deeply tanned she wasn't certain it was me.

While I remained marginalised at Knocke the Allies reached the River Elbe and there on 25 April – the day after our second wedding anniversary – advance American troops met their Soviet counterparts. A fortnight earlier America had spiralled into mourning on the death of Roosevelt, one of the great architects of the victory he was destined not to see.

In Berlin the Russians hoisted the Red Flag over the Reichstag. There was chaos in the streets, with troops deserting in droves and bodies strewn over the pavements.

In his underground bunker Hitler shot himself and Eva Braun, the mistress he had married two days earlier, also committed suicide.

Two days earlier Hitler's Axis partner, Benito Mussolini and his mistress were shot by Italian partisans and strung up by their feet for all to see. The remaining ragbag of German and Italian Fascist troops in Italy finally surrendered.

On 4 May, all German forces in the west formally surrendered to Field Marshal Montgomery on Luneberg Heath. Four days later, on 8 May, the final act of capitulation was signed. It was V.E. Day. The war in Europe was over.

I marvelled that I had emerged unscathed so easily without even trying. I felt a bit of a cheat. My only truly positive contribution to the war effort had been my period with the Air Liaison Section – a matter of some twenty months. But that was how it was with me; the man who just missed out.

So what now? Cedric and Jeremy, in the upper reaches of Whitehall, dithered.

Meanwhile, on 23 May, Parliament was dissolved, Labour members refusing to delay a General Election until after the defeat of Japan. Their argument was that urgent decisions had to be taken on the future of peacetime Britain.

The election was held on 5 July. Collecting service votes delayed announcement of the result until 26 July. By then Cedric and Jeremy had decided to send me back to Royal Artillery headquarters at Woolwich on a thirty-day 'special leave'. I was given to understand that I was destined for the Far East to join the continuing war against Japan.

After a couple of days at Woolwich I was back in Brighton just in time to savour Labour's stunning landslide victory. They had taken 393 seats to the Conservatives' 213 with a decimated Liberal Party and the Independents sharing the remaining 34 seats. It was the first Labour Government to obtain an overall majority.

I had of course voted Labour. So had Sylvia and most of our

contemporaries. We literally danced in the streets when the result was announced, convinced that Utopia was just around the corner, while older Tories – an almost tearful Ada Chillman (nee Guy) among them – wore expressions of apocalyptic gloom.

The Tory Party, which had lost thirteen ex-Cabinet Ministers alone, was left in a state of shock. But it had not heeded the warning signs. It was the first General Election for nine and a half years and a new generation, now mostly in the Services or in Unionised industries, had joined the voters for the first time. We were all aged between 21 and 30, precisely the generation that had been born during or soon after the First World War. Many had grown up fatherless and had watched their widowed mothers struggle to survive on inadequate Government handouts. We had seen our parents face poverty and unemployment, war veterans singing for pennies in the street, the General Strike of 1926 ruthlessly suppressed, the Jarrow Marchers contemptuously dismissed, the class system sedulously preserved.

We weren't having any more of that, not after six years of war, not after struggling to make the best we could of what education we were allowed. We wanted a better, fairer life for ourselves and our children. Speeches and comments by diehard Conservatives showed that they had grasped none of this. They were living in a time warp, expecting society to return effortlessly to pre-war patterns; long live the status quo.

We were castigated for betraying Churchill. But if the ship had to sink the captain was destined to go down with it. Besides, Churchill, great war leader though he had proved to be – and I, too, had been inspired by his fearless decisions and his epic speeches – made his own contribution to the Tory's defeat.

In the run-up to the Election he made a speech that caused huge damage to his party's prospects, claiming that a Labour Government would suppress free expression and 'fall back on some form of Gestapo'. Labour Party policy, he said, was abhorrent to the British people.

His intemperate words startled many in his own party. To my generation they appeared patronising and dismissive. For our part we idealised the Labour victory. To us it meant opportunity for all, no more poverty, free health care, decent homes to live in, jobs that paid adequate wages and publicly owned services run by the people for the people.

Much of it happened, but not all of course. Utopia doesn't come that easy. The war had impoverished Britain and the Government was fighting against long odds.

Sylvia and I celebrated the Labour victory with a trip to London. We stood among the crowds in Whitehall, Sylvia astride my shoulders, waving madly as the new Prime Minister, Clement Attlee, swept by waving back from his limousine. It was a time for optimism. The blackout had ended, the lights were back on, the United Nations had been born and the world was almost at peace again.

But the war against Japan continued. The Philippines, Okinawa and many other islands had been liberated and the 'Forgotten' 14th British Army had driven through Burma to capture the capital of Rangoon. Victory still seemed a long way off, however, and I viewed further service with pessimism.

Then, on 6 August, an American plane dropped the world's first atomic bomb on Hiroshima followed, three days later, by another on Nagasaki. Both cities were totally destroyed and tens of thousands died. It still took another five days for the Japanese warlords to surrender.

15 August, 1945, became VJ-Day. The Second World War had finally ended. It came inevitably, in my 25th year. It had cost the lives of 55 million world-wide, 500,000 of them in Britain and the Commonwealth. My immediate reaction to news of the atom bombs was huge relief. Suddenly I could see a renewal of civilian life. Only later did one consider the implications. A weapon of unimaginable power had arrived capable of wiping out whole civilisations. Global security had changed forever.

There had been talk of my joining the Brighton and Hove Gazette as Chief Reporter following demobilisation so I clinched the deal before returning to Woolwich. The new editor, Leslie Cluett, with the backing of John Chillman and Infield Willis – the new Managing Director, who had replaced his uncle, Henson Infield – had assembled the nucleus of an independent staff and was building a challenge to the rival Brighton and Hove Herald.

Sylvia was still writing her weekly women's page and other material for the Gazette but had also started a new *Argus* feature 'News From The Film World'. Two days after my return to Woolwich she visited the old Gainsborough film studios at Lime Grove to meet Stewart Granger, Anne Crawford and other stars of a new film 'Caravan'.

In December, she covered the first of many Royal visits, Princess (later to be Queen) Elizabeth's tour of the Royal Alexandra Hospital for Sick Children. While Sylvia expanded her areas of interest, I continued to languish in the Army. But phased demobilisation was planned – quite rightly – to avoid the post-war chaos of 1918/19. There was also a lot of mopping up to be done in the battlefield areas.

From Woolwich Cedric and Jeremy despatched me to 492 (H) Field Battery of 128 (H) Field Regiment, RA. They were stationed at Bucken/ Hoya, two villages on the River Weser south of Bremen in deepest Germany. Once again my meandering Army career took me on a solo journey into unchartered territory.

The battery was part of the battle-hardened 51st Highland Division and the camarderie was apparent. Inevitably I was assigned to a Battery office. My office colleague wore the Military Medal ribbon but had lost two fingers in winning it. On reflection, being a journalist, I think that, had I been given the option, I would have settled for the two fingers.

Non-fraternisation with the Germans was in force (even though we had a German girl in the Battery office and couldn't avoid talking to her). I was back in my old role of organising whist drives and other events. Contact with the local Germans was largely for the purpose of flogging recycled tobacco. We were issued with grey circular tins containing fifty Players cigarettes. A widespread practice, in which I unashamedly participated, was to harbour our fag ends then mash up the residual tobacco, pack it back into the tin and sell it as untouched merchandise.

The Treasury must have realised the foreign exchange chaos our flood of fairly worthless German paper money would cause and capped the amount we could exchange. There wasn't much chance of buying goods from the Germans since they had little to trade anyway. I had so many surplus Reich notes I was using them to light my cigarettes. We also had occupation marks but they were fairly useless as well. I still have a stock of both forms of currency today.

One of our duties was indenting for the alcoholic sustenance of the officers' and sergeants' messes. Authorised supply was based, not on demand, but on the number of personnel entitled to benefit. It didn't take me long to recruit a number of phantom officers and sergeants to bring the unit up to establishment and stash away the resultant surplus bottles. I managed to keep my share, carefully padded in a separate kitbag, until demobilisation the following May.

The aftermath of peace in Europe included rehabilitating displaced persons, apprehending war criminals and coming to some kind of territorial accommodation with Russia. In the Far East there was the additional logistical problem of rounding up tens of thousands of Japanese troops scattered around the Pacific. It was not until 2 September that the Japanese signed the instrument of surrender on board the American battleship Missouri.

Three days later British and Indian troops landed unopposed at Singapore. But the responsibility for taking over the dockyard fell to the Royal Navy's destroyer team, led by HMS Rotherham, on which my brother-in-law, Leslie Ellis, was now First Lieutenant and second-in-command. He was the first British Naval officer ashore and it was his task to escort the Japanese naval commander on his way to officially surrender. He also organised the round-up of the 38,000 Japanese prisoners and arranged their embarkation for prison camps in Malaysia and Borneo. It was aboard HMS Rotherham also, with Leslie in attendance, that senior Imperial Japanese Army officers in command of Singapore officially surrendered their Forces in the Naval base.

When he made a survey of the dockyard buildings he discovered a series of former Royal Navy sheds filled with untouched pre-war stores. One contained twenty-three old Charlie Chaplin films – whatever happened to them – which were used to entertain the crew of HMS Rotherham on the voyage back to England. Another shed was stacked to the roof with cases of Bluebell metal polish, no longer manufactured but standard issue in the Navy prior to the war for polishing the ships' 'bright work'. With the end of the war camouflage paintwork could be removed and ships returned to their sparkling glory. My brother-in-law immediately distributed the newly discovered Bluebell among the squadron in Singapore without specifying its source. 'There just wasn't time to go through normal procedures,' he told me.

So he made his own contribution to the surrender of the Japanese and to putting the shine back into the British fleet. It was not until the 1969 publication of John Winton's book, 'The Forgotten Fleet' (Michael Joseph) that the story was revealed.

The sequel came another twenty-five years later when Leslie, now 81, attended a re-union of wartime crew members of the Rotherham – held in Rotherham – at which he was presented with a model replica of one of the Singapore naval sheds. It contained a full-size tin of Bluebell metal polish obtained from the museum stock held by the former manufacturers, Reckitt and Coleman.

While my brother-in-law was rounding up Japanese prisoners in Singapore, I continued to lead a tranquil life in Bucken/Hoya. On 16 December I was informed, much to my surprise, that I was being promoted to paid Lance/Bombardier. I had obviously created an impression. In six merry-go-round years I had gone from Gunner to Lance/Bombardier to Lance/Corporal to Private to Gunner and back to Lance/Bombardier. Not exactly a positive career structure.

Christmas came and went while more momentous events were taking place in the world outside. There were riots and demonstrations in the Arab world against the setting up of a Jewish homeland. In Britain 43,000 dockers staged the first major post-war strike. The Nuremberg trials of the Nazi leaders began. Tito was swept to power in Yugoslavia and de Gaulle was elected President of France. The International Monetary Fund and the World Bank were established and on 1 January, 1946, the first test flights took place at the new London airport.

In Brighton, GI and Canadian brides were setting off for their new homes across the Atlantic leaving behind tearful parents. Over the following months Sylvia's Women's Page became the conduit through which brides and parents kept in touch with each other and with news from both sides of the Atlantic. Dozens of copies of the Brighton and

Robert Hounsome Allen in his pre-war teaching days. The watch chain was probably the one sent to my mother.

In the back garden at Cobden Road, 1916. My mother, Emma (third from left) and my father, Owen. The other two women are Maggie (far left) and, next to her, my father's sister Lily. In front, from left to right are my brother Reg and my sisters Ethel and Eva. Maggie was the girlfriend of my cousin, Robert Hounsome Allen and my guess is Robert took this picture whilst on leave from the Western Front.

Sylvia as a baby with her mother, Rose, and father, Charles (1921).

As a young lad in the back garden at Cobden Road (c.1931).

Our wedding day, April 24th 1943.

At the end of 1944 wearing my RASC badge.

Sylvia and me with our two elder daughters, Rosalind and Alison (1950).

Our three daughters shortly after the birth of Susan (1953).

My week as a down and out in 1957.

Sylvia and me on our night out on the town in 1957.

Walking the Pilgrim's Way in 1960.

In my news agency office (late 1960s).

With Tommy Thomson shortly before the Wessex Export Club's trade mission to South Africa in 1970. Standing between us is Willie the Griffin, the Club's mascot.

Hove Gazette were despatched overseas. Among the brides were some of Sylvia's own childhood friends.

My own future with the Gazette was confirmed and, on leave, I wrote my last story while in uniform: 'During the past week I have been going round asking about re-instatement, resettlement and rehabilitation; three words which dominate many of the problems facing service men – and women – on demobilisation…'

I expected to see my service out at Brucken/Hoya but March, 1946, brought another sudden change: 128 Field Regiment was disbanded and, what were effectively my discharge papers, were signed by the Battery Commander. But I still had another seven weeks to serve and Cedric and Jeremy, up in Whitehall, had one final surprise for me. On April 1st – All Fools' Day – I was on my way to Hanover.

I spent the rest of my Army career guarding food trains from Hanover, through Russian occupied Germany to the British zone of Berlin. There were a few squads working on a rota system. Mine comprised four seasoned campaigners and me, who had never fired a shot other than on the rifle range. But, since I was the only one with a stripe, I again found myself involuntarily in charge.

We made four trips to and from Berlin. We had our own carriage somewhere in the centre of the train, equipped with bunks and a stove and we were each issued with rations for twenty-four hours. The journey never lasted that long despite the clanking stop-go crawl behind an asthmatic engine.

The wagons were sealed and it was our job to ensure that they arrived in Berlin intact. It was an impossible task. There were up to forty-two wagons and we couldn't keep them all in view during unscheduled stops. The train would start again without warning and we would be in peril of being left stranded if we wandered too far away.

Nor were we briefed on what to do if we caught any looters; shoot them, take them into custody, send them packing with a warning? Few trains got through intact. In one case the seal of one wagon was unbroken but it was empty – with a neat hole sawn in the floor. No-one bothered.

There was a Royal Engineers NCO on board, travelling up front with the engine crew. He was at pains to point out that he was in charge of the train and we were in charge of the cargo. I wasn't going to argue with him so near to demobilisation.

Others who had already made the Berlin run briefed me. The true purpose, it seemed, was to eat as little as possible and flog the bulk of our twenty-four hour rations to the Germans on the train's many stops.

Most of the trade took place at the obligatory document-checking stop just inside the Russian occupied area at Helmstedt. There was no shortage of customers. They were desperately short of everything but top of their list was corned beef, coffee and cigarettes (a new outlet for our tins of mashed up fag ends).

Everything went smoothly except on one occasion when we stopped short of the Russian border and two elderly ladies climbed aboard unseen and locked themselves in the toilet. We found them when we got to Helmstedt. Goodness know why they wanted to get into Berlin (their real aim) since every German already there wanted to get out. Our Royal Engineers NCO marched them off to the Russian guardroom. Who knows what happened to them?

Again it may seem immoral to have indulged in such black market activities but the amounts we charged were not excessive and would have cost far more elsewhere. I was operating in two worlds. Back home I was the civilised journalist with a sense of responsibility. In Germany, among the rubble and brutality of war, my corrupted other self took over.

On our final run our officer decided to accompany us. No selling on this trip we told ourselves. But as soon as the train pulled out he handed over his twenty-four hour rations. We had to flog his as well on that trip.

Finally, the Royal Engineers corporal was running a nice little line smuggling German women from Berlin back to Allied-occupied territory on our return trips. One can only guess at the price they paid.

The Soviet guards at the frontier post always inspected the train on the return journey, including our carriage. With their automatics at the ready, they frightened the life out of me. They had the ethnic features of one of the more peripheral soviets of Eastern Russia where human life was valued at rather less than than that of the family yak. Somehow the women on my trips got through except one who was marched off by a Russian guard. One girl got through the border slung between the engine bogey wheels and I co-operated somewhat apprehensively in dressing another girl in the RE corporal's spare battledress, putting her in one of our bunks covered by a blanket and pretending she was ill. We held our breath and got away with it.

The snag with all this black market activity was again what to do with the German marks. When the train reached Berlin, we dashed off to a row of shops that had somehow survived the war but had been reduced to a single storey.

They had little to sell but I bought a very good camera – stolen a few weeks after my return to England – and a wireless set which crackled into permanent silence at about the same time. So there was little gain from my efforts.

Because we were on permanent standby when not on guard duty I saw nothing of Hanover and what I saw of Berlin – towering piles of rubble, a ghostly gloom, shoulder-bowed people shuffling among the ruins, everything at a standstill – suggested that civilised life would be a long time returning.

My train guarding duties ended when I was despatched to a holding camp for my final days before demobilisation. Where it was precisely I can't recall but I remember the unrelieved daily lunch diet of something called MacConachies, a thin gruel in which floated tired cubes of unidentifiable vegetables and small chunks of superannuated meat. Thank goodness I would never have to face that again.

On 16 May, 1946, I embarked on a troopship at some unremembered Continental port and arrived at some equally unremembered British port. From there I was transported to Aldershot to have numerous documents stamped and be given the run of a large shed full of clothes from which to choose my demob outfit. Then I caught the train home.

I didn't look back. I had left six years earlier as a still immature – I now realised – 20-year-old with no baggage and was returning as an adult, married 26-year-old with responsibilities. The immediate reaction was to curse the war as a frustrating interruption to one's career. But there were positive aspects. There had been good times and times of shared adversity, the discovery that kindness existed beneath the roughest exteriors. I had learned independence and the ability to take decisions. I could darn socks, shave in cold water, remain organised under stress and improvise amid chaos. I had also developed, through innumerable kit inspections, an abiding neatness of appearance.

In my Class 'A' Release Book the CO of my last unit, 492 Field Battery, had written: 'Military Conduct – Exemplary. Testimonial – Although L/Bdr Hounsome has only been with the Bty for six months (something wrong there – I was still in Breda at Christmastime), he has shown himself to be a man of initiative with intelligence above the ordinary. He has been employed as a clerk and is methodical and efficient. Previously he served in intelligence work in Army-RAF Co-operation. He has helped to organise the social activities of the Bty and is well liked by all ranks'. OK, I'll settle for that. Maybe I had made a small contribution to the war effort after all. But I never applied for my three medals. I felt I hadn't earned them.

I reached Brighton on a hot lunchtime on 17 May complete with my two kitbags. One contained my personal belongings and my black market camera and wireless set. The other was stuffed with the bottles of spirits that I had lugged all the way from Brucken/Hoya via Hanover.

Sylvia had found a flat to rent at the top of a three-storey Regency terraced house just off the seafront. She wasn't at home – neither of us knew when I would arrive – but I hadn't long to wait. She had been shopping. We climbed the stairs for my first glimpse of the flat. She had done a great job considering the constrictions of rationing, dockets and shortage of money. Her first action after our mutual demonstration of affection was to empty her shopping bag and triumphantly produce her latest discovery at Sainsbury's – half a dozen food tins. Stamped around their circumference was the magic word MacConachies. With admirable self-discipline I never said a word. I couldn't spoil her day.

Today she was out to demonstrate her culinary skills for the first time. She had bought a secondhand Baby Belling gas cooker – about the size of a modern microwave and in common use in bed–sit land at the time. Lunch was fish accompanied by a variety of vegetables – roughly enough to feed an Artillery gun crew for a couple of days. The Baby Belling's tiny oven and the three gas rings were put to full use and within a few minutes the saucepans were jumping up and down and the oven, I swear, was actually glowing.

The poor old Baby Belling had never experienced such overload. Sylvia had left a full box of matches on the hob. Succumbing to the laws of spontaneous combustion all fifty matches suddenly ignited simultaneously and the box took off like a crazed hornet, shooting round the room and ricocheting from wall to wall while Sylvia and I ducked and weaved to avoid being hit. On my first day back in civilian life I was in greater danger of personal injury than during six years of wartime service. It was a foretaste of the rollercoaster ride ahead.

CHAPTER 11

Back to Civvy Street and Journalism

We decided to call on our landlord and landlady, Reg and Winnie Buckland, who occupied the ground and first floors and appeared to be a reasonably affluent 40-something couple. I took one of my illicit bottles of Army whisky, guided by Sylvia's injunction to dispense only conservative measures to avoid any impression of being a couple of lushes. We got on well and they accepted our offering with diplomatic good grace.

A few evenings later ribald singing floated up from below: 'Oh dear, What can the matter be, Three old ladies locked in the lavatory....' I was back at Helmstedt with two old ladies locked in the toilet of our food train to Berlin.

Win and Reg were a pair of hard drinking fun-seekers. We had a few sessions together after that and got to know Winnie's family: her father Charlie Leech and his wife and her siblings, one of whom was Captain Leech – 'Captain' being his Christian name rather than service rank.

Charlie Leech, an East Ender who insisted on addressing Sylvia as Slyvia, had originally earned a nice living making horses' nosebags until he realised that, with the coming of the automobile, he was in a shrinking market. It was the time of the First World War when one of the many commodities in short supply was linseed oil, an essential ingredient of linoleum, the equivalent of today's wall-to-wall carpeting.

Experimenting on his kitchen table with brown paper and other items, he finally came up with a floor covering which eliminated the use of linseed oil. He called it Leenoleum and it was still going strong when the Second World War ended, the business now being run by the rest of the family under the guidance of the aforementioned Captain.

A few years later Win and Reg took a fatal step too far, acquiring the licence of one of Brighton's seafront pubs and spending too much time on the customers' side of the bar counter.

After a few days Sylvia and I departed for a fortnight's post-demob second honeymoon at Coombe Martin in Devon during which we tramped along Woolacombe Sands in a howling gale. Sylvia wore the plastic raincoat I had bought her in Belgium for the first time. The wind ripped it to ribbons. Then it was back to work for both of us.

Others gradually drifted back from war service. Victor Gorringe was ahead of me, now installed as Editor of the *Evening Argus*, with John Chillman as Editor-in-Chief.

Frank Usher became the Gazette News Editor before departing to become a full-time author following the publication of a book 'Exit Without Permit' which he had written while serving in the RAF. He made a successful career writing under the name of Charles Franklin.

Syd Curtis, after a rough time in the Far East, became Crime Reporter of the *Argus*, of which Frank Loder was now Chief Reporter. John Corbyn, suffering from a broken marriage and health problems, was sent off as district reporter to Crowborough to recover from both afflictions. Later he returned to Brighton to join the Gazette staff where his younger brother Ernest was also now working as a sub-editor.

Percy Roberts had a more successful war than me; service in France, the Middle East and North Africa during which he reached the rank of Captain. When it ended he opted to stay on in the Middle East and joined the Egyptian Mail in Cairo. The following year he moved to the Mid-East Mail in Palestine as a reporter while doubling as undercover agent for the Palestine Police. But in1947 he returned to Brighton as a sub-editor on the *Sussex Daily News*.

In 1948 he moved to the *Liverpool Daily Post* but the same year made the far-reaching decision to take up the post of Editor of the Nigerian Citizen. He told me later: 'I had applied for the post such a long time before that I had almost forgotten about it.'

Most of us drifted off sooner or later. What surprised us all, I think, was how easily we slid back into journalistic mode. It was as if we had been away for a couple of weeks' vacation rather than six years.

I was in no hurry to move on. Sylvia and I were having too hedonistic a time to think about the future. Brighton was buzzing and the Gazette was creating a lot of interest and challenging the weekly high ground so long held by the rival *Brighton and Hove Herald*.

Besides general reporting, Sylvia continued her Gazette women's page while, as Gazette Chief Reporter, I began a signed gossip column. We soon became recognised as a couple, being invited around and developing some first-class contacts.

My return to the Gazette – the first week in June, 1946, while I was still officially in the Army – came just in time to report plans for Brighton's participation in Victory Week. My brother-in-law, Leslie Ellis, provided me with one story. He was now in command of HMS Pique, one of two minesweepers to be anchored off Tower Bridge during the celebrations and open to visitors. It wasn't all that far from the factory where once, while waiting to join the Royal Navy, he had learned the art of making ice cream wafers.

Following the celebrations he and HMS Pique joined other naval units in Iceland for an Arctic tour of duty. The war may have been over but for him there were still hazards ahead. But in 1947 he was posted to HMS Royal Arthur, a shore base at Corsham in Wiltshire. My sister and their three sons spent their summer holidays there, renting the local headmaster's house, my sister moving smoothly into the role of officer's wife.

My other brother-in-law, Bill Lewis, JP, was also a useful contact. He was chairman of Southwick Urban Council's housing committee and, in May, 1946, had been elected as the first Socialist member of West Sussex County Council.

His son, John, tells the story that when he arrived at County Hall, Chichester, for his first Council meeting he decided that as the lone representative of his Party he ought to occupy a front row seat. The most convenient was already occupied by a coat and hat which he promptly moved. Shortly afterwards their owner appeared and pointed out that it had been his seat since Heaven knows when. It isn't clear who won the argument but from this unpromising introduction sprang an unlikely lifelong acquaintanceship. On the one hand stood the privileged, dyed-in-the-wool Tory grandee in his castle, the Duke of Norfolk – for it was he who owned the hat and coat – and on the other Bill Lewis, the working class Socialist idealist from the back streets of Brighton.

Bill Lewis left the County Council in1949 after only three years – he probably felt he was swimming against too strong a Right wing current – but the two continued to meet at various civic meetings. The Duke, whose many titles included that of Earl Marshal of England and Lord Lieutenant of Sussex, sent Bill complimentary tickets to race meetings – the Duke was a racecourse steward – and other sporting and social events with which he was officially associated. When Bill Lewis died in 1975 at the age of 71, the Duke was among the mourners. He told John Lewis he was there because 'I don't respect your father's politics but I do respect your father.'

In those post-war years Bill Lewis had many other interests apart from his duties as a magistrate and Southwick councillor. In 1944 he had left Southwick Power Station to become full-time district secretary of AEU 23 Division. A year later he was appointed to the Board of Visitors of Lewes Prison, a position he was to hold for the next twenty-five years. Finally, in the 1960s, he twice stood for Parliament on the Labour Party ticket in the no-hope Hove constituency. In 1947 he gave up his trade union position to join the Brighton engineering firm of Allen West, where my brother had earlier served his apprenticeship, as assistant works administration and safety officer.

Bill's son John, after leaving Worthing High School, followed him into engineering and membership of the AEU, quickly becoming contemporary chairman of the Youth Section of the same 23 Division. But later he was to move to the other side of the negotiating table as he rose up the management ladder, finally becoming Operations Director of a large national company with responsibility for its extensive labour force and factory installations.

Also in 1947 my brother Reg gave up lorry driving and started his own taxi business, at the same time taking up a new, unlikely hobby – philately – in which he gained some local repute and built up a valuable collection. Over the following years my two sisters became pillars of the local Townswomen's Guild. In old pre-war terms the family was moving out of the working class and into the middle class but such clear-cut definitions were to become meaningless over the next half century.

As a reminder of our working class roots my father Owen died in August, 1947, at the age of 75, a victim of throat cancer, attributable no doubt to his life-long addiction to his beloved wrack of ancient briar pipes.

To my great regret my six Army years, followed by my self-centred concentration on re-establishing my journalist credentials, robbed me of the chance to talk with him on a mature level and explore an affinity which I believe existed between us but which was never articulated. He was born in an age and into a social system in which he had no real chance. I still have a feeling of guilt in distancing myself from him.

Following the war and the easing of newsprint rationing, newspapers flourished again, ratching up massive circulations unobtainable forty years later. Television and later the Internet were yet to mount their challenge.

Abroad more conflicts were already stirring. There was a world food shortage and a massive refugee problem. The 'Iron Curtain' was descending across Eastern Europe and the trial of Nazi war criminals continued at Nuremberg. America detonated the first peacetime atom bomb, the United Nations held its inaugural session in London, Japan turned to democracy, civil war broke out in China and the USA initiated the Marshal Plan for massive aid to Britain and the Continent. Proposals for four-Power control of Berlin dragged on. But plans for re-establishing a democratic system in West Germany were well advanced and Churchill advocated a United States of Europe to ensure future peace. In the new Israel many Britons were killed in terrorist acts. The world in fact was spinning on its normal fractious axis.

Economically Britain was counting the cost of war with its reserves gone, an unsustainable international currency and an Empire it could no longer afford. Rationing spread from bread to furniture and from eggs to clothing. There were power cuts, road haulage workers went on strike and professional footballers threatened to do the same for a minimum wage of £7. Church leaders and politicians were worried by a tidal wave of divorce petitions as ex-servicemen and their wives, who had married in haste during the war, now repented in equal haste and not always in peace.

But there were positive signs. We were busy resurrecting our careers and rediscovering pleasure. The theatres, cinemas and dance halls were booming. Society was changing. Britain was embarking on the great nationalisation experiment with the coalmines, electricity, the railways and steel all targeted.

We looked forward to a Welfare State, a National Health Service free to all and the implementation of the 1944 Education Act which would bring opportunities to a new generation. It was a brave programme for any government to take on and almost suicidal given the economic circumstances of the day. The first steps in the inevitable dismantling of the old Empire began with plans to grant independence to India and Pakistan, an event which would be soured two years later with the assassination of one of its great architects, Mahatma Ghandi.

The most urgent need in those immediate post-war years was the provision of housing for the new baby-boom families. In June, 1946, I reported that by the end of the year Brighton Corporation would have completed 300 new houses and flats and 500 prefabs, repaired 25 bomb-damaged buildings and accommodated 1,000 people in 400 requisitioned houses.

The town's waiting list stood at well over 5,500 and was growing by 80 a week. To advance their claims some families resorted to sleeping in cars and tents. As housing committee chairman at Southwick, Bill Lewis would find brown envelopes stuffed with banknotes popping through his letterbox. He promptly handed them over to the Clerk to the Council, making sure the fact was registered.

The Gazette was published on Saturday mornings and the front and back pages weren't put to bed until 10.30 the night before. So we could run late news stories and even occasionally get a hard news scoop. We ran a piece boasting of our exclusives: 'Brighton Drive Against Impure Ices', 'Ghost Dog Eludes Capture', 'There's Danger on the Downs – Whose Job to Remove It?' and 'They're Burning Boots and Shoes At Brighton'.

There were more routine stories: the reopening of the Palace Pier and the Grand Hotel, summer heatwaves and summer gales, local elections, the Trade Union Congress came to town, over 2,000 signed Brighton's 'No Bread Rationing Petition'.

Brighton and Hove's first Regency Festival was patronised by Queen Elizabeth (later the Queen Mother) and George V's widow Queen Mary. The Gazette carried its first full-colour news picture of the Royals walking past cheering crowds at the Royal Pavilion.

Colour pictures of such quality – high tone fidelity and perfect register – were virtually unknown, certainly among the provincial press. It was a pioneering technical triumph which brought a number of tributes.

The Regency Festival, the precursor of the present day Brighton Festival, was an example of Sylvia and me working in harness. I quote from the Gazette: 'On this page we commence two eye-witness accounts of the visit, one an intimate study by 'Sylvia' of their Majesties' tour of the Regency Exhibition in the Royal Pavilion and the other by Gazette reporter Bob Hounsome who saw the Royal visit from the outside.'

There were so many show business celebrities around we were practically tripping over them. I met a 17-year-old Elizabeth Taylor, in town to promote National Velvet, and was fascinated by her extraordinary violet-iris eyes. Sylvia made a hit with Margaret Lockwood, Britain's leading female film star, and interviewed an up-and-coming 17-year-old named Petula Clark.

In the summer of 1947 the Boulting Brothers made Brighton Rock on the Race Hill and the Palace Pier, my boyhood playgrounds. It provided plenty of stories. The following January I attended the film's world premier at the Savoy Cinema. The film made a star of Richard Attenborough whom I got to know quite well during filming. Some fifty years later I wrote to him but maybe he had forgotten me.

In Brighton the Moss Empire-owned Hippodrome was doing capacity business with Crazy Gang shows and Ivor Novello-type musicals but was mostly used as a variety theatre. Many of the performers took to staying at the Salisbury Hotel on Brighton seafront, managed by a livewire Londoner, Vera Rawlings, and her husband Jimmy. They tipped us off about their guests and they got their publicity exposure – a mutually advantageous arrangement.

Later they emigrated to Calamayor in Majorca where Vera became known as 'The Duchess' among the British ex-pats. We visited them over many years until both died in their eighties.

There was a second variety theatre in town – the Grand in North Road. It had been leased, while the war was still on, by Albert Rose, a diminutive East End Jew, who had fought in the First World War and appeared at Collins Music Hall and other variety theatres.

He moved into the agency side of the business and then into advertising but vaudeville was in his blood and when the chance came to take over the Grand for a song he couldn't resist the challenge.

By 1946 he had cleaned up the place and salvaged its reputation. But battling against the big-name muscle of the Moss Empire forced him to promote up-and-coming artistes. Among those who later achieved fame were an art student/singer from Worthing named Alma Cogan, red-haired actress Jean Carson, magician David Nixon and Irish singer Josef Locke.

Then there was the knockabout, shadow boxing comedian who, after completing his act, ambled into Albert's office while I was there one night. He looked dejected and after a few words left again. 'He's thinking of quitting,' said Albert. 'But I think he's got a great future.' He had first appeared at the Grand as one of the turns in a show called 'New Faces Make News', booked sight unseen. It was so awful that Albert had to restructure it with new acts but he retained the knock-about comedian because of his raw talent.

Albert always claimed that he had helped the little comedian restructure his act, encouraging him to introduce new routines and the song which became his famous signature tune. Later he signed him up for pantomime at £20 a week and he became the hit of the show.

Finally the Bernard Delfont office took him in hand and put him on at the London Palladium as a supporting act to the American singer Alan Jones. Next day it was the little comedian who grabbed the headlines. 'A star is born' announced the *Daily Express*. A few days later, when Alan Jones was taken ill, the knockabout was promoted to top of the bill. His name was Norman Wisdom.

Despite all his efforts and the loyal support of his wife Ruby and their two children, Albert never made it at the Grand. There wasn't sufficient demand to support two variety theatres and the public preferred to see the established stars that only the Hippodrome could provide.

The end came in 1950 when the mortgagees foreclosed. Albert finished up in one room – bust – and the Grand Theatre ended up as a repro furniture manufacturing workshop. But Albert bounced back. Seven years later I chanced to meet him again in Mayfair. He had gone back to advertising, was making a good living and residing in North Audley Street.

Another twenty-three years later I also met Norman Wisdom again. He was making some charity appearances on the Isle of Wight and I was there to interview him. We talked briefly of Albert Rose and the early days at the Grand. Norman – Sir Norman now – and I survive but Albert Rose has passed on along with many of the other stars to whom he gave a helping hand.

Max Miller was still at the height of his popularity in those immediate post-war years. The general view was that he was very much under the thumb of his wife Kathleen. But Vera Rawlings told me – and mentioned back-up evidence – of Max spending occasional nights at the Salisbury with someone who certainly wasn't Kathleen. It would have made a national expose story but I never developed it – Vera was too good a contact to alienate and I respected her plea of confidentiality. When Max died in 1963 he left £7,000 to a certain Miss Ann Graham. The Salisbury is now The Brighton Hotel and the meeting place for the Max Miller Appreciation Society!

Max had a tight-fisted reputation but he was good company. He entertained us at length at a late night party we attended at the Black Rock home of Hamish Cochrane, a flamboyant character who appeared from nowhere and eventually disappeared again. He was a prime mover behind a plan to buy the Rechabite Chambers in Brighton –with money supplied by a Brighton and Hove 'Thank You' Fund – and convert it into a centre for ex-service organisations. It was called Churchill House but it never really took off. We were too busy rehabilitating ourselves and finding accommodation for our families.

Another topic peculiar to the times was the rise of the black marketeer profiting from the widespread shortages. At times in the Army I had indulged mildly myself. Now I was often writing expose stories on the same subject. There was the priority milk racket, restaurants taking back-handers for over-the-limit meals (a maximum price of 5s a person was in force at the time), dodgy, make-it-out-of-anything ice cream salesmen and new cars smuggled in from abroad to beat the two-year waiting list. Two new words entered the lexicon – 'spiv' and 'wide boy', along with kipper ties and wide lapels as exemplified by a young Arthur English and Dad's Army's Pte Walker.

My gossip column covered a wide spectrum – show business, politics, the holiday trade and the black market written in the 'Psst, have you heard' style. Arthur Helliwell was writing a similar column in The People with greater emphasis on the racketeers. He lived in Haywards Heath and eventually we met at his suggestion. It didn't occur to me that maybe it was an opening for me to apply for a job with The People. So I passed up the chance. I was enjoying myself working alongside Sylvia.

Les Cluett and I were also running an enterprise on the side producing a series of local year books and a couple of other magazines. They sold well and attracted sizeable advertising revenue. We thought we were going to make a fortune but we were under capitalised and after a couple of years or so gave up.

It was hard work and life was hectic. Then, early in 1947, Sylvia decided we should start a family and she quickly became pregnant. All went well for three months until one night I woke up to find her in a terrible state. She was having a miscarriage. It was a 999 case and she spent several days in hospital recovering. But both physically and psychologically she recovered remarkably quickly and we were soon back working together.

By mid-Summer she was ready for another try. Almost the same thing happened but forewarned the doctor ordered her to bed and pumped Vitamin E into her.

As the pregnancy advanced we realised we were not best placed to cope with a baby; third floor up, a shared bathroom and no space for a pram, not to mention a lack of capital. How did we have so little regard for the practicalities of parenthood?

Thankfully Charlie Leech provided a stopgap solution by offering us the basement flat at his house in Old Steine. It was far from ideal. It had a bath but the bath had no taps. The house was also in a terrace of authentic Regency houses on the holidaymakers' route to the beach and. Sylvia and I would arrive home and plough through discarded cigarette cartons, ice cream tubs and chocolate wrappers in our basement forecourt.

The house was next door to a Lyons teashop. A yard and store shed at the rear of the basement were a popular haunt of street-wise mice which I spent half my leisure time chasing ineffectually with a hammer.

Locally, Winston Churchill was granted the Freedom of Brighton and the Corporation battled with the War Office over the ownership of Stanmer Park, former seat of the Earls of Chichester. The Council won, the 5,000-acre estate was incorporated into the borough and earmarked as the location for the future University of Sussex. It symbolised my vision of better educational opportunities for our children and grandchildren.

Brighton continued to throw up colourful characters. Apart from the show business world, bowler-hatted Harry Cowley was still crusading, Lewis Cohen (later Lord Cohen) emerged as the Socialist founder of the Alliance Building Society (now Alliance & Leicester plc) and the Duke of Norfolk and his intelligent wife, the former Lavinia Strutt, were prominent on the social and charity scene. Another was a musician setting up his own professional band, to whom I gave some publicity. His name was Ken Lyon. His success was blighted ten years later when his 12-year-old elder son, Keith, was knifed to death as he walked across Happy Valley on the Downs above his home. The murder was never solved even after the case was re-opened with an anniversary appeal in 2001.

Then there was Gordon Langley Hall. Les Cluett was also editor of the Sussex country weekly, the *Southern Weekly News*. It still relied heavily on contributions from local correspondents. Gordon Langley Hall became one of them and we began receiving a stream of perceptive stories emanating from the otherwise small slumbering East Sussex town of Heathfield. His contributions were always well written and newsworthy. One wondered at Heathfield concealing so many reportable events.

Sylvia and I met him later when he moved to Brighton and shared a bed-sit with his boyfriend, an ex-Canadian soldier. He was clearly homosexual but subsequent events suggested things were rather more complicated than that. We met a few times, the last occasion being at our flat in Old Steine when he and his friend called at an inconvenient moment. Sylvia was starting her contractions, a female condition with which they were clearly unfamiliar. Afterwards Gordon emigrated to Canada where the astonishing part of his life began.

We realised he was a romancer. He always insisted on giving his date of birth as 1937 but when we met him in 1948 he was certainly older than 11 – more like 21. He was the illegitimate child of Margie Hall, member of a former well off but now somewhat impoverished Heathfield family. His father, Jack Copper, was chauffeur-handyman to the bohemian Vita Sackville-West and her husband Harold Nicholson and he spent much of his childhood at their home, Sissinghurst Castle, over the border in Kent.

His grandmother, Nellie Hall, largely raised Gordon and on her death he took over her role as correspondent to the *Southern Weekly News*.

From Brighton he left for Canada to join a distant relative who was killed in a car crash before his arrival. I next heard of him living on a Red Indian reservation in Canada, where he wrote his first book 'Me Papoose Sitter'.

Later, while working as a journalist in New York, he was adopted by a distant aunt, the fresco painter Isabel Whitney, and turned to writing more books (he had twenty-two published in the end). When Isabel died in1962 his legacy is said to have made him a millionaire and he moved to Charleston. There he began a sex-change course of surgical and hormonal treatment, started dressing as a woman and changed his name to Dawn Langley Hall.

At the same time he met and fell in love with a 22-year-old black motor mechanic, John-Paul Simmons, half his/her age, and outraged conservative Charleston society by announcing plans to marry. Ten months later Dawn claimed to have entered hospital under an assumed name – because of death threats – and given birth to a 7lb girl, Natasha. The sex-change hospital and the gynaecologist who had attended Gordon's own birth questioned the validity of the claim. But Dawn and Natasha, along with Natasha's own daughter, were still together twenty-four years later, living on the shores of the River Hudson. By then John-Paul Simmons was in a mental institution.

CHAPTER 12

The Babies Arrive and Fleet Street Beckons

A few hours after our last sighting of Gordon Langley Hall Sylvia gave birth, in the early hours of 23 May, 1948, to our first daughter, whom she named after Rosalind (*'Then we shall be news-cramm'd'*) of As You Like It.

The birth took place at the Sussex Maternity Hospital at the insistence of the Matron, Miss E.B.Hyslop, one of Sylvia's Women's Page contacts. Several telegrams arrived from a sundry collection of cinema managers, departmental store heads, a hotelier or two, the local head of the British Red Cross and the Mayoress of Brighton.

Rosalind, a forward baby, walked at ten months and showed increasing liveliness as night time approached. We had no idea about baby raising and followed the recommendation of one elderly relative by placing a wrapped penny over the navel – a surefire way, we were told, of ensuring cosmetic perfection. But getting old-style towelling nappies to fit tightly was a skill that escaped both of us. Rosalind's nappies suffered from perpetual droop.

Parenthood coincided with new signs of peace. Eros returned to Piccadilly Circus, Christian Dior introduced the New Look, Princess Elizabeth married Prince Philip, Edinburgh held its first Festival and the 'Austerity' Olympic Games were held in London under the banner: 'The Important Thing in the Olympic Games is Not Winning but Taking Part'. Rosalind's birth also coincided with the establishment of Communist rule in China and the start of the Cold War with Russia. As usual not all the world was at peace.

Sylvia continued working full-time (we needed the money). My mother came to help and she and Sylvia became increasingly attached to each other. We also recruited a part-time help. At other times we would take the baby with us on assignments. One afternoon we at last met Vera Lynn at the Salisbury Hotel. She was enchanted by Rosalind and began bouncing her up and down on her lap. It was all too much for our nappy pinning standards. Suddenly the penny came adrift and we all watched mesmerised as it rolled slowly across the floor.

By June, 1949, life for Sylvia and I became more complicated. The old wives' tale that breast-feeding mothers can't conceive has no gynaecological foundation. On 22 June, 1949, 13 months after Rosalind was born, our second daughter, Alison, arrived – this time at a private nursing home. When Sylvia's contractions started we casually caught the trolleybus there!

Alison was a more placid baby but even so it was like having time-lapse twins and everything was in short supply. There was no maternity leave or benefit, disposable nappies and automatic washing machines belonged to the future and we had two extra mouths to feed. Clearly, Sylvia would have to give up full-time work although she continued her women's page and the Gazette children's column for a time.

When Alison was only a month old another chance appeared to move to Fleet Street. I had written a story about a Burma Reunion for those who had served in the Far East during the war. It was a fairly routine story but it was seen by Frank Owen, the editor of the *Daily Mail* and a Burma Reunion enthusiast. He sent me a hand-written letter – which I still have – congratulating me on the piece. 'It is accurate and friendly to everyone concerned and in revealing the reason for Percy Thompson's generous act it is dramatic'. (Percy Thompson having donated £2,000 to kick-start the first reunion). 'A fine piece of journalism. Come and see me one day', he wrote.

The letter was dated 20 July, 1949. I marvel that I didn't grab the chance. It wasn't until 12 August that I bothered to reply and another fortnight after that before I turned up at Northcliffe House off Fleet Street. Frank Owen was busy as editors always are; all shirtsleeves, broadband braces and tie adrift. But he found time to spend a good half-hour talking about my background and about journalism. I had plenty of opportunity to ask for a job and I have no doubt he expected it. Why, then, didn't I seize the chance? How different a course our family life might have taken.

Maybe I was enjoying life in Brighton too much. Or maybe there was still that lingering sense of self-doubt. Then again, I wouldn't be 30 until the following October and the start of another five-yearly cycle. Perhaps my guardian angel decreed that further development must wait until then; and so it proved.

At Christmas I was approached by Leonard Knowles, then both a Labour member of Brighton Council and Industrial Correspondent of *The Star*, the national evening paper. Would I like to join the staff? Now the time was right and so was the salary. The deal was clinched in the office of the editor, A.L. Cranfield. The starting salary: £655 a year.

I was to be the paper's staff reporter based in Brighton and covering Sussex; the best of all worlds. I like to think Leonard Knowles suggested me, out of the local reporters available, on journalistic merit. But was there an ulterior motive?

Leonard was one of those journalists from whom I had learned my trade in the Golden Fleece before the war, when he represented both *The Star* and its morning sister paper, the Liberal News Chronicle. Now, though based in London, he still lived in Brighton.

He was a complex character, pompous and a little intimidating but with a soft centre. Politically, he had started out as a Liberal then crossed to Labour during the time I knew him, standing, unsuccessfully, for the Party in Brighton Pavilion constituency at the1945 General Election. Ultimately, when the Labour Party was in the grip of the militant left, he joined the Conservative majority on the Council and became its leader. Yet he had an impractical side. He always rented his various properties and never sought the financial security which house purchase and adequate savings would provide.

My starting date on *The Star* was 1 January, 1950. It was the beginning of a renewed exodus from the *Evening Argus* editorial department. Among the departures was the film critic, the late Peter Black, whose fearless opinions sometimes caused apoplexy among the local cinema managers. He joined the *Daily Mail* and became its television critic — many would argue still the most gifted yet to emerge. Another to leave was Derek Granger, the highly respected theatre critic and dream of a writer, who moved to Granada TV and went on to produce several celebrated programmes, including Brideshead Revisited and many episodes of Coronation Street.

Of the Gazette staff, Jim Pegg, as already reported, became a sports sub on the *Daily Telegraph* and *Sunday Times*. Ernie Corbyn went to Reveille, then a widely read magazine and became Managing Editor. He also had a book published – 'All Along The Line'. Tony Chapman, who followed me as Chief Reporter, also joined Reveille as chief sub. Then there was Syd Curtis who left to join the *Evening Standard*, also as Brighton correspondent.

Our Regency basement flat was no place to cope with two babies and my move to *The Star* coincided with our being allocated Council accommodation in one of a stretch of new bungalows high up overlooking the South Downs. Because of our income we were charged the full economic rent without subsidy and found ourselves among middle-rank professionals. Our immediate neighbours were a police inspector, William Tapsell, and his wife, Penny, who had two daughters roughly the same age as our own two. Our families would continue to weave in and out of each others' lives over the succeeding years. It was in their home, too, that I watched television for the first time, the flickering, black and white image of the FA Cup Final on a tiny screen, without realising that in time this new medium would reshape newspaper journalism.

One drawback was our remoteness from shops and other facilities, especially when pushing two babies around in a large twin pram. But there were also advantages. At last we had a bathroom with taps and even central heating.

My new job warranted the purchase of a car. All I could afford was a 1935 Austin 12/4 belonging to the veteran days of running boards, louvred bonnet flaps, starting handles and a throttle lever on the steering wheel. It had been a taxi, had seen better days and cost me £100. Yet it defied snowdrifts and below freezing temperatures while parked on the edge of the Downs. Had I held on to it, it would have fetched a handsome profit when veteran cars became collectables.

Wartime rationing remained in force. There were power cuts and strikes and in September, 1949, the Government was forced to devalue the pound by 30 per cent. But it pressed ahead with nationalisation and the concept of free care from the cradle to the grave was born. Sylvia and I duly collected our subsidised ration of dried baby milk and orange juice.

Nine days after I joined *The Star* Clement Attlee called another General Election. He scraped back with a majority of five and survived for only twenty months before being supplanted by a Conservative Government led by Winston Churchill, now 77 years old.

Joining *The Star* meant a change of routine. Work started early with phone calls to police and emergency services for any overnight stories.

Around 10 am I met up with Syd Curtis, now with the *Evening Standard*, and Bob Chapman, representing the *Evening News*, who later became Science Correspondent of the Sunday Express. Together we attended a morning briefing by Detective Chief Superintendent Charlie Ridge, head of Brighton CID, on the latest activities of the area's criminal element. In fact it was not so much a briefing as the tossing of morsels of information of the barest kind. The police generally still regarded the Press with suspicion but there was also an indefinable undercurrent. Everyone was impeccably polite and Charlie Ridge was positively unctuous.

When, in 1951, Charlie went on a senior officers' course at the Police College at Ryton-on-Dunsmore he asked me to let him have some ideas on Press-Police relations. I received a letter from him at the College thanking me for 'the very great and splendid effort you have made on my behalf....I am in full agreement with most of what you say.' He intended to read my notes out to his colleagues during a discussion period and promised to buy 'the Boys' (i.e. we three musketeers) a round on his return. But when he did return our Press briefings followed much the same morsel-tossing routine.

Stories frequently required pictures and I teamed up with Freddie Wackett, a dream of a cameraman who had served as a war photographer in South-East Asia on the staff of Lord Mountbatten. We remained good friends and I used his services off and on almost until his untimely death from cancer just as he was about to retire.

I continued in Brighton for two years. Few of my cuttings of the period have survived and many of the stories were pretty routine stuff. But two stand out.

Around Christmas, 1950, I happened to meet Kate Hemsley over lunch. At the time she was working as a 'hello girl' at the manually operated Brighton Telephone Exchange. She told me that the Brighton Medical Officer of Health and his team had visited the exchange that morning and ordered the staff to be vaccinated immediately by their GPs against smallpox. It was an emergency. One of their colleagues, Elsie Bath, had gone down with the disease.

The story needed checking out but I caught the late edition and the authorities realised they would have to go public. So I not only had an exclusive but I had the satisfaction of bringing the case into the open; or perhaps the credit for that should really go to Kate, one of the first five members of the public to be told of the outbreak.

On 17 December the medical fraternity realised they faced a serious outbreak when a Brighton taxi driver was admitted to Bevendean Isolation Hospital and diagnosed with the disease. They then confirmed that his daughter, the girl from the telephone exchange, who was in the same hospital awaiting diagnosis, was also a victim.

The source of the outbreak was traced to the girl's boyfriend, an RAF pilot, who had flown home from India. What dramatised the outbreak was the popularity of a film, 'Panic In The Streets', which was showing at the cinemas. It centred on the search by public health officials for a drifter who, unknown to himself, was carrying the bubonic plague and infecting contacts as he moved around.

In addition, the Brighton outbreak, the first smallpox case for many years, suddenly highlighted the greater danger of tropical diseases being brought to Britain. In contrast to slower sea voyages, rapid air travel meant that carriers could arrive before the incubation period had elapsed and the disease had manifested itself.

By the time the Brighton outbreak was identified a large number of people had already been in contact and possibly infected. Apart from the telephone exchange women – two more of whom were struck down – there were the taxi driver's passengers. The laundry handling his household washing had to be closed and nearly 2,000 customers contacted. One of the laundry staff, as I remember, was a Sunday School teacher, creating a further link in the chain.

With nurses and other staff and patients at risk, Bevendean Hospital was sealed off. Two patients had attended weddings so that brides and grooms and their guests had to be contacted. A greengrocer's shop in Downs Terrace became involved through a couple of nurses. All the greengrocer's customers were rounded up, ration books posing a further source of infection. The chain of contact spread. Some local travellers to London were treated like pariahs and there were rumours of panic on the streets of Brighton and neighbouring Hove which had also become involved. When the taxi driver died, undertakers and crematorium staffs refused to handle the body or coffin and health department staff had to take over.

I could understand their apprehension. I had to circulate freely to gather news of the outbreak. And right in the middle of it Sylvia and I woke up one morning to find our two daughters smothered with spots. Panic. In no time we had the MoH, Dr Rutherford Cramb, and his team in our bungalow carrying out inspections and tests. The diagnosis was chicken pox but it sure gave us a fright.

By the time the outbreak was halted 127,000 people in Brighton and Hove had been vaccinated. The number of victims was limited to thirty-five, of whom ten died. It was considered a textbook operation. On 1 February, 1951, the first nine nurses walked arm-in-arm out of Bevendeam Hospital after thirty-four days and the building was completely evacuated so that it could be disinfested. The eighty-five staff were given fourteen days' leave.

That same year brought the Festival of Britain, the end of petrol and soap rationing and wartime identity cards. In October the Labour Government was ousted and replaced by the Conservatives under Churchill's leadership.

Another important story during my time in Brighton was the case of an American hypnotist, Ralph Slater, the first stage hypnotist, I believe, to be sued by one of his 'victims'. He appeared at Lewes Assizes accused of negligence, breach of contract and assault by a 23-year-old shop assistant, Diana Rains-Bath, one of the volunteers to be hypnotised by him on the stage of the Brighton Hippodrome. Backed by her father, Major J.G.Rains-Bath, the girl was claiming damages. She alleged that Slater had treated her roughly and that she had been miserable and frightened for weeks after the show.

The Star made it the front page lead on each of the three days of the hearing. Covering it was a two-handed job and Tom Watson joined me from head office.

Slater lost the case. As a hypnotist and an American he was on to a hiding. Miss Rains-Bath was awarded £1,000 damages for negligence, £25 for assault and £107 special damages, a total of £1,132, plus costs.

The Ministry of Labour cancelled Slater's work permit, forcing him to abandon three scheduled shows. I got a good interview with him at his hotel the following day and won kudos from *The Star* newsroom.

He was in bad shape but he subsequently appealed and the Court of Appeal set aside the £1,000 negligence and £107 special damages. They gave leave for application to be made for a fresh trial and the matter dragged on to the following December when Miss Rains-Bath dropped her re-trial option. She ended up with only £25 assault damages. A bitter Ralph Slater was ordered to leave the country. As so often happens in such cases the only winners were the lawyers.

There was one other case of personal interest during my Brighton stint. Les Cluett was suddenly hauled before the magistrates. Out of consideration for any of his surviving relatives I refer to his offence euphemistically as a transgression into female sensitivities. I knew that he was something of a womaniser but he had now overstepped the accepted limits. He was heavily fined and his career in Brighton was over. He decamped to his native Poole in Dorset. But our association had not yet run its course.

Soon after the Slater trial I moved to *The Star* head office in Bouverie Street, a turning off Fleet Street. My replacement in Brighton was to be Leonard Knowles. In a letter to me he wrote 'in confidence, and whatever you may hear elsewhere, the idea is to tighten up the general matter of <u>news administration</u> (his underlining), etc. Although after eleven years of going up and down (to London) it will make things easier for me...the change was not, I can assure you, of my seeking.'

I didn't know what to make of it and still don't, especially as I find among my souvenirs, a letter from the Deputy Editor, Charles Carrdus, 'noting that you would like to join the Head Office when we start the re-organisation'. I can't even remember asking! So was Leonard protesting too much? Was he being demoted? Had I so impressed or maybe disappointed Head Office that they wanted me in London at all costs? But I went and lasted the course.

Leonard was getting on a bit and was a member of the Town Council so the move suited him, although I'm not sure how I would have fitted in council work with staff work.

There was no way I could afford to move the family to the London area so I simply stated that I would continue living in Brighton – after all the editor, A.L.Cranfield, also lived there! It said something that the company agreed to pay my train fare. It was only 4s 5d daily return on the workman's train when I started but fares climbed steeply by forty per cent over the next seven years. So the agreement made a vital difference to my income.

Sylvia was now pregnant with our third daughter. Working in London meant that I could no longer afford to keep a car. It left Sylvia marooned, pregnant, with two small daughters and without my presence for several hours a day. A solution was needed.

I was also no longer able to visit the remote West Sussex village of East Marden where my father was born. Only two Hounsomes now lived there. One was Lucy Hounsome, daughter of my father's brother Harry. The other was Aunt Lily who had returned to East Marden when Harry's wife died in childbirth.

Cousin Lucy had followed a common practice of staying on at the village school, becoming a monitor and then an unqualified teacher. When the school was earmarked for closure in 1945 – 100 years after its foundation – she was given leave to attend the Bishop Otter teacher training college in Chichester. She qualified and became a teacher at Westbourne infants' school, a few miles from East Marden, until her retirement. I had to wait until my own retirement before taking up the family history again. But throughout the intervening years it remained very much in my mind.

On the international stage there was rioting against white rule in South Africa and the rise of the Mau Mau in Kenya. Eisenhower was re-elected President of the USA while at home Britain tested its first atom bomb and Parliament voted for equal pay for women.

As the new boy at *The Star* head office, my contributions were limited to down-page stories and stock overnights. I must have been doing something right, however, because while on holiday in November, 1952, I received a telegram from the office: 'Congratulations Stop. Good Overnight. Star News Room'. I have no record of the overnight but it must have been something special.

That particular holiday was special for another reason – Sylvia gave birth to our third daughter, Susan, late in the evening of Sunday, 16 November.

She had opted to have the baby at home and while she screamed and cursed the midwife – husbands didn't attend the birth in those days – I listened in the sitting room and vowed never to put her through that again. But women seem to have a built in psychological trip-wire when it comes to maternity; a remarkable sense of certainty and fortitude before the event and an amnesiac post-natal condition which wipes out memory of the labour pains, all necessary for maintaining the reproductive urge. By morning Sylvia was sitting up in bed nursing the baby with a satisfied smile. Our other two daughters clambered aboard while I cooked breakfast and joined them; unhygienic but marvellous for family bonding.

Early in 1953 we were surprised to discover that Sylvia's father had somehow managed to buy a terraced house to safeguard his own future. The Council house where he lived with 'Auntie' Jess was in her name and he had no claim on the tenancy should anything happen to her.

When the ground and first floor of the house fell vacant, we moved in. Now there were nearby bus routes, local corner shops, a public park and a school. There were disadvantages – no proper bathroom, no access to the garden and no electric power or other mod cons – but we struggled on.

The 1950s may have been the decade of post-war consolidation and stabilisation but rich it certainly wasn't. The annual average wage was

£320 and, although I was bringing in substantially more than that, we could afford few frills – a week's holiday on a Sussex farm, on which we also took my mother, was the height of our luxury. But we were happy and I was making progress on *The Star*.

A minor breakthrough came one morning in 1953 when the rush was on to fill the front and back pages of the first edition. Two cows were found improbably wandering in Hainault High Street in Essex. A quick call to the local police fleshed out the details but I decided to embellish them a little.

I quote: 'When a policeman on patrol in Hainault saw two sloe-eyed females ambling forlornly along the High Street he decided that, if only for their own good, they should be taken into custody.

'They were obviously lost. So he rang the PDSA Sanatorium at Ilford. Which wasn't an odd thing to do for the females were two black and white Friesian cows. Mirabel and Pansy are still at the Sanatorium waiting to be claimed. With a spacious meadow in which to graze and a roomy stable for sleeping, they are taking the whole episode with a placid calm – it's nice to get away from all those other girls for a while.

'The Sanatorium staff and fellow inmates too, have accepted the new arrivals in a fraternal if mercenary spirit. For Mirabel and Pansy are paying for their keep by yielding an average three gallons of milk a day......'

A fairly trivial piece but it caught the eye of the legendary Chief Sub (and later Assistant Editor), 'Jock' Black, who came bustling in to the reporters' room to congratulate me; which was no mean accomplishment. 'Jock', who could pack more expletives into a single sentence than any other person I have ever met, was normally stinting in his praise, a person whose right side was the place to be on.

The next break came when I was sent off to Edgware Road, Marylebone, to cover what appeared to be a minor bus collision. In fact it had crashed into two shops, killed two people and injured twenty others. For some reason I got a beat on it and it made the front page lead – my first since reaching London I think.

The third break came on 2 June, 1953, the day of the Coronation of Elizabeth II. I was given the comparatively minor job of standing among 30,000 schoolchildren lining Victoria Embankment on the Royal procession route to Westminster Abbey. Again I quote: 'I stood on the banks of the timeless Thames today and watched the dawn of a new era....I saw a young Queen who will lend her name to an age, drive to her Coronation through the cheering ranks of those who will shape that age.

'Here, together in one symbolic tableau of colour and jubilation, I saw the young Elizabeth and her New Elizabethans – the children who will grow up and find their destinies before her reign is out.....'

It was fulsome stuff perhaps but what the occasion demanded. And it earned me my first by-line. I stood among the girls of Aylesbury School, Bromley, and quoted one of them, Teresa Stone of Bickley. What kind of destiny did they, and particularly Teresa Stone, find I wonder?

Nationally and internationally 1953 was quite a year. Stalin died and so did the matriarchal Queen Mary, wife of George V. The Korean War ended and the European Union was formed. Princess Anne was born and stiletto heels were inflicted on us.

One big story on which I got a front-page exclusive, was the delivery of a letter to the Piccadilly home of Mrs J.R.Bassett from her son Guy Burgess. He was the British diplomat who had disappeared with colleague Donald Maclean two and a half years earlier just before both were exposed as Russian spies.

I managed to get an exclusive interview with her and her husband, Lt-Col Bassett. They refused to reveal the full contents of the bulky hand-written letter, but were convinced it was genuine, even though it was posted in London, presumably by a go-between.

The Burgess-Maclean saga was still rumbling on and this was the first indication that Burgess was alive. So it was an important story, the letter indicating that both men were well and living in Russia (later confirmed when the 'third man', Kim Philby, also defected). Today's tabloids would have paid handsomely for the Burgess letter but *The Star* wasn't into chequebook journalism.

CHAPTER 13

Buying a House with 2s 7d

The following year, 1954, brought the Vietnam War, more strikes and the breaking of the four-minute mile barrier by Roger Bannister. But for me there was a more pressing domestic development. It came one afternoon when Bernard Murphy, our larger-than-life Irish news editor, who had made his name reporting the Nuremburg war crimes trials, called me into the Newsroom. Sylvia was on the phone. The call over, he must have seen the look of panic in my eyes. 'Everything all right?' he asked. 'My wife's just bought a house,' I replied, 'and I've got two shillings and sevenpence (about 13p) in the bank.' Sylvia had a more intuitive, cavalier view of life than me. I left early that day to sort things out.

It was a nice little house: only twenty-eight years old, semi-detached, six rooms, bathroom, long garden with an apple tree and a hop plant climbing over the potting shed. It was situated on a large estate developed in the Twenties and Thirties on the back of the old village of Patcham on the outskirts of Brighton.

Sylvia had beaten the sale price down from £2,050 to £1,850 – barely enough to buy a clapped-out second hand car today but a small fortune in those days. We negotiated a 95 per cent mortgage but that still left a deposit of £93 plus legal and incidental costs – a total of £250 I reckoned; and I had 2s 7d.

My accommodating bank manager – a genre still existing in those days – agreed to lend me £100, secured by the surrender value of a small life policy and *The Star* offered to lend me £150 interest free for eighteen months. We were a property-owning, middle-class family at last!

It was also my 35th year and the start of another quinquennial cycle.

It was certain to bring a new twist or two but began unpromisingly when our eldest daughter, Rosalind, was rushed to hospital in a coma after a vicious streptococcus infection. It was a fraught few days but fortunately she made a full recovery. One of the happiest and most fruitful five-year periods for the whole family followed.

My career on *The Star* continued to blossom. I was now writing mainly celebrity gossip stories for the Diary page, behind-the-news features, off-beat stories – frying an egg in a Friday heat-wave on the pavement of Friday Street was typical – and tongue-in-cheek humorous stories – the wedding of one of the cast of the Guys and Dolls musical written in the present-tense Bronx style of Damon Runyon ('I am in London today and am walking round and about Harry the Horse's place in Harley Street when who comes along but Harry in person. He has a dreamy look on his puss and is holding on to the arm of some doll I never see before...')

I was now also radio critic, amounting to a few paragraphs which I phoned over each morning from East Croydon station on my way to the office.

Scheduled air services were taking over the traditional role of ocean liners as the main form of trans-Atlantic crossing. They cut travel time from four days to a few hours and as a result more show business people were making the trip. I began interviewing them either at London Airport or at their hotels. In the case of 59-year-old Buster Keaton – 'the original dead-pan, sad-man' as I described him – I managed to extract a three hundred word story during a ten minute taxi journey across London with him and his 35-year-old third wife. Buster ranked up there alongside Charlie Chaplin and Harold Lloyd among the original Hollywood greats, learning early in life that he got his greatest laughs by never laughing himself.

London Airport – now Heathrow – was a more relaxed place in the mid-1950s. All buildings, many of them single-storey, wartime constructions, were sited round the periphery. There was no central terminal (although the first was opened during the period of my visits), no vast crowds, no armed police or security restrictions (airport bullion burglaries and plane hi-jacking hadn't yet been attempted). Arrival and departure procedures were fairly primitive with passengers crossing the aircraft aprons in the open. On one occasion, while awaiting the arrival of Glynis John from America, I intercepted Pandit Nehru, the then Prime Minister of India, as he ambled across the concourse on his way back to India and got an exclusive interview. It couldn't happen today.

I found that two enterprising journalists, realising the potential, had set up the first Airport freelance news agency which they later extended to Gatwick. I had last seen them at Gatwick, around the time of D-Day. For Mike Richardson and Bill Brennan, brother of Bernard Brennan, air correspondent and later news editor of the Sunday Express, had been fellow Mustang pilots with 168 Squadron.

Early air passengers whom I interviewed were John Wayne and Gina Lollobrigida, both staying at the Savoy Hotel. It was given to few journalists, I suppose, to interview Miss Lollobrigida in her bedroom.

When a four-week strike by electricians and engineers halted newspaper production in March, 1955, I caught later trains to London and one of my occasional travelling companions was John Chillman who had been superseded as Editor-in-Chief in Brighton by Victor Gorringe. He was now working for the Press Association. I was not in possession of the circumstances of his departure but it saddened me. He had given both Sylvia and me our chance in journalism. Another travelling companion was Leslie Holmes whom I had interviewed when he was one of The Two Leslies variety act (the other was Leslie Saroni). Then he had suddenly given up the stage and was now Circulation Manager on the News of the World.

One big story during the strike was the resignation of the ailing Sir Winston Churchill as Prime Minister. His successor, Anthony Eden, promptly called a General Election for May, the Conservatives winning with an increased majority of fifty-eight. But disaster for Eden was to follow.

With the newspaper strike over I was back on the celebrity beat. Meeting the stars never created an urge to join their rarified life-style or to move to London. Catching the train back to Brighton was like a journey back to reality; married life, three children and environmental reminders that I was still the slightly insecure son of a one-time shepherd boy and a domestic servant.

About this time I had a call from Tito Burns, one-time band leader now on the management side of showbusiness. He had a new singer, he said, who was going to be a sensation. Tito's reputation commanded respect and it would make an overnight Diary piece if nothing else. At his office, next door to the Windmill Theatre off Piccadilly Circus, he introduced me to Jane Hilliard. She had been born in Littlehampton but was working as a telephone exchange 'hello girl' in Bristol and singing part-time with a local band. She was 21 and a good-looking blonde. And that was it. Tito decided she needed re-branding with a new name. He suggested Janie; but how about a surname? It was a hot summer's day and I was dreaming of the Sussex countryside and East Marden village. 'Marden,' I said. 'How about Marden?' 'Fine,' said Tito and so Janie Marden was born, neither she nor the villagers to this day aware of the connection.

As it happened she went on to achieve fame throughout the 60s and 70s in top TV and stage appearance. She sang with Cyril Stapleton's Show Band, appeared in a West End H.M.Tennant show with Dora Bryan, was a vocalist in some of the Morecombe and Wise shows and was in constant demand.

Other Star assignments during 1955 ranged from the funeral of Sir Alexander Fleming, discoverer of penicillin, to a front page story on an £11,000 London bank raid. I interviewed Dr Edith Summerskill, then Chairman of the Labour Party, as she headed off with a Party delegation for Yugoslavia. I also ghosted a three-part series on the experiences of a Brighton housewife and mother, Mrs Betty Ashley, as a member of a National Assembly of Women delegation to Communist China.

In Britain a new postwar generation was rocking and rolling to the sound of Bill Haley and His Comets and with money to spend was seeking a new image, expressed particularly in the Teddy Boy tendency. The upper classes were continuing in their immutable way as I discovered at Henley Regatta. A call came from Bernard Murphy. 'Get down to Henley,' he said with some urgency. I was on a story in the East End at the time. 'The Russians are rowing at the Regatta for the first time,' he explained.

I rushed back to the office, phoned Sylvia ('Won't be home tonight'), grabbed a spare toothbrush and razor, got spare money from the cashier's office (no credit cards in those days) and headed for Paddington.

Henley-on-Thames was bulging with public school boys having cream teas with their proud parents and elderly former oarsmen wearing their old, too tight school blazers and caps; quintessential England. I booked the only remaining hotel room – the bridal suite at the Red Lion. Then I went in search of the Regatta secretary to bone up on rowing terms and to find out about the Russians.

There was no chance of speaking to them, they were brainwashed and guarded by an accompanying political commissar. So round to the tradesmen's entrance of their hotel to buttonhole the kitchen staff: 'What are they like, what have they ordered for breakfast?'

I phoned the story over next morning for the first edition. 'Stay on and let us have a follow-up story,' ordered Bernard Murphy. Which was just as well, as by then the Russians were threatening to withdraw because their boats were strike bound in London Docks. Later the Stevedores' Union released the boats, the Russians withdrew their withdrawal and they went on to win some of their races. *The Star* feature writer, Margaret John, had been taken ill. I was ordered to stay on a further day to provide a fashion story as well.

I knew even less about women's fashions than I did about rowing and if that wasn't enough the Press weren't allowed into the inner sanctum of the Stewards' Enclosure. I was forced to stand outside and ask the crème de la crème what they were wearing.

'Oh, you don't want to mention me,' they would say. 'OK,' I replied and turned away. 'Well, if you *must* know,' came the hurried rejoinder. So I found myself writing about Empire lines, organzas and satins and outrageous hats.

At quieter moments I liked to meet activists at London University Students' Union. It provided occasional stories but it also acted as substitute for the undergraduate life I never experienced. Similarly contact with the Central School of Speech and Drama sustained my interest in the theatre.

The Central School was enjoying a vintage period under the inspired leadership of the principal, Gwynneth Thurburn. It also moved from its cramped rooms high up in the remoter regions of the Albert Hall to a vacant theatre in Swiss Cottage. The students included such future giants of the theatre as Dame Judy Dench, Vanessa Regrave and the late, tragic Mary Ure.

Among those to whom I gave their first, brief Press mention was Wanda Ventham since she was a Brightonian like myself. She chose as her 'passing out' performance, if I remember correctly, an excerpt from Sally Bowles in 'I Am A Camera'. I followed her career with interest afterwards to the point where she became Rodney's mother-in-law in Only Fools and Horses.

I was continuing my stint as radio critic and on one occasion wrote something complimentary about that popular radio sitcom of the day, 'Life With The Lyons'. It featured the former Hollywood stars Ben Lyon, his wife Bebe Daniels and their two children Richard and Barbara. There was an interesting sequel later.

Throughout this period I had been working on our newly-acquired house. A lot of improvements were needed. There were no power points and the bathroom was fitted with a lethal, antediluvian gas geyser. There was no airing cupboard, the kitchen was a mess, the garden was overgrown and the roughcast exterior walls were a grimy white. But by 1956 the work was complete and loans repaid. We even acquired our first twin-tub washing machine, our first refrigerator (second hand, a gift from Ethel) and our first television set.

During the same period there were further family fragmentations. My brother-in-law, Leslie Ellis, who had been made up to Lieutenant Commander, found that, after waiting the required eight years, he had been passed over for further promotion. Slimming down following the war, the Royal Navy had a surfeit of Lieutenant Commanders. Leslie was expendable. His eldest son put it down to natural wastage. Sceptic that I am, I take the less charitable view that in the final throw the old school tie triumphed over the ability of an erstwhile lower deck rating whose mother wasn't even married.

So, at the age of 43, Leslie left the Navy and started a new career with Massey-Harris Ferguson (later Massey-Ferguson) the agricultural machinery manufacturers, firstly as Establishment Officer running their agricultural college and then in personnel management.

The family moved to Coventry and my mother chose to go with them, again a wrong choice on her part probably – she was now approaching 75 – because it meant moving to another area with which she had no association. But perhaps she felt she had no option.

In 1956 there were more visits to the airport and to hotels, interviewing celebrities from actresses to Football Pools jackpot winners.

As a boy I had at times sneaked into Stanmer Park on the outskirts of Brighton, then the private seat of the Earls of Chichester, in search of conkers. Now I met the Dowager Countess of Chichester, widow of the sixth earl, who had once lived there but now had a home in Chelsea. She was awaiting the arrival of her great-grandchildren, the 11-year-old ninth earl and his older sister together with their mother who lived in Argentina.

It had been a tragic era for the family. The sixth earl had died in 1926 and his elder son, the seventh earl, only nine days later. The eighth earl (the seventh earl's younger brother) was killed in a road accident in England in 1944 while serving with the Scots Guards, just fifty-three days before the birth of his son, the ninth earl. This quick succession of deaths – three in eighteen years – and the consequent drain in death duties had forced the family to surrender their beautiful 6,000-acre estate to Brighton Corporation.

I also nearly met Marilyn Monroe that year. I was among journalists waiting at London Airport, along with a swarm of sightseers and officials as she posed at the aircraft exit and swanned across the parking apron. She wore a form-hugging woollen beige dress, a matching trench coat and, despite the drizzle, designer sunglasses and clutched a bouquet (courtesy of the airline) and a sweater (courtesy of the manufacturers). Loping alongside her, clutching her arm and wearing a rictus smile suggesting he would rather be somewhere – anywhere – else was her bespectacled husband-of-a-fortnight, the distinguished playwright Arthur Miller. Also waiting to welcome them was Sir

Laurence Olivier, his wife Vivien Leigh and Mr Milton Greene, vice-president of Marilyn Monroe Productions, Inc (President Miss Monroe). Miss Monroe was contracted to make the film 'The Prince and the Showgirl' with Sir Laurence.

So inadequate were airport facilities for dealing with visiting VIPs in the 1950s that, as I wrote afterwards, 'At a press conference in an airport lounge a police bodyguard (a rare exception, that) stepped in to save the famous figure being flattened in the crush to less undulating contours'.

For the same reason we were led into a prefabricated staff canteen with a serving counter occupying the whole width of one end. Miss Monroe and Sir Laurence, with their partners, appeared on the other side of the counter. We were seated for a question and answer session. But someone broke rank and rushed up to the counter. There was a stampede as we all followed. I ended up nose tip to nose tip with Arthur Miller, trying to cock an ear to what Marilyn Monroe, trapped between the cheese rolls and ham sandwiches, was saying next to him. I was at least close at hand. What sort of story those less agile journalists behind us managed to lace together I have no idea.

After each question, there was a consultation between the two stars before Sir Laurence answered for Miss Monroe, who simply smiled beatifically. 'She says she is here for about 14 weeks,' explained Sir Laurence.

Had she seen a press conference like this before? 'She says it's very orderly,' replied Sir Laurence continuing his ventriloquist act.

'She is serious about Dostoevsky,' we learned for some obscure reason. 'She doesn't like using a microphone because it is an ordeal. All this is an ordeal.' So it went on.

Mr Miller watched his wife with some concern. Since we were nose tip to nose tip, I felt it incumbent to ask him something but 'Written any good plays lately?' seemed a touch impertinent. So I settled for 'What's it like being married to a film star?' Mr Miller with quiet tolerance replied, 'Well, of course, it's not like this every day, thank goodness.' That was my exclusive bit. With that they all exited left, shepherded by a police inspector, Miss Monroe and her new husband heading for a Georgian manor retreat hired for them in the Berkshire countryside. So I never did really meet Marilyn Monroe.

It wasn't a tranquil time for the Oliviers. Vivien Leigh suffered her second miscarriage three weeks later. The psychological effects of that and her fear that Olivier might have an affair with Monroe caused further tensions in an already tense marriage. In fact far from having an affair with Monroe, Olivier was driven to distraction by her tantrums, rudeness and disregard for shooting times. Instead he began an affair with Joan Plowright and it fell to me, shortly after Olivier and Leigh were divorced in1960, to write up the story of this one-time Scunthorpe schoolgirl who was to be his next bride.

Six years after her visit to England Marilyn Monroe, that haunted sex symbol, was dead. Vivien Leigh, herself 'a sexual dervish' according to her friend Margaret Leighton, took another lover but never ceased to love Olivier until she, too, died seven years later in 1967.

On another occasion, in 1956, I broke the news to Mrs Kitty Brasher at her Kensington home that her son Chris had won his appeal against disqualification in the 3,000 metre steeplechase at that year's Olympics. His gold medal was confirmed – the first for Britain in an individual track event in twenty-four years.

Also in the race was John Disley who later joined forces with Chris Brasher to establish and run the London Marathon. In 1957 John Disley married Star journalist colleague Sylvia Cheeseman who herself had run for Britain in two Olympic Games and gained a bronze in the women's 100 metre relay.

When I had to demonstrate a new type of security bag that set off a deafening hooting sound when snatched by a bandit, Sylvia acted as the stooge from whom I had to grab the bag and escape. The fact that I was then an unfit 39 and she was an Olympic sprinter lent a touch of absurdity to the enterprise.

The beat-the-bandit bag had been invented following a regular spate of snatched wages bags from messengers every Friday in the days when earnings were still paid weekly in cash. The snatchers still exist but now their targets are handbags and mobile phones.

In September, 1956, I was sent to Southampton to welcome Liberace, arriving aboard the Queen Mary on his first trip to England.

He had decided to travel in style, bringing his mother, brother George, sister-in-law and manager with him. They were met not only by a batch of journalists but a trainload of fans —mostly middle-aged, middle class women – and thousands more when his train pulled into Waterloo. It made the front page. Noel Coward was also aboard the Queen Mary and he and Liberace were among the last celebrities – and certainly the last as far as I was concerned – to cross the Atlantic by liner.

With all these celebrities the urgency was to get a story for the earliest possible edition. Full-page, in-depth interviews weren't my brief. I was after a scintillating gossip piece – three hundred words or so; some personal background, why one's quarry was in England and above all an angle, something to catch the reader's eye and preferably exclusive. Sometimes one was driven to desperate lengths, as when Diana Dors flew in after five months' filming in Hollywood. I was one of a battery of reporters waiting to meet her at London Airport. The story was the break-up of her marriage to her Svengali, Dennis Hamilton, and her alleged affair with Rod Steiger. She was seated on a chair in the open air with the Press boys semi-circled round her. I was slightly to her rear and I noticed this queen of glamour was wearing odd stockings, one with a seam, the other without.

So I began my story: 'Diana Dors flew into London Airport today wearing odd stockings and no wedding ring'. Well, it made an angle, a small exclusive touch. As the rest drifted away I quizzed her about the odd stockings. 'Have you ever tried dressing on an aeroplane?' she replied. An outsize topaz had replaced her wedding and engagement rings. 'A present from someone, I won't say who, about seven years ago, before my marriage,' she explained.

The transient nature of these encounters leaves only superficial memories of the stars: Elizabeth Taylor's violet eyes, John Wayne's laid-back, laconic style, Diana Dors' bubbly joie-de-vive, Marilyn Monroe's figure, Rita Hayworth's sheer beauty.

A newcomer to *The Star* in 1956 was Peter Brooks who brought me news of Bob Black. He had left the Press Association before the war to join the new *Evening Gazette* in Reading. He returned there after war service and, when the *Gazette* folded, set up a freelance news agency in the town along with two partners, Fred Radford and Henry Maude. Peter himself joined the agency and then moved on to *The Star*.

When the Reading agency partnership broke up, Bob moved back to Brighton with his family, as *Daily Express* correspondent, until 1965 when he was appointed Brighton Corporation's Publicity Officer. He died in 1987 aged 74, an old colleague sadly missed, to whom I owed a great deal; curious how our lives followed similar patterns, even to each having three children.

Another newcomer to *The Star* in 1956 was a replacement Editor to take over from A.L.Cranfield who had reached retirement age.

Ralph McCarthy had been Night Editor of the Manchester edition of The Star's sister paper, the News Chronicle. He was a good Editor with a tendency to have bright ideas without understanding the practical complications of translating them into column inches. He seemed to like my style so that, as time went by, I caught the full force of his immediacy approach.

One early story which drew his appreciation was an interview with the 85-year-old actor A.E.Matthews while he was rehearsing at Golders Green. I was gathering details about his ex-actress wife. Bow Street Magistrates had dealt with a summons against her for a parking offence and, in her absence, the mystery of her age had arisen. A policeman reckoned she was 30 but Mr Matthews was vague on the subject. 'She looks 24, could be 30 or is it 36....I shall have to ask her when she comes back. At present she's in Devon having a rest from me.'

Would it help if he remembered the wedding date? Before the war? 'Couldn't have been the Boer War,' he mused. 'Or was it?'

'It was quite a considerable time ago,' he admitted. 'It seems longer to my wife than it does to me.'

A copy of the marriage certificate finally gave the wedding as July 16th, 1940, and the bride as Patricia Lilian, aged 31.

If 1956 had been a vintage year for me the same was true in wider terms. Towards the end of the year the Prime Minister, Sir Anthony Eden, had colluded with the French and, it was suspected, the Israelis, in a co-ordinated invasion of the Suez Canal zone in response to the Canal's nationalisation by the new dictator of Egypt, Col Nasser. It was a major folly, incurring the wrath of the United Nations and alarm in the United States which threatened economic reprisals. There was an ignominious retreat, Eden's health collapsed and a month later he resigned, to be succeeded by Harold Macmillan. Whatever his achievements as Foreign Secretary and Prime Minister it is the Suez fiasco with which Eden will always be associated. Nearly 50 years later another Prime Minister seemed in danger of being similarly haunted by the reckless decision to go to war in Iraq.

Apart from the Suez fiasco, 1956 had seen the Melbourne Olympics, the re-election of Eisenhower as President of the USA, Russia's ruthless suppression of the Hungarian uprising and anti-occupation demonstrations in Poland.

Social mores were continuing to undergo change in Britain as illustrated by a feature I wrote early in 1957. It dealt with the efforts of the clumsily named National Council for the Unmarried Mother and Her Child. Illegitimate births, as they were still called, had already reached 30,000 in England and Wales and continued to bring shame and ostracism on most of the unfortunate mothers. In the contemporary climate I was allowed to use only the Christian names of the women I interviewed.

Rehabilitation wasn't easy. 'For the most part these women are not brazen hussies and their sense of shame is still one of the biggest factors to be overcome,' the Council's general secretary told me. How attitudes were to change over the next 40 years!

A cultured 30-year-old with a well-paid professional job told me, 'I have never been so hard up.' But she would never give up her baby son. How are they now, in the twenty-first century I wonder, she in her mid-70s, he in middle life?

Housing was a big worry. One girl I interviewed wrote to me later. She and a friend, both with babies, were sharing a single room. She wrote: 'Everyone encourages us to keep the babies. The big question is where? Every rented accommodation we try has a 'No Babies' reservation'.

On another assignment in 1957 I was sent to the Old Bailey to produce a 'colour piece' on the QC who was causing a stir as the senior counsel for the defence in the high-profile case of Dr John Bodkin Adams, an Eastbourne GP. Dr Adams was accused of murdering one of his many elderly patients, Mrs Gertrude Hullett, under whose will he was a substantial beneficiary.

The QC in question was Geoffrey Lawrence whom I had last encountered in Brighton 20 years earlier when he was a young barrister and I was a junior reporter. I was able to recall the comment of that old court reporter Pat Maguire: 'My boy watch that man, one day he will be a judge.' Now he was already Recorder of Canterbury. He had a magnetic oratorical style. 'Certainly no-one, other than his brothers (both also in the legal profession) can make such polysyllables as "cerebral" and "respiratory" sound more like something out of Keats', I reported.

Dr Adams was acquitted – another feather in Geoffrey Lawrence's judicial wig. It is known that a number of other elderly patients of Dr Adams died in suspicious circumstances, leaving him money in their wills. He may have been an earlier version of that later GP serial killer Dr Harold Shipman, though nothing was ever proved. Dr Adams was subsequently fined £2,400 for forging documents and prescriptions and was struck off the Medical Register, only to be restored in 1961. He resumed his practice in Eastbourne where he died peacefully in 1983 aged 84.

By way of contrast I next attended the third wedding of Jolie Gabor, mother of the three glamorous Gabor sisters – a collective Hungarian Rhapsody, one might say – bringing their combined number of marriages to thirteen. Daughter Eva was missing. She was still in California negotiating her third divorce.

Jolie's age? 'I believe she is 54,' daughter Zsa Zsa confided to me, 'but please make her 49.' Or should that have been 60? Jolie's latest husband – 'He came here and lost his freedom in a hurry,' explained Zsa-Zsa – was Count Edmond de Szigethym, described as 'a Hungarian freedom fighter'. He was also the thirteenth husband.

Another interview was with Hollywood star Jane Wyman, first wife of future US President Ronald Reagan, who flew in 'to see old friends and have a look round'. Then there was that suave comedy actor,

Wilfred Hyde White, at 54 arriving at London Airport with his new wife, glamorous 35-year-old American Ethel Drew.

There was no shortage of variety. Four features followed on 'The Changing Face of London' and a night out at Stonehenge to witness the Druids ceremoniously welcoming in the summer solstice.

That summer I also met Princess Joan Aly Khan (daughter of an earlier Lord Churston) at her Sloane Square home for her reaction to the news that the will of the third Aga Khan had nominated her son (and his grandson) Karim as his successor, thereby leapfrogging Karim's father. At the age of 19 Karim became the spiritual leader of twelve million Ismaili Moslems.

Long hours, the constant race against time and family commitments were taking their physical toll and two assignments during 1957 finally caused my body to rebel.

One Friday afternoon Bernard Murphy announced that I was to spend a week as a down and out in London – starting on the Monday; no option, no thought for preparation, another of McCarthy's instant action ideas. Four features were required.

On the Monday I turned up unshaven, wearing my gardening clothes, a motheaten scarf, string for laces and a distinct lack of enthusiasm. Murphy offered some encouragement. He knew a Roman Catholic hostel that offered free accommodation, except that it was closed for renovation.

Help came from a bowler-hatted City type who, with some hesitation, gave me sixpence in response to my pleading and two women volunteers in the Tothill Street WVS (now the RWVS) shop. At first they turned me down but as I limped off one chased after me. 'Come back a moment,' she said, 'we want to give you a little something. We aren't supposed to do it so don't tell anyone.' But it was too good a story to leave out. That was when I begged for the first time since incurring my mother's wrath for scrabbling for money beneath the Palace Pier.

The WVS ladies gave me a florin. With the City gent's sixpence and my 'starting out' 1s 7d I had enough for my first night's bed in the Great Peter Street hostel run by the Salvation Army (or Sally Army as it was known to the down and out fraternity). But there was another snag. I needed to produce some identification – and being undercover I couldn't do so. The man queuing in front of me was sympathetic. He passed me a crumpled document. 'Here, this will get you in,' he said. It was a railway warrant issued by Pentonville Prison for a man discharged a few days earlier. So now I was a jailbird.

Then I was in: a clean bed for the night, a twopenny cup of tea and a free breakfast in the morning. My first feature was building up nicely. Again, I couldn't help recalling those boyhood years when I watched the inmates of Brighton Workhouse begging from racegoers and worried that I might one day be forced to join them.

My fellow guests at the hostel ranged from rheumy old men and prison lags to Hungarian refugees and provincial artisans working in London for whom it was a cheap form of accommodation. From them I learnt about other hostels – the slightly cheaper, LCC-run Bruce House near the old Covent Garden, privately run doss houses with dubious reputations and, as a last throw, the LCC Reception Centre in Camberwell known as 'The Spike'. Accommodation there was free but had to be paid for by work the next day. I turned down this option as a journalistic cul-de-sac.

I also heard about the Silver Lady Mission free meals services – a mobile soup kitchen on the Embankment and a canteen in Kennington. I discovered how to earn a few pence – selling evening papers, dishwashing at hotels and, the one I opted for, helping out at Billingsgate fishmarket.

The market was centred round the Monument, alongside the Thames where the Great Fire of London started. To get the fish to the delivery lorries the porters had to push their loaded coster carts up steep little hills. So the cry went out 'Up the 'ill' at which point one of the collection of down and outs would step forward and lend a hand; the reward – sixpence a time. It meant getting down to the market at 6.00 am and being the best sprinter.

There were other adventures and some haunting stories and the series created quite a stir. By using various hostels, taking full advantage of the Silver Lady services and heading for Billingsgate, I was making a small profit by the end of the week. But the hardship and poor diet played havoc with my health.

It was ironic that Harold Macmillan, who had succeeded Eden as Prime Minister, chose this moment to make his now-famous 'Most of our people have never had it so good' speech. I had just seen the other side of the coin.

A week later Ralph McCarthy sent me off to spend a night out on the town to see how the other half lived. For the only time in my journalistic career an Editor told me to spend as much as I liked! By co-incidence it was our fourteenth wedding anniversary and McCarthy agreed that I should take Sylvia with me.

It was quite an anniversary: caviar sandwiches and champagne cocktails at the Ritz; cabaret at the Café de Paris with more champagne and Sophie Tucker providing the cabaret; Princess Margaret's favourite nightclub and more champagne.

We stayed at the Strand Palace and had our evening meal at the Savoy Hotel Silver Grill (rather than the more 'high society' Mirabelle or Caprice) for a particular reason. The Strand Palace was the hotel we had originally chosen for our wartime honeymoon. During my down and out week, I had also approached the staff entrances of both hotels seeking work as a kitchen washer-up – unsuccessfully in both cases. Now, back again, we were being feted – the Savoy even rustled up an anniversary cake when they learned of our special occasion. Another example of how clothes and circumstances make the difference between rejection and acceptance.

We ended the night at 4.00 am drinking coffee with our taxi driver on Victoria Station concourse.

The next pressure point came in July, 1957. It arose from a famous gang raid on Maples, the up-market furnishers in Tottenham Court Road, four years earlier, when £38,000 in cash and jewellery was stolen – quite a sum in those days.

A few months later five alleged gang members, including a Maples' night superintendent, appeared at the Old Bailey. All pleaded guilty except Alfred Hinds, a 38-year-old building contractor and father-of-two, who had eight previous convictions but had gone straight for eight years. The Lord Chief Justice, Lord Goddard, decided to take the case – demonstrating its seriousness – and was to describe Hinds as 'a most dangerous criminal'.

The prosecution claimed Hinds was the gang leader and the 'jelly boy' responsible for blowing the strong room safe. He was sentenced to twelve years' preventative detention. From the start he protested his innocence, insisting he was at home at the time of the raid, but the Court of Criminal Appeal refused him leave to appeal. The Home Secretary also refused a plea from a number of MPs for an inquiry.

Hinds started a protracted campaign to right what he claimed was a miscarriage of justice. He read law books and produced a booklet entitled 'An appeal to any member of the public who may consider it a duty to cause an inquiry to be made'. His loyal wife Lila organised eight petitions to the Home Secretary. By 1957 Hinds had been on hunger strike at Pentonville and twice escaped from prison to advance his case, once remaining free for two years. He kept hitting the headlines.

Ralph McCarthy decided to take up the case. 'Should Hinds's plea for an inquiry now be met?' asked *The Star*. 'Can a leopard change his spots? Is he the victim of circumstances and his own past record? Has an innocent man been convicted?'

The job of providing the answers landed in my lap; four features needed in double quick time.

For five days I travelled up to the Leytonstone home of Lila Hinds who held copies of all the court transcripts. She was an intelligent person and we established a close rapport.

One of Hinds's complaints was that Lord Goodard had made a late change of date for the hearing inconvenient to his counsel. A new counsel was appointed but Alfie (as I came to call him) saw him for only four minutes before proceedings began.

There were numerous other complicated issues. Only one of the other accused – the Maples' night superintendent – identified Alfie as having taken part. Alfie claimed that an identity parade in front of the superintendent to support his claim was refused.

The prosecution claimed that two tiny fragments of jute impregnated with black bitumen were found in a pocket of Alfie's suit similar to material in a piece of fuse found in the keyhole of the strongroom door. It was also claimed that mahogany dust, indistinguishable from that taken from the rifled safe, was found in Alfie's trouser turn-ups and shoe welts. Alfie claimed to have answers to these allegations. Some of the evidence, he also claimed, had been planted by Det Supt Herbert 'Iron Man' Sparks.

So it continued: four whole features extracted from a mass of material in a few brief visits. In essence I was acting as a one-man appeal court, combing through a mass of trial depositions which really needed a legally trained mind. I had no solicitor to advise on the legal implications and I worried that I had misread or misinterpreted the evidence.

Alfie later acknowledged that my articles had given him renewed hope and a determination to fight on. He made one further escape but his real chance came when Bert Sparks – his sworn enemy – retired and wrote his memoirs, including references to the Maples robbery and Hinds's guilt. Alfie sued for libel and the jury awarded him the then large sum of £1,300 in damages, swallowing up the bulk of Sparks's life savings.

Alfie was immediately released although his conviction was never quashed. He and Lila retired to the Channel Islands where he died in 1992. Far be it for me to express a view on his guilt or otherwise. I simply presented the evidence.

It was a draining experience on top of my down and out adventures and my body finally erupted, sparked by a minor operation that necessitated a week in hospital being fed a variety of drugs. A fortnight later the eczema from which I had suffered mildly, on and off, suddenly flared up. Hospital treatment ran to a variety of creams and potions but the condition simply grew worse. I felt exhausted and depressed. There was medical talk of changing my job and possibly becoming an in-patient.

Luck came my way, ironically, through another McCarthy bright idea. Bob Wraight, our theatre critic, who sat next to me, heard of a nursing home in Hastings which had had remarkable success in treating arthritis sufferers by nature cure methods based on the Schroth 'dry diet and wet pack' system. McCarthy decided to feature it.

Three guinea pig sufferers were selected for treatment at the nursing home for six weeks. Bob Wraight complained that insufficient time had been given to select the volunteers. The rigorous regime demanded resolute willpower. One patient gave up while another, a former engine driver, cheated by surreptitiously meeting his wife who fed him with beef tea. One patient, a 50-year-old former nurse, did go the distance, however. Her limbs were swollen and distorted at the start and she hobbled in using walking sticks. She was taking ten aspirins a day to ease the pain. Six weeks later she came out, the swellings gone and fit enough to ride a bicycle. I was impressed.

Through this I met Dr Douglas Latto, one of three remarkable brothers, who monitored the project. He and Gordon were highly qualified doctors while Conrad was a surgeon. All three were life-long vegetarians who believed in nature cure as a corollary to orthodox treatments and were still practising in their 80s. Dr Douglas, also a noted philatelist, seemed to survive on about three hours sleep a night.

Under his guidance I tried out the Schroth treatment for my eczema. I took three weeks' sick leave and plunged into the unknown. The 'wet pack' treatment involved sleeping through the night wrapped in a wet sheet and swathed in eiderdowns and hot water bottles. It required sterling co-operation from Sylvia to mummify myself each night. Once bodily warmth took over it was surprisingly comfortable and sleep inducing.

I was warned that the condition would become more severe initially with the release of toxic waste and so it proved. I was covered from head to foot and shedding skin like a fish discarding its scales; a disgusting sight. I was thankful for the loyal support of the family. I withdrew into myself and my willpower was tested to the limit.

I gave up all my old eating and drinking habits and switched to Dr Latto's strictly controlled diet. The main ingredients included fresh and stewed fruit, real yoghurt, honey, figs, dates, wheatgerm, a raw salad with a few nuts and raisins, two slices of wholemeal bread and butter, lightly cooked vegetables, potatoes in their skin and dried brewers' yeast.

For protein there were two ounces of cheese and four eggs a week.

Absolutely banned – and I went without for 18 months – were tea, coffee, alcohol, condiments, sugar, citrus fruits, tinned fruits, meat and fish and nibbles between meals. Cigarettes were also banned but I was a twenty-a-day man and it was one step too far for my stretched willpower (that required further drastic action twenty-five years later). My only liquid intake was small quantities of diluted apple juice.

The third part of the treatment, a little later, comprised occasional two-day fasts. Obtaining some of the ingredients wasn't easy. Nature Cure, Alternative Therapy, Organic Food and Vegetarianism were still unfamiliar subjects. My treatment was considered positively eccentric. But it was working.

After three weeks I was able to end the 'wet pack' treatment and return to work. I still wasn't a pretty sight but thankfully the visible parts of my body were clear. My energy was also returning and so was my optimism. It wasn't easy sticking to my diet and refusing offers of food and beverages but I lasted out.

Bernard Murphy was understanding with job allocations but at one point I was sent off to London Airport again, this time to meet another Hollywood icon, the late Jayne Mansfield. I managed to knock out 450 or so words in time for the Late Final and, despite the pressure of time, it merited a front page show with a by-line. It is worth repeating in part, if only to demonstrate the extent of my mental and physical improvement under Dr Latto.

'Miss Jayne Mansfield, the Hollywood platinum blonde whose reputation has been built up on the generosity of her outward contours, made a perfect two-point landing at London Airport today and proceeded to talk about things like inner sweetness and bigness from the inside,' I wrote.

'But her arrival left no doubt that sex makes all the difference. One of her fellow passengers was ex-world lightweight boxing champion Jimmy Carter. Like Miss Mansfield he has a 41-inch chest. But no-one seemed interested in poor Mr Carter. It was clearly Miss Mansfield's 41 inches that everyone had come to see. That's life.

'While Mr Carter, who had to bash his way to the top, wandered off in unmolested solitude, Miss Mansfied, who you might say busted her way through, was mobbed as she stepped off the plane….'- and so on.

Miss Mansfield, in London for the premiere of her latest film 'Oh For A Man', didn't seem short on that score. Her bachelor escort was Lord Kilbracken. 'I think he's awfully sweet,' she confided. But her heart, she explained, belonged to ex-Mr Universe Mr Mickey Hagerty whom she later married. Looks weren't the things she looked for in her ideal man, however. 'Inner sweetness, inner devotion, tenderness and serenity, big inside and dedication to making a woman's life beautiful. These were the real qualities,' she said. Mr Hagerty had a lot to live up to.

I got a call next morning to meet Jayne at the Dorchester Hotel in Park Lane. She, and her publicity-conscious manager, were delighted with the story. I was welcomed to coffee and received a smackeroo kiss from Miss Mansfield. Sylvia giggled when I told her. The next day *The Star* published a reader's letter appreciating my 'irreverent reporting'. It commented: 'I laughed like a drain. Can't similar Press treatment be administered to some of our political windbags?' A tragic postscript to all this was Jayne Mansfield's early death, decapitated in a car crash back in America.

Ralph McCarthy was determined I should continue to earn my keep. His next idea was the stirring story of the RAF Battle of Britain airfields and their squadrons. Off I went to the Air Ministry to wade through mountains of library material; great if you were researching a definitive book and had the time but I was expected to come up with five snappy features in a week.

I concentrated on five airfields – North Weald, where I had once been stationed, Biggin Hill, Hornchurch, Northolt and Tangmere. Apart from the outstanding exploits of their Spitfire and Hurricane pilots, they endured German air raids which had called for heroism from their ground staffs and local villagers, many of whom were killed.

In October, 1957, another assignment was thrown my way – five features please on 'The Story of Brighton'. They were boldly trumpeted in advance on the front page; a circulation-boosting idea I suspect. I had been absorbing the story of Brighton from my early schooldays and, except for changing a few dates and facts, I wrote the whole thing straight out of my head.

I don't know how Leonard Knowles, based in Brighton, reacted to this. In his place I think I would have been a bit peeved but it was not for me to quibble.

In December I was off to Smithfield Market to see how cheaply I could purchase a turkey at the Christmas auction. I bought a 20-pounder for £4 10s, rather ironic considering I was still on my vegetarian diet.

But my taste buds had adjusted to the new regime and I was making remarkable progress in general health and in the treatment of my eczema. It had effectively vanished except for one remaining small spot which also soon disappeared.

In the years that have followed I have benefited from both orthodox and alternative treatments and the medical profession has come to recognise increasingly the importance of balanced diets, natural foods, allergic reactions and the validity of a holistic approach.

That December I received a personal 'Dear Robert' letter from Ralph McCarthy: 'I am glad to tell you that your salary will be increased by £100 a year from 1 January, 1958. Although there is no general salary revision this year (and for that reason I ask you to treat this in confidence) your work has been so outstanding that I have succeeded in putting through this increase'.

It had been quite a year. But there would be no let up. McCarthy's letter added: 'Thank you for all you have done. Now on to further effort, greater success'. It sounded ominous!

CHAPTER 14

Pilgrims, Spiritualists and Lyons

Some of my 1958 stories have a contemporary ring. I began one feature with two questions: 'What is it that makes a husband want to be present when his wife is having a baby? Why does a wife want him there?'

They arose because German millionaire Heinrich von Thyssen had just helped his wife, former fashion model Fiona Campbell-Walter, give birth to their daughter. Only a few years earlier when our own three daughters were born it never occurred to me to be present. The idea was way off the cultural and moral scale of the day.

The social fabric was continuing to change. University intakes were double what they were before the war. Two-thirds of the population now had TV sets and radio listeners fell by 4.5 million in eight years. The cinemas were also hit, the Rank Organisation closing148 with more to follow.

The novel Lady Chatterley's Lover was adjudged not to be obscene, women peers were allowed into the House of Lords, Ruth Ellis became the last woman to be executed in Britain and the year saw the end of that peculiar English species, the debutante, when the annual Presentation at Court was held for the last time. Christopher Cockerell introduced the hovercraft and the Munich plane crash decimated the all-conquering Manchester United football team. There were riots in Notting Hill, Cyprus and the Middle East. There was a new Pope in the Vatican and Britain and Iceland were involved in the Cod War. The world was going about its normal business.

A local story in which I was glad to have played no part centred round conspiracy and corruption allegations within Brighton Police Force against the new Chief Constable Charlie Ridge, two detectives, a local bookie and a licensee. It dated back to the time when I represented *The Star* in Brighton, Charlie Ridge was head of CID and I compiled my thesis on Press-Police relations for him to present at the Police College.

In court the allegations included bribery, protection of crooks and back-handers to allow a club, known as The Bucket of Blood, to breach opening hours. There were also allegations that stolen groceries were delivered to Charlie Ridge's house, just off the main London road at Preston village, by a five-ton lorry shortly after midnight. A policeman was said to have witnessed it but mysteriously failed to report it.

In the end two detectives – one of whose children went to school with ours – were jailed for five years for conspiracy to obstruct the course of public justice while the bookie got three years. There was also a bit of a clearout of the CID but Charlie Ridge and the licensee were both acquitted. In the aftermath Brighton Watch Committee sacked Charlie without a pension. Five years later the House of Lords decided the dismissal was invalid and Brighton Council, in the High Court, agreed to pay him £6,424 and his pension.

By then Charlie Ridge was 63. As far as I know he enjoyed a blameless retirement. His must have been the shortest reign of a Chief Constable in the entire history of Britain's Police Forces.

In July Ralph McCarthy thought it would be a good idea if I walked the Pilgrim's Way from Winchester to Canterbury – some 126 miles – in a week. I was given three days; little time for research and none for booking accommodation. I was forced to 'cheat it' as they say, leapfrogging from one area to another and walking only short distances for appearance's sake.

What saved the day for me was a copy of Hilaire Belloc's book 'The Old Road' recording his negotiation of the Pilgrim's Way fifty years earlier – taking rather longer than a week it must be said – and a set of inch-to-the-mile OS maps on which I traced out his route. I was so ill prepared I had to enlist the help of three Winchester schoolboys cycling ahead to guide me on to the starting point at Nun's Walk alongside the River Itchen. Somehow I managed to produce six features of around 500 to 700 words each. That was one assignment at least I wouldn't have to repeat. Or so I thought. I was reckoning without the short memory and fertile mind of Ralph McCarthy.

The following year, 1959, followed much the same pattern and again some of the topics had a familiar ring forty years later. British Rail, for example, was having a hard time. When I started commuting to London the trains ran on time – unless there was a pea-souper fog. Fares were cheap, carriages were clean and there was always the restaurant car to patronise or, if it coincided with your travelling time, the luxury of the Brighton Belle Pullman.

But gradually travelling conditions changed and protests began. Among the protesters were members of the North-East Kent Railway Travellers' Association whom I joined for a feature on their complaints. These included late arrivals, signal failures, engine breakdowns, and crowded carriages. The same complaints were still being made forty years later. I also joined the Militant Commuters of Kent in the buffet car of the 5.14 pm from Cannon Street along the Thanet Line. 'We're running eight minutes late,' said the official timekeeper. 'Good Lord, we're early,' said a cynic.

Ralph McCarthy had yet another idea that summer. A High Court judge had adjudicated in favour of a claim that a spiritualist medium had induced a woman to leave him the bulk of her estate by giving her messages from the 'other world'. Down came the order; four features on Spiritualism please. This was how I came to interview Lord Dowding, architect of the Battle of Britain, and his wife, both long-time believers. My inquiries covered the range of spiritualist beliefs, practices and manifestations from seances, 'proxy sitters' and re-incarnation to levitations, materialisations and ectoplasmic phenomena.

I had the full co-operation of the College of Psychic Science and it was there that I had my own private sitting with a 'deep trance' medium, a Mrs Elizabeth Bedford who looked like somebody's grandmother and probably was.

We sat informally on chintz armchairs beside a purring gas fire. I was told in advance that her voice and larynx would be used by a 'control' called Messenger (an Elizabethan judge named Thomas Owen who died in 1598 and is buried in Westminster Abbey).

Mrs Bedford began by telling me things about my life and my

antecedents which, as far as I am aware, she could not possibly have discovered by terrestrial enquiries. The details astonished me. My father had died (an easy one that). He had suffered for about two years and his cheeks were very thin when he died (he was a victim of throat cancer). Then she added: 'Since he has passed on you have thought a great deal about him and wish you had understood him better.' Too true.

My mother was still alive, she said, but had not been well (she was in the early stages of dementia and had returned from Coventry, after living for seventeen years with my older sister, to Southwick where my younger sister Eva and her husband had found a care home for her to be looked after).

I learned all this before Mrs Bedford went into a trance. For the next hour a strange voice, speaking rapidly and with only occasional pauses, imparted a staggering mass of facts and advice. Afterwards I found I had taken down sixteen pages of shorthand notes.

My father wanted me to do all I could for my mother. She had been guided to a house (the care home?) and had my sister near her. I was buying my own house, he knew my wife and liked her (easy enough maybe). I was an author? A writer? She could, one supposes, have discovered I was a journalist from someone at the College but I doubt such duplicity.

She went on to tell me I had moved about two years previously (over three actually), that the house was 'handy for the schools' (correct), that I had three daughters (correct). One of them, she added, had done very well at school (my eldest daughter had just gained a place at grammar school). I was told that I remembered only one grandparent (correct – Grandma Woods).

Finally I was asked if I wished to enquire about anyone else. I thought of my old school pal, Don Beattie. I mentioned the name Don only. He was here, I was told, a boyhood friend. We had joined up. He was in uniform but not of the R.A.F. 'He was blown to bits,' I was told. 'But he is very happy and doesn't want to come back.' I knew his brother and sister I was told (correct). His mother had also passed on (which was news to me).

As I wrote at the time: 'Allowing for the possibility of clever deduction and intelligent guesswork, for a few wrong facts and generalisations, I was left with a residue of revelations which it seems impossible to dismiss or to account for by any natural laws'.

What did it all add up to? Where is the proof? I quote Lord Dowding: 'I never use the phrase "proof of survival". Proof for one person is not proof for another. I talk about "conviction of survival".' He warned: 'Spiritualism is not an easy path to tread.'

I retain an open mind. But, if one believes voices and manifestations are possible from beyond the grave, one is into the Hereafter and the limitless possibilities of an infinite Universe.

That year I interviewed 20-year-old film actress, Janette Scott, and Canadian wartime fighter pilot, Jackie Rae, on the eve of their wedding. I always considered her one of the most beautiful women I met. Time goes by. I next saw her a matronly, but still attractive, 60-something, appearing on the TV 'This Is Your Life' tribute to her mother, the late Thora Hird.

Reference to 'This Is Your Life' recalls another of Ralph McCarthy's impossible demands. There was a rumour that Eamonn Andrews, the presenter of the programme in 1959, was returning to the land of his birth as head of Ireland's TV Authority.

Bernard Murphy came out from the editorial conference at 10 am asking for a 1,000-words in time for the lunch edition. What was more he wanted it written in the style of 'This Is Your Life'. Down from the Library came a pile-high mass of cuttings to sift through. I managed it but it left me a gibbering wreck; one of those moments when I nearly gave up.

Christmas, 1959, brought one significant personal development. It must have been four years since one of my 'Sound Choice' radio reviews praised the popular 'Life With The Lyons' sitcom. It had brought a letter of thanks from Bebe Daniels and the following Christmas a bottle of Dry Fly sherry arrived. Further bottles followed on successive Christmas Eves, although my radio reviews had been dropped in favour of 'Televiews' (it was thought at the time that the advent of universal television would mean the end of radio).

I wasn't surprised, therefore, when no sherry arrived in 1959. But when I returned on 27 December there was another bottle waiting with apologies. The original bottle had been broken in transit.

It inspired me to fill the time travelling backwards and forwards to Brighton by writing a suggested script for the show. I sent it off in mid-January along with thanks for the sherry and a reminder that we had met many years earlier at Hove Greyhound Stadium. Then I forgot about it. A couple of weeks later, however, a letter arrived from Bebe. She wanted to see me about some script writing for their new series on which they were about to start work.

Because of my commitment to *The Star* it was agreed that I would have time only to work on every other programme – eight in all – alongside their regular scriptwriter Bob Block. For sixteen weeks I juggled with two jobs.

Bebe Daniels devised the plots and sent outlines to Bob and myself. Every other week, after a day's work on *The Star*, I headed for Bebe and Ben's home in Holland Park, to spend the evening stitching the script together.

I left just in time to catch the midnight train back to Brighton, leaving Bebe Daniels to put her stamp on the dialogue and produce the final version. Bebe, now middle-aged but still glamorous, was a nightbird who preferred working during the small hours, wearing a colourful bandana and hammering away on her portable typewriter, its canvas cover bearing the signature 'Bebe' embroidered in red.

It was a hectic schedule. I would arrive home sometime after 1.0 am, tumble into bed and arise in time to catch the 7.20 am train back to *The Star*, sleeping all the way. In addition I had to attend rehearsals and the teatime recordings before an audience. I saw little of the family during the peak periods but did manage to take them with me for one recording and my youngest daughter still remembers being held aloft, wearing her Davy Crockett hat, by Ben Lyon during the warm-up.

I was able to cope with the long hours because of my improved physical state since my nature cure dietary changes. The experience also demonstrated that, when it came to comedy script writing, I had a lot to learn. But it was a beginning and at least I had my name in the *Radio Times*. Bebe Daniels was sufficiently impressed to promise to use me again if and when they embarked on another series (they were by now thinking of retiring but she seemed fairly certain that they would opt for one more time).

Most of my work on *The Star* was now feature and Diary writing and I was able to slot the two commitments together without too much difficulty. But there were times when it was a close run thing. There was the time, for instance, when I was despatched to Eastbourne to interview Sir Percy Sillitoe, gang-busting ex-Chief Constable of Sheffield, ex-head of MI5 and now head of Security Express.

He talked about law and order in much the same vein in which it was being discussed forty years later. 'The police are doing a splendid job,' he said, 'and are as efficient as they can be in the prevailing circumstances. But the great problem facing the police today is manpower.'

His solution: 'Put the policeman back on the beat...form a Traffic Corps so that the police can get on with the job of detecting and preventing crime.'

There was another week when the 'Life With The Lyons' arrangement was in greater jeopardy. Ralph McCarthy received, as did other editors, an appeal for publicity for a 'Pilgrimage of Youth', led by London University students, dressed in medieval costumes, as part of World Refugee Year. Participants would set out from Winchester on Good Friday, and walk the 126-mile Pilgrims' Way, arriving at Canterbury the following Friday. Money would be collected for the charity on the way. McCarthy decided *The Star* should take part.

So I walked the Pilgrim's Way again, only this time I would walk every inch. A daily progress report was required for publication.

We were sent on our way with a special service at the shrine of St Swithun in Winchester and encouragement from the Mayor of the City and from Christopher Chataway MP, Vice-Chairman of the World Refugee Year UK Committee.

Only twenty-two volunteers turned up for the start – a mixture of students, sixth formers, boy scouts and a Non-Conformist minister who knew how to swear – but we picked up a number of others on the way. As the only one who had made the walk before I became unelected guide, a 40-year-old competing with lusty young students and teenagers, sleeping makeshift in village halls, schools and ARP centres. While the students headed for the local hostelry at the end of the day I had to knock out some 700 words to phone over to *The Star* at 7.30 next morning and on top of that I had to start work on a new script from Bebe Daniels. I arrived home exhausted on 22 April – two days before our seventeenth wedding anniversary.

After finishing work on the Lyons series in June, 1960, I was despatched to the 39-nation Berlin Film Festival and was staggered by the transformation of West Berlin. The rubble mountains and deep despair I had witnessed fourteen years earlier had vanished, replaced by new shops, offices and houses. The cafes were full and there was a new confidence in the air.

My main contribution from the Festival was an exclusive interview with Hollywood producer Stanley Kramer and the two women in his life – actress Donna Anderson, the one he discovered, and assistant producer Anne Pearce, the one he married. Kramer's film 'Inherit The Wind' was America's challenge at the festival and also starred Spencer Tracey, Frederic March and Gene Kelly. As we sipped iced coffee beneath one of the striped pavement umbrellas on a sun-soaked Kurfurstendamm I couldn't help recalling my last visit. But now the talk turned to the problems of combining marriage, career and coping with fame. Donna Andrew, still only 20, had been whisked off her honeymoon to face the glare of film festival publicity. 'It still frightens me,' she said.

Anne Pearce, married to Kramer for ten years, mother of two and the film's assistant producer, spoke from experience. 'You can't really generalise about marriage and career,' she said. 'In the end the husband must come first. It's a question of communication.' The controversy rumbles on. Next day Kramer and his wife flew to London for the British premiere on 'Inherit The Wind'.

In June that year I was also sent to St Patrick's Roman Catholic Church in Soho Square for the wedding of a rising young pop star, who had changed his name from Tommy Hicks to Tommy Steele, and his bride Ann Donoghue.

Another feature dealt with the concern being shown – even then – at the fatigue experienced by married women already juggling with home, children and career. 'Probably the mother of small children is the most likely of all women in today's society to suffer from fatigue', wrote a Canadian woman consultant Dr Marion Hilliard. 'The wife who tries to manage a home and also go out to work is a close runner-up'. The argument continues.

I was also asking if divorce was becoming too civilised and casual, not realising how prevalent it would become. It is worth noting that in the September of the same year former suffragette leader Sylvia Pankhurst died at the age of 78. Women had come a long way in their quest for recognition and equality, as my own Sylvia could confirm. But there was a long way still to go.

On 14 October I was back at Tito Burns' office for what proved to be, although I did not know it, my last celebrity interview for *The Star*. It was to mark the 20th birthday of another up-and-coming rock 'n' roll star.

He was wearing a new gaberdine jacket – a present from his Mum – but I was more concerned about his wealth. Tito explained that his star's allotted weekly wage had just been increased from £10 to £15 to help pay for his new car. 'I'm No Millionaire' ran the story headline and, to be fair, I calculated that, although he was already raking in large dollops of money, his expenses and entourage costs meant that he was getting only about £7,000 out of every £100,000 earned; pretty small orange juice compared to his later earnings.

The 20-year-old, who had been earning only £5 a week two years previously as plain Harry Webb, had now metamorphosed into the evergreen Cliff Richard. Both he and Tommy Steele carved out illustrious careers, Cliff ending up with a knighthood and Tommy Steele with the OBE.

I was in my fortieth year at the start of another quinquennial cycle and wondering why another change of direction hadn't occurred. I was doing well and there was the prospect of more work with the Lyons. Perhaps that was it, a new career as scriptwriter. The house purchase loans had been paid back, the decorating finished, our two older daughters were now both at grammar school and, with our youngest also at school, Sylvia was finding time to ease her way back into journalism.

Being a wife and mother was still labour intensive and mobility was difficult but, since 1958, she had been making extra money by milking the Sussex country weeklies, spotting stories where a new angle could be followed up and then bombing them off to the daily and Sunday nationals. She used the manufactured name of Sylvia Medwin which she was to use off and on over the years. She didn't make a fortune at it but she was getting back in the groove and even, on a couple of occasions, received congratulatory telegrams from the *Daily Express* and the *Sunday Express*. Then in 1960 she began undertaking some part time work for the *Evening Argus*.

One way and another prospects looked good. What I didn't know was that, even as I was attending the Berlin Film Festival, secret meetings were taking place that would dictate a drastic and unexpected career switch.

CHAPTER 15

Death of a Newspaper
and the World of Television

Three days after my meeting with Cliff Richard our world imploded. It was Monday, 17 October, 1960, and I was having a day off. Norman Batchelor, *The Star*'s crime reporter, phoned me at lunchtime. 'Get up here quick,' said Norman. 'Something big's happening.'

I caught the next available train and reached the office just in time for a full editorial meeting. Ralph McCarthy broke the news. We had just published the last issue of *The Star* and the next morning's issue of our sister paper, the News Chronicle, would also be the last. There was stunned silence. Then the questions began.

It was just nine days since my 41st birthday but there was no doubt that anonymous accountants had already settled the death of the News Chronicle and *The Star* during my 40th year.

Then the facts emerged. We had been taken over by Associated Newspapers, publishers of the rival *Daily Mail* and *Evening News*. There was little secret that the News Chronicle, still regarded as the Liberal Party flagship (the Party then seemed in terminal decline), was losing money. But *The Star* was profitable – it just had to go as part of the deal.

Suddenly one hundred Fleet Street journalists were out of work. Only ten were taken on immediately by the Daily Mail group. I was not one of them.

Then came details of the financial pay-off. There was no redundancy pay in those days and the grace-and-favour pension that went with the job now vanished as fast as bath water down the plughole.

The Cadbury family, majority shareholders in the papers, pledged that all the money raised by the sale of the papers and the company sports ground at Morden would be used to compensate the staff. For editorial personnel that meant three months' salary plus a lump sum related to length of service – £300 in my case, quite a useful sum in those days.

The closure had us shaking our heads in disbelief. It was at that moment that I resolved that somehow, sometime, I would be my own boss, no longer subject to the whim of employers and moneymen. This, I was convinced, must be the opportunity I was looking for. After talking it through with Sylvia I decided to try to establish myself as a freelance writer. With the money from *The Star* and the prospect of more script writing with the Lyons I reckoned I had a chance.

I soon had three magazine articles published in 'Today' (successor to the former 'John Bull') with a couple of other possibilities agreed. The old Sunday Chronicle commissioned me to cover some Saturday League football matches and a Public Relations consultant I knew was passing me some work. My friendly bank manager loaned me the money to buy a car. It looked promising.

Then, from out of the clear blue sky, I was hit by a double thunderbolt and the dream began to crumble.

First came news that, although our promised three months' salary would be paid, a minority shareholder was opposing the extra compensation money. He argued that any profit from the sale of the two papers should be paid to the shareholders. There was an air of confidence that he would be beaten. In fact he not only gained an injunction but also won the succeeding court action. It would be two and a half years before any payout was made and then, for most of us, it was a much-reduced amount.

At the same time the Inland Revenue demanded £146 10s excess income tax. The 'Life With the Lyons' shows had been syndicated to Australia which brought an extra £40 a programme my way to add to the original BBC payments. Now the Inland Revenue had caught up with me.

It was time for a rethink. I was 41, married with three growing daughters, a mortgage, a car loan to pay back, no company pension, no guaranteed work and £146 10s owing to the Inland Revenue. I had about six weeks' salary still to come but there was no sign of the promised £300 compensation money and no word from Bebe Daniels about a further series. I was broke, unemployed and approaching middle age. No time now to set up as a freelance; time, instead, to panic.

I began wishing I had been less single-minded and had paid attention to the NUJ vacancy list, threadbare though it was. I had rejected the one Fleet Street offer I received. It came from the News Editor of The People. Having read my exploits as a down and out, pavement egg frier and readiness to dangle 200 ft above the Thames in a bucket (as I had done at one point) he suggested I became their stunt man! But at 41 I wasn't going down that road.

Preston Benson, The Star music critic and Father of the NUJ office chapel, who was trying to find work for everyone, sent me a note referring to rumours of more newspaper and women's magazine closures. 'It has put the wind up everybody', he wrote. 'You're well off to have escaped. It's a street of fear now in quite a big way'.

But now I wasn't sure that I *had* escaped from the Street. Things were desperate. I did get to see Charles Wintour, editor of the *Evening Standard*. 'Of course, you're a writer, aren't you? I'm afraid I can't afford you,' he said. If only he'd known. But I wasn't going to grovel. End of interview.

But my guardian angel came to my rescue once more. Preston Benson, aware of my changed situation, rang me. Southern Television had a job in their newsroom for a News Film Organiser and he had recommended me for it.

I shot down to Southampton and met Director of Programmes, Roy Rich, his deputy Berkeley Smith and Dick Clark, Head of News, who would be my immediate boss.

The salary was about £500 a year less than I was getting from *The Star*, quite a sum in those days. But there was no option. I took the job.

So we enjoyed Christmas after all, even if it meant at least a temporary end to my freelance dreams.

Gradually Star colleagues also found jobs. John Rodgers, a seasoned sub-editor, joined me in the Southern TV newsroom. Bernard Murphy joined the BBC and then emigrated to a newspaper job in Houston,

Texas. Very few landed new jobs in Fleet Street. Others went into Public Relations, among them Ralph McCarthy and Peter Brooks, and some into Government department Press Offices. Norman Batchelor headed for Seaford in East Sussex, working for the local weekly and stringing for the *Daily Mirror*. Bob Wraight ended up in Cambridge where he continued as art critic, author, dealer, painter and proprietor of the Magdalene Street Art Gallery which achieved a high reputation, particularly among the city's undergraduates.

Bill King, who had started as a copy typist, graduated to news editor's secretary and finally to journalism, emigrated to the State newspaper in Perth, Australia. When it was learned that an early American spacecraft would pass over Perth at night he suggested, in his column, that the city should turn on all its lights. The astronauts radioed back that they could identify the city, so publicising Perth around the world. Bill was invited to join the Western Australia civil service as a result and ended up as First Secretary back at the State's London office in The Strand. On retirement he was awarded the MBE.

Those who suffered most from the abrupt closure of *The Star* were the older staff members. Although due for a substantial compensation sum – which they eventually did get despite the action – they saw their anticipated pensions evaporate with very little chance of another full time job. Leonard Knowles, Brighton town councillor, pillar of local society but not even a house owner, was one of them.

He survived, at least partly and possibly entirely, by writing up some of the big Sussex stories he had covered for the *Evening Argus*. When he died almost all his savings had gone and his widow, who worshipped him and the civic gravitas he generated, was forced to seek Social Security aid; one of the saddest of all *The Star* stories.

What we all missed was the special camaraderie of the editorial department. Although we scattered to all corners, we kept in touch and, over 40 years later, we survivors were still meeting in the Cheshire Cheese in Fleet Street every 17 October, the anniversary of the paper's closure.

I began work at Southern Television in Southampton on 28 December, 1960. It was another beginning. But if the past six years had been rewarding, the next four were equally turbulent. There was the immediate disruption to family life. Sylvia wasn't happy about leaving Brighton. It meant separation from relatives and friends and would end her burgeoning move back into full-time journalism. Every marriage has its times of stress and this was one of them. But she had some justification.

Southern TV's employment conditions were specific. Apart from producing two references, I was expected to reside within a reasonable distance of Southampton and subsistence allowance meanwhile would be limited to six weeks. It hardly left time to sell our house and buy another in Southampton.

Removal expenses would be met but that left legal and other costs to be paid and I was already cash starved. It helped, at least, that I could stay with my cousin Freda in Southampton during the week while we organised our move.

When we did sell our house the purchaser paid cash and wanted us out immediately. We ended up in a mobile home on the edge of the New Forest while we negotiated the purchase of a house we had found in Southampton. Caravan life suited and appeased Sylvia, however, and she and our youngest daughter entered into the pastoral spirit and went gypsy. I had the task of taking our older two daughters with me on the daily 30-mile journey to Southampton and dropping them off at their new grammar school. It was a stressful time, in the midst of which I was doing my best to settle into the unaccustomed world of television.

While we were in the caravan a letter arrived from Bebe Daniels inviting me to work on the next (and, as it turned out, the last) series of 'Life With The Lyons'. A few weeks earlier I would undoubtedly have taken up the offer. Now I had to turn it down; another near miss for the Very Nearly Man.

I soon realised that, whatever my official job description, I was in fact the news editor (a position later added to my title) and deputy to Dick Clark. News items landed on my desk for assessment and it was left to me to order stories and arrange film or photo coverage from our list of freelance journalists (mostly local paper staffers) and cameramen across southern and south-east England. I went on a tour to meet many of them and I like to think that I gave a start to some in their own television careers.

The technical side of producing a news programme fascinated me. Writing three-words-to-a-second scripts to cue in with an accompanying film and remembering to think in terms of spoken dialogue, rather than the written word, was a new experience. I enjoyed sitting in with the film editor in the race against time to produce an acceptable sequence (editing was done manually on an editing machine using acetate to join up film sections). Another aspect was flogging filmed stories, when they were big enough, to ITN for the national bulletin.

My efforts merited two salary increases – by £50 and £100 – within eighteen months. I also won kudos for my first television documentary. It was based on the development of the heart-lung machine that enabled open-heart surgery to be performed for the first time. Southampton Chest Hospital, as it was then known, was a leader in the field and we had one of its top surgeons in on the news bulletin to discuss it. I suggested using an operation as the centrepiece of a programme covering the philosophical and physical role of the heart down through history.

I spent the next weeks researching the project, starting with the ancient civilisations who regarded the heart as the life force and keeper of the soul. Then came the Renaissance, when it became the symbol of love. Above all there was William Harvey, physician to the Stuarts, who finally broke through the misconceptions and realised the heart was just a pump and discovered how it worked.

After that came the clinical, surgical and diagnostic developments which had to precede the use of the heart-lung machine. Finally I sat through an entire operation at the Southampton hospital for the final details.

At the centre was the diagnosis of a 12-year-old Milford-on-Sea girl, Jacqueline Furnell, who had a life-threatening hole in the heart problem and faced an operation to correct the defect.

The programme, using just about every technique then known to black and white television, ran for an hour and was counted a success. It was sold on to ITV stations covering London, the Midlands, the Grampians and the North and also received its share of Press publicity.

Berkeley Smith wrote a special letter of thanks. 'An outstanding success', he wrote. For my efforts I was paid an extra £25!

Nearly 40 years later I re-discovered Jacqueline Furnall, now Mrs Cook, with a family of her own and still living in the same Milford-on-Sea house. She was the picture of health. What she didn't know was that, because of the newness of the operation, we shot an alternative sequence of an operation on a young boy as a safeguard. He survived also.

Roy Rich and Berkeley Smith were surprised when, just before the programme was broadcast, I handed in my resignation barely nineteen months after joining the company.

'I won't pretend that I am not disappointed and that is a compliment to the work you have done for us but I appreciate your position and readily wish you well in the calculated gamble you propose to take', wrote Roy Rich.

And from Berkeley Smith: 'I am very sorry to receive your resignation…your going will be a great loss …'

The 'calculated gamble' was my decision to go freelance again. Leslie Cluett, my former editor in Brighton, provided the opportunity. After his brush with the law in Brighton he had opened up a freelance agency in Poole. He had been bombarding me to join him for some time, partly because he was competing with another agency in neighbouring Bournemouth.

I carefully checked out his current standing, particularly his relationship with women. He was still living with the woman he had met in Brighton, whom I knew, and who was acting as secretary/book-keeper to the agency. So I took the plunge and joined him in September, 1962.

It may seem to have been madness to abandon the new and expanding medium of television. But there were several reasons for my decision. I never quite established a rapport with the general run of Station personnel who were of a different genre, drawn mostly, I imagine, from the film world. The News Room was an isolated island of journalists. John Rodgers had the same impression and soon decamped to Canada where a daughter was already living and where he landed a job on the State newspaper.

There was also a frustrating shortage of resources. I had not been told that Southern Television was preparing to launch its first early evening magazine programme, finally dubbed 'Day By Day' (eventually becoming 'Coast to Coast'). Priority was being given to making it a success. In charge was an up-and-coming film editor who later made his name as an internationally acclaimed film director. His name was John Boorman. When it went on air 'Day By Day' caused a stir with its special features and time-lapse shots of burgeoning flowers.

Logically, the news bulletin should have been incorporated into the programme. Instead I had the feeling that we were the poor relations. I could usually get hold of a cameraman when required but we were allocated a sound crew, at most, every other day. Stories crying out for sound treatment and live interviews seemed always to occur when we had no sound crew.

The culminating moment came when a Southampton-based liner — the Berangaria as I recall — ran aground in the Solent with a full complement of passengers. It was one of the biggest news stories of my time at Southern TV. But John Boorman nicked it for his programme. He was the one who had the facilities to send anchorman Barry Westwood out in a boat with a sound crew. I felt I was knocking myself out against the odds.

Later the news bulletin was incorporated into the magazine programme and later still, in Meridian Tonight, became the main thrust of the programme, with feature material taking a supportive role, in line with a traditional newspaper format.

Promotion prospects were another uncertainty. Dick Clark, as Head of News, seemed a permanent fixture. I was also in the wrong trade union. Dick orchestrated the programme from the control room at transmission time. I stood behind him learning the technique but unable to touch the controls without evoking strike action. To touch the controls I had to be a member of the ACCT — another link with the film world. But I was in the National Union of Journalists.

I already knew I wasn't extrovert enough to be a success in front of the camera – the one role that really appealed to me. So should I switch unions after thirty years?

The only realistic advance would be to the backroom staff at ITN and that would mean returning to life in London from which I had so recently escaped, only this time working a shift system.

Another consideration was that, despite my two salary rises, I was still well below my income level with *The Star*. When we moved to Poole I had to ask for a £40 sub from the special Hardship Fund set up by the NUJ's Central London and Evening Papers Branches and the advance of a similar sum from the compensation I would eventually receive from Daily News Ltd (erstwhile owners of *The Star*).

Domestic considerations also influenced my decision to leave. Sylvia was desperate to get back into full-time journalism – not easy for a 40-year-old mother who had been out of circulation for a few years. The local *Southern Evening Echo* praised and splashed a full page feature she wrote on the New Forest but her application for a job was turned down. They still had no women reporters on the staff.

Then the late Alan Smith, our stringer in Salisbury, fixed an interview on the weekly Salisbury Journal, where he was chief reporter. Sylvia hot footed there and talked herself on to the staff, travelling backwards and forwards from Southampton every day.

Our respective jobs meant that neither of us was reaching home before 7.00 pm. We worried about our daughters becoming latchkey kids. It didn't help that the older two girls were now at a co-ed grammar school and it was not unusual to find a batch of spotty, testosterone-fired schoolboys camped on the doorstep.

Had I taken wrong turnings? Maybe I should have tried harder to remain in Fleet Street but in the next ten years several more old-established newspapers disappeared and, faced by the competition from television, those which were left had to change their style. Would I have been lost in the maelstrom?

Later Southern TV lost its licence to Television South which then gave way to Meridian. In the process, most of those I had known on the news side vanished along with Roy Rich and Berkeley Smith. So did I detect the hand of my guiding spirit yet again?

Much had been happening in the world since the death of *The Star* – a royal marriage and two royal births and John F. Kennedy was elected President of the USA (only to be assassinated three years later). There was another new Pope and a new Archbishop of Canterbury, the Berlin Wall went up, Russia threatened to site nuclear missiles in Cuba and then backed down in face of American threats. A clutch of Russian spies was unmasked and ballet star Rudolf Nureyev defected in Paris. Elizabeth Lane became the first woman High Court judge and Angela Mortimer beat Christine Truman in the first all-British Wimbledon women's final since 1914. Sir Winston Churchill died and so did Marilyn Monroe.

At the same time Sylvia and I were approaching middle age and our twentieth wedding anniversary.

CHAPTER 16

Freelance and a Sudden Death

One condition I laid down before joining Les Cluett was that a job must be found in the area for Sylvia. The *Bournemouth Echo*, again, had no women reporters and she joined, instead, the weekly *Bournemouth Times/Poole Herald/Christchurch Times/Swanage Times* series owned by the Southern Newspapers group and started another women's page.

Our two older daughters joined their third grammar school in two years – a disruption about which I feel guilty to this day. Our youngest daughter joined them a year later. 'Aren't you lucky?' commented a neighbour as they set off together for the first time. Yes indeed.

Everything went smoothly in the agency at the outset. Les Cluett was an accredited correspondent to all the news outlets at the time except the Express Group and Southern Television so, trading on my connections, I added these also. Accreditation was a pre-requisite before the media would accept one's telephone transfer charge calls – the only way, laborious though it was, of transmitting copy in those day (fax machines and the Internet were still years away).

We doubled our turnover in the first month, a promising start and, domestically, Sylvia and the children were settling in well. We even had a family holiday in 1963, helped by the fact that in April I was finally paid my promised compensation from *The Star* – almost eighteen months after its closure.

The Cadbury family honoured their pledge and pitched in their share of the sale proceeds. But independent shareholders held on to the £200,000 apportioned to them as a result of the court case – and who can blame them? Some £500,000 of the residue had to be set aside to meet existing pension commitments and those over 50 with ten years' service rightly received their full compensation amount. But, by the time the actuaries got down to my level, I received £150 instead of the original £300 and from that had to be deducted the £40 loan I had received to help me move to Poole. But £110 was better than nothing!

Dorset and South Wiltshire were proving a steady source of stories, ranging from courts martial to early UFO and corn circle claims and from holiday news to an occasional murder.

One of my first contacts was the Town Clerk of Poole. John Hillier turned out to be the son of the same William Hillier, Chief Constable of Hove, with whom I had passed the time of day all those years ago while we waited for Hove Magistrates' Court to convene.

For her part, Sylvia met up with Miss Bournemouth Regatta. She was thinking of running for Miss World via Miss United Kingdom. I tried to talk her out of it. I had followed previous contestants around while with *The Star*. There were high odds against winning, I pointed out. Losing would be a big let-down.

But she was not to be deterred and, of course, went ahead and won; Ann Sydney, the unknown hairdresser from Poole, was catapulted into fame as Miss World, 1964. Over the next few years she became, for me, a useful source of stories. At one point we were both flown up to Newcastle – I forget why – to be interviewed on local television.

I missed out on one big story, however – her brief fling with Bruce Forsyth while he was appearing in a summer show in Bournemouth. The Bournemouth agency beat me to it. My excuse is that the leak came from Bournemouth. Ann herself had given me no inkling; never get too close to your news source.

Ann had a fabulous first year, touring the world under contract to the International Wool Secretariat and appearing alongside Bob Hope. Afterwards she turned to show business for a career, appearing in a few plays, landing minor parts in a couple of films and becoming a regular pantomime Principal Boy. In between she moved to Australia where she had a disastrous marriage and transferred to Las Vegas where she formed a cabaret duet with another Poole ex-patriate, Penny France. She married unsuccessfully twice more.

We remained friends with Ann over the years, meeting up when she returned each Christmas to appear in pantomime. The last time was in

March, 2000, when she returned for a thanksgiving service for her mother who had died while visiting her in America. In her mid-fifties Ann retained her magnetic looks.

I had to cope emotionally in 1963 with the death of my mother. Sylvia and I had made the 200 mile round trip as often as possible to the rest home where she was living only to find that she no longer recognised us. I realised, as I was to realise again many years later, how cruel dementia is and how devastating for the relatives. My mother had lingered on in the home for five years. Her death at the age of 83 was a happy release and, with it, I understood how much I owed her.

By now tensions began to appear in the agency. Despite the promising start I realised I was doing too much of the leg work and we weren't making as much money as we should. It was clear that Les Cluett and his partner, as she would be called today, were having domestic problems. They would be missing from the office for a whole day, later for two. She would put in an appearance on her own to cope with the administrative work. We had a few part-time telephonists to call on when there was a rush of stories but things were reaching a climax in the agency.

It came early on Sunday, 7 June, 1964. I received an urgent call from Les Cluett's partner. I dashed over to their home to find him sitting up in bed reading the *Daily Mirror*. He was very dead, yellowed from an overdose of barbiturates. His partner hovered in the background frozen with shock. Then the questions rushed in: what to do, who to inform and then, where did it leave me? Practical considerations took over. I called the police and ambulancemen who were soon crawling all over the place. Bizarrely, in the midst of the turmoil, a phone call from the *Daily Telegraph* asked if we could let them have the results of a national yachting championship taking place in Poole Bay that day, plus intro. Somehow I managed it and arrived home that evening drained and bewildered.

There was a big family discussion about the consequences of Les Cluett's death. But my mind was made up for me the following morning when I found what amounted to a 'Sorry, there's no other way' suicide note addressed to me in the office. It left me his share of the business. Whatever the domestic and emotional problems leading up to his suicide I have often wondered whether they included a feeling that he had let me down. He was only 53.

An inquest followed from which, thankfully, I was spared. His partner departed and I was left with the aftermath, very much alone. It was a hectic period. I worked twelve or sixteen hours a day over the following weeks, keeping the flow of stories going while sorting out the office finances and filing system. Then I set out again under my own name – Hounsome of Poole as I became known. I was still barely solvent but I was, at last, my own boss with my own freelance business.

I was not only working harder on news stories but, thanks to my earlier contacts, other commissions were coming through. Shortly before Les Cluett's death I had been called in by a Fleet Street advertising agency to provide a Press and Public Relations input to an advertising campaign it had been contracted to run for Devon County Council to attract more industry to the County.

The Government was offering financial help to selected areas of high unemployment – including Devon – designated Industrial Development Districts.

Based in Poole I was ideally situated halfway between London and Devon and I set about liaising closely with the Council's Press Officer and Industrial Development Officer. I wrote the text for a sixteen-page glossy brochure and arranged a Press Conference in London to launch the campaign. I subsequently made several trips to Devon, ferreting out material for Press Releases to emphasise the quality of life in the County and the satisfaction of firms already operating there.

At the end of the campaign I received a congratulatory letter from the advertising company's own PRO who had been busy with other accounts. He had only recently arrived from his native New Zealand. His name was Des Wilson. Afterwards he became Director of Shelter, President of the Liberal Party and holder of many other positions (and, incidentally, twice stood for Parliament in the same Hove constituency where my brother-in-law, Bill Lewis, had also once stood).

In 1964 I wrote two features for the then top-selling magazine 'Tit-Bits' on the adventures of a 17-year-old local model and singer, Paula

Dalby. She was the only girl aboard her father's 41-ft yacht on a world cruise when they were shipwrecked at night on a remote coral reef in the Caribbean. As the boat sank they clambered into inflatable dinghies and, after two hazardous hours, reached a deserted island from which a fishing boat eventually rescued them. The articles appeared as by Paula Dalby 'in an interview with Robert Hounsome'. We shared the fee 60-40 in my favour I seem to remember.

It was October and my 45th birthday and that meant the start of another five-yearly cycle. I awaited the changes that were bound to follow.

I had been so concerned with career and family affairs since *The Star* folded that I hardly noticed a further social upheaval taking place, led by a thrusting post-war generation of writers, artists, pop stars, theatricals, photographers, fashion designers and new university radicals.

This was the Swinging Sixties. Couples began living together without the formality of marriage and the spreading use of the contraceptive pill heralded a new sexual liberation. Flower Power and the mini skirt were taking over, Twiggy was discovered and the King's Road was the place to be at. It was the rock and roll age of Elvis Presley, of Beatlemania and the Rolling Stones. Mods and Rockers fought their battles on the beaches of southern England and the first North Sea pirate radio station, Radio Caroline, began broadcasting. But the Windmill Theatre, proud of its record of never having closed in the war, finally did, its statuesque nudes overtaken by the new age of strippers and girlie magazines.

Dr Beeching closed a quarter of the British Rail network and over 2,000 stations, Prime Minister Harold Macmillan, having survived the Profumo scandal, was superseded by Sir Alec Douglas-Home who had renounced the Earldom of Home to do so. Tony Benn also surrendered the title of Viscount Stansgate in order to stay in the Commons.

Our daughters were into the pop scene and wearing strange clothes at weekends. I was called on to act as chauffeur for a Rolling Stones gig and similar events. Waking up in the morning we found recumbent bodies in sleeping bags littering the sitting room floor. Sylvia took a shine to one teenager, Alex Cummings, brought home by our middle daughter. She said he made her laugh. He wanted to be a journalist but had been unable to break through on the local evening paper. She fixed an interview with the editor of her weekly series. He took him on trial and she helped him with his early efforts.

A week after my 45th birthday the British public voted in a Labour Government after thirteen years of Tory rule but with another wafer thin majority of just five seats. Harold Wilson took over as Prime Minister, having promised the 'white heat' of a scientific revolution. Almost immediately he was forced to accept a loan of £1,080 million from eleven nations to prop up a sliding sterling.

It was an uncertain moment. Although I had my news outlets and the continuing work for Devon County Council, I had no back-up capital to rely on. Not for the first time I had a cash flow problem. I might well have sunk without trace but for the loyal dedication of a succession of women employees and two young journalists. Typical of them was Yvonne Williams who had been one of the part-timers we used for phoning copy through to the national press on busy days. When I found myself without any secretarial back-up, I turned to her for help.

She subsequently became my part-time bookkeeper for the next fifteen years or so. She had more business experience than me and it was really through her that I learned – slowly – the need to think, firstly, as a businessman and, secondly, as a journalist; to give profit precedence over news values.

At times during the early days, when I was bumping against my overdraft ceiling, she would mysteriously conjure up a loan to pay the wages, which we repaid some days later with a little interest. I never asked the source of these loans. But they were lifesavers. I kept the family in ignorance of how close run things were in those early days.

My first full-time secretary was Lorraine Rostron, a pulchritudinous but efficient blonde, who stayed with me until 1970 before becoming a full-time model and eventually setting up a model agency with a partner. The equally efficient Jean Hoare (later Jean Robinson) followed and remained with me for a further ten years. Other faces float through my memory but their names have been forgotten. I remember their loyalty with gratitude and wonder that, despite hard work and modest wages, they stuck with me. There were even brief periods during college vacations when my daughters helped.

I am grateful also to the two young reporters who worked for me before going on to better things. David Mead joined me from the local weekly newspaper series at the end of 1964 and Roger Scott from the local *Evening Echo* sometime in1965. It would have been almost impossible to operate a full-scale press agency without a team of this size.

Copies of only a couple of dozen or so of the hundreds of press stories we had published have survived in my possession. The rest have mysteriously disappeared. Most of them were routine, some were off-beat and a few were front page headline breakers.

There was the court case involving a serious sexual assault on a fostered boy living in the macabre-named but elegant Dorset village of Gaunts Common. It merited a big spread in the *Sunday Mirror* with follow-ups by the rest of the media. The case attracted national concern, bringing demands for changes in the surveillance of fostered children.

One regular source of news was the number of people trapped while climbing the easy-looking but treacherous cliffs along the east Dorset coast.

The man called out to rescue them was volunteer coastguard Gerald Plant, a lovely man who lived with his wife Gwen and daughter in a clapperboard house in West Lulworth and worked as a civilian at the local Army camp. We became good friends and Gerald made sure that, after all the necessary emergency calls had been made, I was the next to be informed.

This paid off particularly in the most serious incident – the discovery of a man who had been trapped in the mist on a narrow ledge for two days. While Gerald was lowered down the cliff face, the rest of us – police, press and passersby – waited on the surface. Then the call came through on the field telephone that Gerald always carried with him, asking for me. Thanks to him I was able to interview the man, while he was still halfway down the cliff, in time to catch the Sunday papers with the full details including his identity. Of all the interviews I have conducted, that was the strangest.

There were times, on barren news days, when a degree of invention was necessary as on the Monday morning when, leafing through the local weeklies, I came across the Dorset Sunday League football tables. Nestling at the bottom of the lowest division of all was the village of Wimborne St Giles – seat of the Earl of Shaftesbury – with an appalling record, every match lost, no goals scored and something like 120 conceded.

I arranged a lunchtime meeting with team representatives, and especially the overworked goalkeeper, at the village pub and suggested the idea of claiming to be the worst team in Britain. They agreed almost with pride. The national papers fell for it and then came the demand for a follow-up. So I thought up the idea of challenging any team to *lose* against them.

The Black and White Minstrels, then at the height of their popularity, took up the challenge. They arrived at Wimborne St Giles, a village hardly heard of previously, trailing television cameras, microphones and national press men in their wake. In goal was the late Leslie Crowther. After the match – I forget the result – the players were entertained to tea in the village hall. Then they all departed – Black and White Minstrels, journalists, cameras and microphones – and Wimborne St Giles sank back into anonymity; an example of a completely manufactured story that proved a nice little earner. It was another thirty-seven years before the village hit the headlines again with the mysterious disappearance of the current Lord Shaftesbury on the Mediterranean coast.

The most unusual story of my news agency days was a macabre form of suicide. From a contact I learned that a man had been found shot dead in a remote agricultural cottage in the hamlet of Mapperton, a few miles from Poole. A girl was involved. The information was sparse but potentially explosive.

Despite minimal police co-operation I obtained the address of the farm worker's cottage into which the 15-year-old girl had stumbled after the incident. Shocked and in tears she had recounted her story to the couple living there while they waited for the police to arrive. From them I heard what had happened at the cottage half a mile further up a dirt track from their home.

The dead man, some years older than the girl, had befriended her family. On the evening of the shooting he had taken her on his motorcycle to the cottage on the pretext of taking photographs to illustrate a non-existent murder mystery being written by a friend.

In one of the rooms he set up his camera on a tripod and produced a revolver, the trigger of which he linked to the camera exposure cable. He explained to the girl that the revolver was loaded only with blanks. When she pulled the trigger it would simultaneously take a picture. Then he lay down on the floor in full view of the camera and instructed the girl to aim the gun at him and pull the trigger. There was only one deviation from the truth. The revolver was in fact loaded with a live bullet. The girl pulled the trigger and the man died instantly.

I had one major problem. The next day was Good Friday when, in those more pious days, no newspapers would be published. I put the story over to the *Evening Standard* and *Evening News* and the local television and radio stations, all of which gave it a good show, even though there were still missing details.

All I could do then was ring round and leave a memo with the daily and Sunday newspapers duty staff and hope that one of them would take the bait. It turned out to be Fred Redman, News Editor of the *Sunday Mirror*. He wanted an exclusive interview with the girl and her mother for that Sunday and was sending down a reporter. By then I had tracked down the family's home in Poole. There was no-one at home so I had left a message at the neighbouring butcher's shop. Soon afterwards the mother phoned me and poured out more details.

My job now was to cosset daughter and mother and talk them into an interview with the *Sunday Mirror*. Dusk was settling in by the time the reporter arrived. She was a young Australian. Together we gradually got them to agree to move to the Burley Manor Hotel in the New Forest where I had already booked accommodation.

For the moment my job was over. I went home and discovered that my eldest daughter had known the girl all along; they were fellow members of a local drama and elocution group!

There was no time off the following day – Good Friday. Those were the days when the national dailies had staff reporters based at Southampton. Early in the morning they descended on me like a bounty-hunting posse – all except the *Daily Sketch* man who was stuck with a story on the Isle of Wight.

It was a delicate moment, keeping them happy while not compromising the *Sunday Mirror*'s exclusive. I added just enough extra details to pacify them, though they remained far from happy.

They disappeared to be replaced by a disgruntled Chief Detective Superintendent Green, head of Dorset CID, pacing round my office complaining bitterly that the *Sunday Mirror* had hi-jacked his star witness. Did I know where she was? I knew they had been down but that was all, I explained. Unscrupulous people, these Fleet Street journalists.

That afternoon the *Sunday Mirror* reporter turned up at my office to type her feature, leaving mother and daughter in the New Forest. Shortly afterwards the *Daily Sketch* replacement reporter, who had been despatched from London, arrived. I gave him the same details I had given to the other staffers that morning. As he prepared to leave he looked across at the *Sunday Mirror* reporter. 'Your secretary's having a busy time,' he commented. I didn't say anything.

The *Sunday Mirror* ran a centre page spread, complete with pictures. There were efforts by some other papers to catch up. One impossible request: get the film from the camera. But a check with the police revealed that there was no film – proof, if any were needed, that death was premeditated.

It may have been that story which inspired one angry newsdesk man to ring my home when my youngest daughter – only 12 at the time – was alone. She reminded me many years later, though I had forgotten it, that he had lambasted her till she was near to tears, ending with the threat: 'Someone's neck's going to be on the line and it will probably be yours.' To my credit, so she told me, I rang the caller when I returned and tore him off a strip for distressing her.

Another regular news source was the exiled Prince Carol of

Romania and his wife, Princess Jeanne, who were living at Upton House, a rather grand but run down mansion set in 930 acres of land sweeping down to the remoter shores of Poole Harbour. It had been built in 1816 by one of the merchants who had grown fat on the Poole-Newfoundland trade and had been given to the Corporation by its final owner in 1961.

In the same year the Council, not quite sure what to do with this potential burden on the rates and partly bedazzled, I suspect, by the presence of Royalty in their midst, granted a 21-year lease to Carol at a modest annual charge of £800. The sum covered rent, rates and insurance, although there were certain renovation commitments. In September that year Princess Jeanne gave birth to a son, Alexander, although, to the surprise of many, at Poole Hospital rather than a private nursing home.

By the time I arrived in Poole the family were already settled in and Princess Jeanne was gracing the local social scene accompanied by a 'lady-in-waiting'.

Although she spoke, when she remembered, with a fractured French accent, Princess Jeanne had been born Thelma Jeanne Williams in Nashville, Tennessee. When she met the Prince he was leading a quiet life in Paris. The Prince's roots were in France and I remain curious as to why they ever left there.

They visited the Continent and the Middle East 'looking into social and humanitarian problems in the Arab World' as the local paper put it and the Prince was elected Grand Master of the Sovereign Order of St John of Jerusalem.

But behind this façade the Carols gave every appearance of being short of cash and could afford to live in only a part of the mansion. There was talk of Prince Carol having a £30 million estate frozen behind the Iron Curtain with much of it accessible in Western banks. But nothing came of it, not at that time anyway.

I got to know them and at first had some sympathy for them, particularly for Prince Carol, a victim of the complicated love life of his volatile father, King Carol II, and the rigid social mores of pre-war Romania.

While still the Crown Prince, the future King had married commoner, Zizi Lambrino, in 1918 and renounced his succession to the throne. But four months later the marriage was dissolved on the orders of the reigning Hohenzollern monarch, Ferdinand I, and Carol was reinstated. But by then Zizi was pregnant and on 8 January, 1920, gave birth to the young Carol. The pair were banished to Paris, where Zizi spent the rest of her life, and the young Lambrino grew up with the stigma of illegitimacy hanging over him, even though he was a great-grandson of Queen Victoria.

His father next married the beautiful Princess Helen, daughter of the King of Greece, and in October, 1921, she obliged by giving birth to his second son, Michael, whose legitimacy was in no doubt.

But that marriage also foundered, Crown Prince Carol eloping with another commoner, Elena (later better known as Magda) Lupescu, who was already married. Once again he renounced his right to succession and, when King Ferdinand died in 1927, it was not the Crown Prince who ascended the throne and certainly not the young Carol Lambrino but Lambrino's 5-year-old younger half-brother, Prince Michael.

The following year the ex-Crown Prince divorced Princess Helen and his enduring affair with the red-haired Madame Lupescu came to scandalise European high society and feed the gossip columns for the next twenty-five years. Yet astonishingly, in a coup in1930, Carol grabbed the throne from his son Michael and, with Madame Lupescu always at his side, reigned disastrously as Carol II until 1940. War brought the Nazis and his dethronement and the reinstatement of Michael. When the Russians moved into Romania in1947 Michael was dethroned for a second time and the Honhenzollern dynasty came to an end.

When his father died in 1953 Carol Lambrino was at last able to apply, through the French Courts, for his birth to be legitimised and his status re-designated as HRH Prince Carol. His application was granted in 1955 and in December the same year he married the lady from Nashville as his second wife.

It was the stuff of which romantic novels are made and had Princess Jeanne exploited this aspect of their lives instead of pursuing regal pretensions, which they were economically incapable of living up to, they would probably have earned sympathy and support.

Instead the cracks began to appear. Stories emerged from local tradesmen of goods and services not paid for. The son's nurse sued for unpaid wages and contributions to the household expenses. Later came a claim for unpaid fees from the son's tutor.

Their reputation locally declined further when it became known that they had issued a notice to their 60-year-old gardener to quit the cottage he and his wife had lived in for twenty-nine years.

The complaints couldn't be ignored and adverse stories began to appear in the press. I wasn't responsible for all of them but it was on me that Princess Jeanne concentrated the blame. I became *persona non grata* and visits were met with threats of trespassing charges. When Mike Dove, Chief Reporter (later News Editor) of the Sunday Express, came down to do a follow-up story on their problems, I had to take him to the gate and leave him there.

In 1969, after neglecting to appear, the Prince was fined £10 in Glasgow Sheriff's Court for failing to make an annual return for a private property investment company of which he was a director and which had been the subject of raised eyebrows. Two other directors were similarly fined although three others were acquitted.

By this time Poole Council had become increasingly concerned about the Carols' tendency to run up rent and rate arrears and their failure to observe repair covenants. Under pressure, Prince Carol surrendered his lease and he and his wife departed in 1969 for some other part of the country.

I retain some sympathy for the Carols – the Prince himself had been unjustly treated over the years and it may be that Princess Jeanne was motivated by a desire to invest his royal designation with some substance. But I have sympathy, too, for the small people who suffered financial difficulties as a result of unpaid bills.

Today Upton Country Park, as it is now designated, is flourishing, with magnificent grounds open to the public and the refurbished mansion used for conferences, courses and private functions.

If these stories were the highlights, there were more mundane commitments which were also useful money spinners for the agency – such as yachting in Poole Harbour and Bay and greyhound racing at Poole Stadium.

There seemed to be more national yachting championship events taking place in Poole Bay in those days, as well as the Olympic trials and there was greater interest among the national dailies and Sundays.

I knew absolutely nothing about the sport but somehow managed to flam my way through the various stories ordered by the nationals. In fact it was through yachting that I later found a further career change.

For a few years the agency prospered. But the newspaper scene was already changing.

Harold Wilson had gone to the country again in March, 1966, and was returned with an increased majority of sixty-nine. But the Government had been forced to declare a state of emergency to counter a seamen's strike and, by July, Britain was on the brink of runaway inflation. Bank rate was running at seven per cent and there was a squeeze on lending and wages, prices and dividends. Purchase Tax went up, holiday currency allowances went down and Enoch Powell coined a new quote. 'Britain,' he said, 'was the sick man of Europe.'

Political turmoil and economic restraints on the one hand and the expansion and technical development of television on the other were eroding newspaper prosperity. Circulation figures and advertising revenues suffered and the weaker publications went to the wall, particularly among the Sundays. Who, today, remembers the Sunday Chronicle, Sunday Despatch, the Empire News and Reynolds News? A casualty among the Dailies was the *Daily Sketch* while, later, the *Daily Herald* – mouthpiece of the Labour Party – re-emerged as *The Sun*. The *Evening News* and *Evening Standard* retracted and became largely Greater London regional papers.

It was this upheaval which opened the way to a new breed of owners, in particular the Australian Rupert Murdoch and the Canadian Lord Thomson. Newspapers would never be the same again. Ultimately, too, it led to the near annihilation of the old-style, paternalistic family ownership of the provincial press and its replacement by large public company multiples.

The turmoil had a serious effect on agency revenues. Newspaper contents were changing, with a greater emphasis on features at the expense of news. There were fewer outlets to sell to and a reluctance to order stories. The lucrative market for early-edition 'overnight' stories for the *Evening News* and *Evening Standard* dried up.

Fortunately I was already diversifying. The expansion of the staff had left me time to use my previous television experience to script occasional locally-produced commercial films. They included a corporate film for ICT Computers on a new high-speed document processing plant and another, 'Dynamo Of The North-West', for Liverpool Corporation. One of the most enjoyable and worthwhile was for the Pestalozzi International Village in East Sussex, with its collection of Tibetan refugee children. On another occasion I spent a day scripting the installation of the first computer – the size of a large room – at Ford's Dagenham plant.

There was another documentary for Southern Television on a YMCA Camp. The commentary was by Dickie Davies who had been talent-spotted, while serving on the entertainment staff on a cruise ship, by Roy Rich. He was introduced as a newsreader during my time at Southern. Later, of course, he became better known as anchor man of ITV's long-running Saturday afternoon 'World of Sport' programme.

When Southern TV introduced a Sunday teatime news bulletin I drove up to Southampton every other week to edit and lace up the programme. It lasted until permanent staff took over but it was an interesting period being back in my old job.

CHAPTER 17

Public Relations, Marriages
and a Con Man

By 1967 I was moving further into the Public Relations business. As a result of contacts I had made through reporting yachting events, I was approached by Frank King and George Davies, two club sailors and business partners, who had recognised the potential of glassfibre in boat hull construction. It was strong, durable, flexible, relatively cheap and required less maintenance than traditional timber hulls.

In 1959 they formed a new company, Southern Ocean Supplies Ltd – later renamed Southern Ocean Shipyard Ltd – and enlisted the services of a well-known Dutch yacht designer, E.G.van de Stadt, who also grasped the significance of the new material.

The company's first 30ft cruiser, the Pioneer, was an immediate success and, by the end of 1966, two hundred had been sold worldwide. Another series, the 36ft Excalibur, was equally successful. Turnover grew by 20 per cent with exports accounting for threequarters of sales.

The 53ft Gallant, then the world's largest glassfibre series yacht, caused a stir at the 1966 Earls Court Boat Show and it was at this point that I was asked to provide some much needed Public Relations and Press publicity.

It was a straightforward assignment. The material was there. It simply needed channelling in the right direction. Press publicity rolled in. A Caribbean charter firm ordered five Gallants (one subsequently appearing on a series of West Indian stamps). Naval Lieutenant Les Williams ordered another, Spirit of Cutty Sark, for the 1968 Single Handed Trans-Atlantic Race. Yet another, owned by the Vice-Chairman of the Tory Party, Richard Sharples, won the Lloyd's Register of Shipping Trophy for the best boat built that year. Tragically

Sharples, a devoted family man, was assassinated only five years later while serving as Governor of Bermuda.

There were other SOS series, reaching a peak with the even larger Ocean 71 which could be fitted out as a racing yacht or a luxury cruiser. One, Ocean Spirit, won the two-handed Round Britain Race in1970. It was co-owned and jointly sailed by Leslie Williams and Robin (later Sir Robin) Knox-Johnston, the first man to sail solo, non-stop round the world. A luxury version, 'Treena', was ordered by TV's Galloping Gourmet, Graham Kerr, and named after his wife.

By now the company had moved to a larger quayside yard and it was there that Graham Kerr was 'captured' for a TV 'This Is Your Life' programme. Publicity flowed in for 'Treena' and other Ocean 71s including features in the national press, yachting magazines and foreign publications.

Soon after being engaged by the yacht company I was approached by the Powell Duffryn Group's Public Relations Department to act for them on the south coast – one of a team of local representatives they were establishing across Britain. At the time Powell Duffryn was a large trading organisation owning a variety of companies whose products and services ranged from engineering to shipping, timber to coal and fuel oil and stevedoring to waste disposal and air conditioning.

My area was one of the busiest, including four large companies and one or two smaller offshoots and stretching from Weymouth in the west to Dover in the east.

The coal and fuel oil company sponsored show jumping events at three agricultural shows across the south. My attendance was required to generate Press publicity and ensure that the trophy and the presenting director turned up and were properly looked after.

The same company sponsored annual concerts for schoolchildren by the Bournemouth Symphony Orchestra at Bournemouth, Southampton, Portsmouth and Brighton. This again meant organising on-the-spot Press publicity. It was a contrast to my first job with that rather smaller coal agency in Brighton all those years ago.

With the slump in the newspaper business, Public Relations offered a brighter prospect and I set about gradually changing the organisation to meet the new requirements. Firstly, and with much regret, I disposed of the services of Dave Mead, who wasn't married at the time and then of Roger Scott, who was. But I retained both until they were able to land new jobs.

Dave left in 1967 to join British Leyland's publications department before moving on to the Press Association's wire service. But his hobby was painting birds and he became so successful at it that he later turned professional.

Roger stayed on until 1968 when he joined the *Daily Mail*, first in Northern Ireland and then as north of England correspondent, contributing a long succession of features and important exclusives until his retirement.

I also became involved in two other enterprises away from newspaper journalism, in both cases at the instigation of the Mayor of Poole, Freddie Rowe, a self-made millionaire. Fred was one of a group of council members and officials who were in the process of recreating Poole into the modern, rapidly expanding, diversified and high-value town it is today.

They planned a new undercover shopping mall to include a large indoor sports centre – only the second non-profit-making, municipally supported enterprise of its kind in the country.

It fell to Fred Rowe to spearhead the public appeal towards the building costs and I was called in to help with the Press publicity in an honorary capacity.

Fred next hosted a lunch to launch the Wessex Export Club. Similar clubs were being set up across the country by the Board of Trade, as it was then called, through the medium of the British National Export Council, to boost Britain's external trade.

The idea was to bring businessmen together to promote exports, discuss the problems and procedures involved and, most important, to arrange overseas trade missions. Companies participating would have doors opened by consular officials in the host countries and half their mission expenses would be reimbursed. The lunch was attended by one hundred and twenty companies, fifty-two of which formed the Export Club.

The Chairman was Josh Sieger who, later, was awarded the CBE. He had been involved in many enterprises in the past, including the development of radar and large screen television. Now he was founder-Chairman of an eponymous firm specialising in industrial detection systems capable of identifying the minutest concentrations of dangerous gases and vapours in an ambient atmosphere.

I was invited on to the Export Club committee. Later I also joined the Sports Centre management board and finance committee and the governing Charitable Trust.

Sylvia and I were simultaneously dealing with further family developments. For a period our three daughters were at grammar school together. But between 1965 and 1969 all three departed along different paths.

Our middle daughter, Alison, married in 1968 and presented us with our first grandchild, Jenni. Our eldest daughter, Rosalind, having completed her 'A' levels and a secretarial course, disappeared for a couple of months backpacking round Europe with a girlfriend. After briefly working for me and for a local solicitor, she set off again, this time for three months. Back in England she left for London – with a former schoolfriend as flatmate – to become secretary to the principal of one of the London University colleges. Our youngest daughter, Susan, started a business studies National Diploma course.

There was a transitional period when I continued to run the news agency and the PR business and it was during this period that I met up again with Percy Roberts, my pre-war fellow junior reporter on the *Brighton Evening Argus*. Following his post-war return to North Africa he had, by 1951, risen to Managing Director of the *Nigerian Daily Times*, which became part of the West African media interests of the pre-eminent Daily Mirror Group.

The Group Chairman, Cecil King, on a tour of the group's overseas empire, was sufficiently impressed by Percy to promote him to Managing Director of the Mirror's interests in the Caribbean. By 1962 he was back in Britain climbing further up the Group ladder. When we lunched together in London he was Managing Director while I was still the Group's accredited freelance correspondent in Dorset. Looking back at our time as juniors together we couldn't but recognise the irony of the course life had taken.

Percy was convinced he had reached as far up the ladder as he would get. But by 1977, after Cecil King had given way to Hugh Cudlipp and there had been a couple of group take-overs, Percy was finally appointed Chairman. Sylvia and I had lunch with him and his wife Paula at the Mirror's Holborn headquarters. I was no longer running the news agency but I like to stretch a point and claim to have been the only Mirror stringer to have dined with the Group Chairman in his private suite. Sylvia and I subsequently visited Percy and his wife at their home in Ross-on-Wye and continued to keep in touch by exchanging Christmas cards.

In 1969 I reached 50, the start of another five-yearly cycle. I had handed over the news agency business to the Bournemouth freelance outfit – for a small monetary consideration I seem to recall – and changed my business from Hounsome Press Agency Ltd to Robert Hounsome Associates.

The second half of the Sixties brought new challenges and changed attitudes. Abortion was legalised, illegitimate births were multiplying, 'the irretrievable breakdown of marriage' became legitimate grounds for divorce and homosexual activity in private among consenting males over 21 was legalised. Soccer hooligans were causing mayhem and drug addiction was becoming a national problem. It was also a period when thousands of immigrants flooded into Britain, provoking Enoch Powell's inflammatory 'Rivers of Blood' speech. An outraged Edward Heath, who had replaced Alec Douglas-Home as Conservative leader, sacked him from the Shadow Cabinet. The Race Relations Act became law and Tony O'Connor became the country's first black headmaster.

Hippies were exhibiting the potency of flower power and preaching peace, London became the Hip City and fashion centre of the world. England won the World Cup, the 70mph speed limit was introduced along with compulsory breath tests and the Government announced the intended switch to metrification.

I was so busy at this time that it was Sylvia, I now realise, who was keeping things together domestically while continuing her own journalistic career. It was even more difficult because her father's health unexpectedly deteriorated, leading to his death in 1967 at the age of 67.

On 17 October, 1969 – the ninth anniversary of the closure of *The Star* – Rosalind was married to an Italian from Sardinia whom she met in London. Her flatmate married another Italian.

When the children were younger we had always managed to scrape an annual family holiday, however frugal. Now, stressed out, we ventured on our first overseas package holiday, to Majorca.

My two office stalwarts, Yvonne and Jean were still with me and my Public Relations consultancy was now established. As far as I know, it was the first independent PR business anywhere in Dorset. I also became a member of the Institute of Public Relations.

The Swinging Sixties gave way to what might be described as the Schizophrenic Seventies, scarred by industrial strife and raging inflation and coloured by a younger generation.

In January, 1970, the age of majority was reduced from 21 to 18, giving our three daughters the right to vote. Then on 11 May, 1970, our eldest daughter gave birth to our second grandchild – another girl, Sonia.

Three weeks later a 15-strong trade mission, sponsored by Wessex Export Club and backed by the British National Export Council, set off for South Africa. I accompanied the mission as the appointed secretary.

I accepted the job because of the chance to witness apartheid in action. It was no sinecure. The participating companies – only six of which came from the Wessex area – were receiving substantial Government support. So set procedures had to be followed. There were travel and itinerary arrangements to make and a bi-lingual brochure to produce.

In the cause of publicity I persuaded the members of Swanage Women's Institute to create a four-foot high red and green felt effigy of Willie the Griffin, the Wessex Club's motif. It seemed a good idea until we made an unexpected night stop at Mombassa on our flight out and, half asleep, had to unload all our hand luggage – including, in my case, the unwieldy Willie. But it proved its worth as I and Tommy Thomson, head of a Poole engineering company and the mission leader, hawked it round from Mayors' Parlours to Press receptions and trade cocktail parties. Just before returning to England we presented it to a children's hospital.

These visits, together with 'mothering' the mission members, kept me busy during the three-week tour which took in Johannesburg, Cape Town, Durban and Pretoria.

But I did find time to marvel at the breathless beauty of the Cape itself and to visit a Zulu tourist-trap village. I also toured Soweto native township with a civil servant guide. She astonished me with her enthusiastic pride in the place but its dusty, depressingly basic uniformity and no-hope atmosphere appalled me. Here was someone too close to the acceptance of white supremacy to realise that, inevitably, the overwhelming endemic majority would one day prevail. Already the taut, introverted atmosphere in the white-dominated commercial centres was tangible. I maintained an outward neutrality only with great difficulty.

The mission was a commercial success. Contracts worth £115,900 were signed and another £1,008,000 worth were subject to completion.

In the General Election two days before our homecoming in June, 1970, Harold Wilson's Labour Government suffered a surprise defeat by the Conservatives, led by Edward Heath.

Sylvia's career had also taken a new twist. She was made editor of a freesheet, Shoppers' Newsguide, produced by Southern Newspapers in opposition to one launched by the Bournemouth freelance agency. It ran for eight months until the agency ceased publication. Shoppers' Newsguide also closed as a result and Sylvia resumed her normal role on the regular weeklies.

Domestically our eldest daughter gave birth to a second daughter, Tania, in 1971 and in February of the following year our second daughter followed suit with another granddaughter, Nova.

Then, in August,1972, our youngest daughter, having obtained her Business Studies National Diploma, married a boy she had met through College friends and moved to Guildford. She was not yet 20.

From being a five-strong family with a house bustling with

teenagers, by the beginning of 1973 our daughters had flown and we had four grandchildren. We were a fifty-something couple living on our own.

Professionally we had plenty to occupy our time. Sylvia had progressed to Chief Reporter of her local weekly and was Mother (Chairman) of her NUJ Chapel (office sub-branch). I also remained an active member of the NUJ and in January, 1973, was appointed Branch Chairman, with Sylvia as my Vice-Chairman. The Branch was larger than it had ever been.

It was a frantic period, coping with professional pressures, maintaining contact with our daughters and, when appropriate, providing them with such practical and sometimes emotional and financial help as we could.

In April our eldest daughter left, with her husband and their two daughters, to live in his native village of Milis in Sardinia. To us Sardinia was a remote Mediterranean island noted for kidnapping and village vendettas – both exaggerations as it turned out – and we were naturally concerned about the family's welfare. Anxious for first-hand knowledge, we followed that summer for a fortnight's visit.

Facing the prospect of making regular visits for years to come, we bought a secondhand Volkswagen Dormobile for the long journey down through France and Italy. It was a disaster. All went well until we reached the outskirts of Chalon-sur-Saone – about two thirds of the way – when there was a loud bang and we cruised to a standstill.

Through the AA's French associates we were towed to the nearby village of Rully and parked in a compound full of motorway crash wreckages. There we learned the shock truth. The Dormobile engine was declared irreparable.

While the AA sorted out the problem we explored Rully village and pressed our noses against the window of an intimate little restaurant, salivating as we watched the diners regaling themselves. We couldn't join them. I had only a limited amount of French money and those were the days before credit cards and when currency controls were at their strictest. I promised Sylvia that one day we would return to Rully.

A replacement car arrived next day and, after transferring everything from the Dormobile, included numerous items belonging to our daughter, we set out to make up lost time. We had to make a further unscheduled stop at Nice airport to change vehicles again. We had pre-booked a place on the early morning ferry from Civitavecchia, way down the Italian peninsular, for Sardinia and made it with a couple of hours to spare. The AA had saved us from disaster. Besides arranging the two replacement cars, they delivered our broken down Dormobile back to Poole.

Situated on the edge of Sardinia's fertile south-western lowland, Milis is a typically deceptive Italian village grouped round a main square dominated by a pink palace owned, at the time, by an absentee mainland countess. But it had a lush landscape deriving from the springs where the water, filtering down from the northern mountains, broke cover. Orange trees lined one of the approach roads. There was an orange orchard, fields of water melons and tomatoes, wild-growing pomegranates, fennel, rosemary and myrtle and prickly pear cacti (which I learned how to harvest using a bamboo cane split at the top to grasp and twist off the pink-fleshed fruit). There were luscious grapes from which Vernaccia, the local golden coloured wine, was made and which was distilled down to produce the colourless but corrosive local firewater known as aquavita.

It was an island of contrasts, scenically and culturally. It was not unusual to see sheep being driven down the village streets alongside modern cars and old ladies in their traditional dark clothes and headdresses sitting with teenage college students in their casual wear. It gave the impression of a generation being leap-frogged.

The welcome from our son-in-law's extended family was overwhelming and we struggled to cope with the hospitality at meal times. Talk in the village bars was conducted at a high decibel level in the local Sard dialect.

I helped to harvest a field of melons that our daughter's father-in-law had bought. Along with tomatoes and other fruit they would be transported to northern mountain villages where they were sold or bartered for the locally made cheeses, breads and wine. One variety of cheese depended on being colonised by a particular type of maggot and

I watched, fascinated, as one villager devoured large chunks complete with their writhing inhabitants.

The Aga Khan and the international jet set had recently discovered the Costa Smeralda in the north but the package tour fraternity was largely limited to a holiday complex in the south. So it was still possible to find sweeping high-duned bays, almost deserted but which always seemed to have a beach bar-restaurant.

It was manana land where time tended not to matter and there always seemed to be a colourfully costumed festa in one town or another. At the height of summer the mid-day heat was so oppressive that a siesta behind closed shutters was obligatory.

We had an unexpected meeting while on a weekend visit with our daughter and her family to a remote waterside fishing village on the Costa Smeralda, across from the millionaires' playground.

We booked into the only bar-hotel in the village and were in the bar when Sylvia noticed a couple of English lads behind us. One was an ex-boyfriend of our youngest daughter from their college days in Poole. He was backpacking round the Mediterranean and happened, briefly, to be in this particular spot. He stayed on, lodging with our daughter for a few weeks. Some years later he re-surfaced as author and scriptwriter. His name was Mark Wallington, best known for his early book '500 Miles Walkies' – an account of his travels round Britain with his dog – and 'The Missing Postman', his TV play featuring James Bolam of 'The Likely Lads' fame, which won acclaim.

We flew back to England wondering why we were returning to the pressure-cooker world at home. Little had changed. More wage increases were followed by further inflation, followed by more strikes.

Industrial unrest resulted, in December, 1973, in the three-day working week and Ted Heath called another General Election under the slogan: 'Who runs Britain, the Government or the miners?' The electorate seemed not to know. They gave Labour 301 seats, the Conservatives 297 and the Liberals, Scots and Welsh Nationalists 23.

Ted Heath tried to do a deal with the Liberals but failed and on March 6th, 1974, Harold Wilson was back in Downing Street with a minority government. It made little difference, inflation reaching a post-war record of 16 per cent and the FT Index slumping to below 200 points for the first time in 16 years.

My business held steady although it, too, was caught up in the wages-prices cycle. I had to sit down every three months and adjust my fees upward to meet the inflationary spiral. A further strain was the growing practice of client companies to delay settlement of accounts in order to limit their own overdrafts and the crippling interest rates they attracted. Where they had once settled in a month, the period now stretched to one, two, three and finally four months.

Small businesses like mine were faced with building up our own overdrafts — at a penal interest rate of 26 per cent — or finding extra working capital. I chose the latter. It meant limiting my own out-take and cashing in various life insurance policies which, in any case, were trailing behind inflation in value.

At the same time our youngest daughter's marriage collapsed in divorce after only two years.

We survived the competing pressures and I celebrated my 55th birthday on October 8th, 1974. More significant changes were due.

On 11 October another General Election was held. This time the Labour Government scraped back with a paper-thin majority of three, the result reflecting the dilemma of a nation divided.

Soon afterwards Sylvia and I paid a second visit to Sardinia. This time we took the journey more leisurely, staying at Rully in France and enjoying the promised dinner in the village restaurant.

Then we headed for the French Alps and took the scenic Napolean route to Nice before catching the Sardinian ferry from Genoa, avoiding the long journey down to Civitivecchia.

My two main memories, apart from seeing our daughter and grandchildren again, were being transported to a local football match on the back of a donkey-drawn cart and being introduced to the Sardinian custom of taking a lamb into the home for fattening up for Christmas. Fortunately we left before its short life ended.

On the return journey we drove, for the first of several occasions, via the Italian northern frontier town of Aosta and then through the Grand St Bernard tunnel into Montreaux in Switzerland and on to the

French mustard capital of Dijon. Later, as a variation, we took the Mont Blanc tunnel to Chamonix.

Back in England life was much the same, with more strikes and the cost of living still rising but one surprise was the election of Margaret Thatcher as leader of the Conservative Party in place of Edward Heath. The grocer's daughter had beaten the Grocer, as Private Eye dubbed Ted Heath.

Sylvia and I had other things on our minds. Through our trips to Sardinia we had caught the continental travel bug and Sylvia spotted what she reckoned was the answer – a newspaper advertisement headed: 'Own your own mobile home abroad'.

We wrote off and were referred to the company's Dorset representative whom we met at a hotel in Bridport. She was a tweedy country type accompanied by a husband who looked like a retired bank manager. She produced a glossy brochure and rattled off costings like an animated cash register. One snag, however; the main site for the homes was in the Algarve and what we wanted was somewhere in France en route to the Sardinia ferry. Then an invitation came to join a 'site inspection' weekend to the Algarve. 'Why not?' we thought. We had never been to Portugal.

We were quite a large party and were introduced to various people in Portugal and taken on a tour of the site and shown the footings and walkways being dug out. The operation appeared above board but Sylvia and I didn't quite take to the owner. Sylvia had sharp words at one point and mentioned that we were journalists. We were also adamant that we wanted a quick delivery in the south of France. It was these two facts that surely saved us.

I was sufficiently impressed by the company's offices in London to hand over £3,000 – the cost of a mobile home – on the promise that it would be delivered to the south of France by Easter. No problem, we were told. A site had been found at Opio between Grasse and Cannes.

It arrived, even though it was late. We had also arranged for the company to act as our letting agents when we were not using the home. There was a frisson of doubt when the £100 for the first week's letting failed to arrive. On a business visit to London I called at the company's offices and found them deserted. We were philosophical. We had lost £100 but we had our mobile home and we enjoyed the first of several holidays in the south of France.

Ironically the main purpose of our buying the mobile home – as a staging post to Sardinia – had ceased to apply. Our eldest daughter was pregnant again and returned to England with her husband and children so that the new baby could be born there.

By then unexpected changes had taken place at Sylvia's office. She had tried to resign as Mother of her office Chapel of the NUJ in March but was prevailed on to serve for a further year. Her former protégé, Alex Cummings, who, after training on the paper had had spells with the freelance agency in Bournemouth and a period freelancing in Spain, had returned and was chief reporter on the associated *Christchurch Times*. When the editor of the weekly group moved on to edit the local *Evening Echo* in July, 1975, Alex was the successful applicant for the job. Sylvia also applied but who was going to appoint a 53-year-old grandmother? The following month our eldest daughter gave birth to our first grandson, Carlo.

Sylvia's former protege was now her editor and she his chief reporter. As Chapel Mother, it was her job also to negotiate with him over salary and working conditions! The situation was handled with diplomacy and discretion on both sides and was eased six months later, in March, 1976, when Sylvia finally relinquished her position as Mother. As for Alex, he later moved on successfully to higher managerial levels.

We enjoyed our holidays in the south of France. The mobile home site was set among pine trees with two swimming pools, a restaurant and laundry and ablution facilities. The rent was high but this was paid for, along with the bulk of the cost of our own holidays, by our lettings at £100 a week. There was no shortage of takers, many of them through our youngest daughter who, by now, had returned to Poole and was working for one of the big banks.

We ranged the south of France from St Tropez in the west to Nice in the east and on to Ventimillia and other nearby points over the border in Italy. We visited Monte Carlo where we recalled 'The Man

Who Broke the Bank at Monte Carlo', the old music hall song we sang as kids without thought of ever getting there.

Cap d'Antibes was our regular bathing rendezvous and we mixed with millionaires. Sylvia struck a new fashion note on our first visit to St Tropez. She had forgotten to change out of her bedroom slippers.

The village of Opio also had its interesting aspects. Visiting the local mini-supermarket for the first time, I found myself sandwiched between two local residents – film star Dirk Bogarde and stuttering humorist Patrick Campbell.

Soon after our first trip I learned how lucky we were when two heavies from Scotland Yard Fraud Squad turned up unannounced at my office. The owner of the company selling the mobile homes had departed hastily for South America with lots of customers' purchase money. I was the only one who had actually received delivery of a mobile home. It had been a sublime con operation which would probably have been uncovered had he reneged on our early delivery stipulation. Our newspaper background had probably worried him also.

In Britain inflation seemed out of control. Unemployment reached 1.5 million but that summer brought the greatest heatwave of the century. Harold Wilson resigned as Prime Minister to be succeeded by Jim Callaghan who faced a country being torn apart by extremists, with revolutionary militants on the left and flag-waving nationalists on the right. There was fighting on the streets and subversion in the air.

The National Union of Journalists was not immune from the new militancy. As early as 1973 Sylvia, as Mother of the Chapel, had had to lead the weeklies' staff in a two-day strike in pursuit of a wage claim.

A year later she was presiding over meetings dealing with further strike proposals. There were the first signs of doubt as the staff began to worry about the viability of their papers which were by now losing money.

That October Sylvia and I retired as Vice-Chairman and Chairman respectively of the Branch. But we continued our commitment to the Union, although we were troubled by the growing extremism. Chris Whitfield, a colleague of Sylvia, recalls her nagging the staff to 'get off our backsides and do something'.

After that year's annual delegates meeting, Chris was one of the prime movers in the formation of AJAX – Allied Journalists Against eXtremism.

In 1977 our sixth and last grandchild, Jody, arrived – a third daughter for our middle daughter. I was now 57 and Sylvia 55. We managed a final trip to our mobile home in Opio but were now facing the prospect of having to dispose of it. We weren't popular with the site owner. We were, I think, the only occupants to rent out to holidaymakers and he had little enthusiasm for late arriving visitors asking for gas bottles. He imposed increasingly difficult conditions so that the operation ceased to be viable. Time to move on anyway. I sold the home for the original purchase price; an interesting experience.

June that year brought the Queen's Silver Jubilee celebrations but it also brought violence on the picket lines outside the Grunwick film processing laboratories over trade union recognition. The miners voted for £135 and a four-day week and the railwaymen pitched in with a 63 per cent claim. London undertakers walked out leaving eight hundred unburied bodies and further industrial action blacked out the State Opening of Parliament.

The following year Sylvia celebrated her 57th birthday and decided to go part-time. But she continued to play a full part in Chapel affairs.

The NUJ was discussing the 1979 pay claim. Sylvia's weeklies were still losing money but the Chapel initially supported limited strike action if it became necessary.

Callaghan warned the Trade Union Conference that the ensuing winter would be make or break time and could settle the result of the next general election but his warnings were largely ignored and the unions marched on relentlessly into what became known as 'The Winter of Discontent'.

A meeting of NUJ provincial delegates voted for sanctions in pursuit of their pay claim and, if that failed, for strike action. But pockets of dissent appeared in areas where employers made comparable offers that were swiftly accepted. Southern Newspapers, proprietors of the *Southampton, Bournemouth and Weymouth Evening Echos*, came up with an offer of 15 per cent on gross salaries. Here, too, staff accepted the offer despite possible Union disciplinary action.

It placed the staff of Sylvia's weekly series in a compromised position. A strike that halted publication, while the local Echo continued publishing, would leave the weeklies in an even weaker position.

When their staffs, too, were offered 15 per cent – though on net rather than gross salaries – the Chapel vote 8-7 in favour of accepting with 5 abstentions (including Sylvia who, now a part-timer, was in a particularly awkward situation). At Southampton, 15 striking journalists picketed their evening paper colleagues.

By January, 1979, the employers' organisation had offered a general 14.5 per cent increase and more staffs accepted. Hardliners thought acceptance would mean other striking members were being sold down the river, however.

Then came the retribution. Staffers who had ignored the strike call were expelled or fined. Sylvia and her weekly colleagues were among those expelled despite the dilemma of their situation and hers in particular.

Everything was then thrown back in the stewpot. Journalists in Coventry and Birmingham had the strike declared illegal because of alleged balloting irregularities. The Union was granted leave to appeal to the House of Lords and a debilitating three and a half years' legal wrangle ensued.

Expelled members retained their membership until the appeal was heard. It was a case of suspended animation. The Bournemouth branch and its subsidiary chapels began to fall apart. Many members ceased paying their subs but I was determined to keep Sylvia's up to date, even though we were now having difficulty finding someone to pay them to!

Meanwhile the *Times* and *Sunday Times* suspended publication indefinitely in face of industrial action. Schools were closed and hospitals turned patients away. Food and petrol supplies were disrupted, rubbish piled up in the streets and cemetery workers refused to dig graves. The domino effect caused thousands of other workers to be laid off. In March the Government lost a vote of confidence by a single vote. The next day the Prime Minister called a General Election.

Clearly, the Labour Party's historic links with and financial dependency on the trade unions restricted attempts to limit the influence of the militant left in industrial relations. So it was Mrs Thatcher, a more formidable foe, who strode into Downing Street quoting the words of St Francis of Assisi: 'Where there is discord let there be harmony, where there is despair let there be hope.' Empty wishes; from my standpoint, harmony turned out to be a mirage and hope a mockery for the disadvantaged over the next twelve strident years of her reign.

I have always believed that the Labour Government might well have continued in power had acceptance been given to 'In Place of Strife', the trade union reformation White Paper introduced in 1969 by the then Employment Secretary Barbara Castle – no faint-hearted Socialist herself. The same applied to the 5 per cent pay limit proposed by Chancellor Denis Healey in 1978. But both were rejected by the unions and, in the case of 'In Place of Strife', by some 100 Labour MPs, led by the then Home Secretary, James Callaghan. Ironically, it was Callaghan who led the Labour Party to defeat and the start of its many years in the wilderness.

In October I celebrated my 60th birthday and wondered what the start of a new five-year cycle would bring. Earlier that year my brother Reginald had died after a relatively short illness at the age of 74. Again I regretted not having seen more of him.

It was a confidence-sapping time for British business, with high unemployment and inflation and my industrial clients were feeling the draught. The *Times* returned to the newsagents in October following agreement between management and unions. But it was an isolated case of conciliation. The miners rejected a 20 per cent pay offer and steel workers struck for the first time since 1926. Mrs Thatcher announced that state benefits for strikers would be halved. The stage was set for the battle ahead.

By April, 1980, the government's economic policies had led to unemployment reaching 1.5 million and inflation by 21.8 per cent. As the policies bit deeper, manufacturers reported order books falling by as much as 40 per cent. The unions blamed Mrs Thatcher and Mrs

Thatcher blamed the unions. The Labour Party was riven by intercine warfare, leading to the formation of the breakaway Social Democratic Party.

Small businesses like mine were caught in the middle and I began losing clients struggling to counter the recession. Powell Duffryn diverted payment and responsibility for public relations to its individual companies who had no enthusiasm for this new burden.

I was 60, the mortgage was paid, a small annuity had matured and I had a substantial working capital invested in the business. The children had left, Sylvia was still writing her women's page. What was the point of carrying on?

The determining factor was a deterioration in my health, resulting from a head-on car crash a few months earlier. It left me with a fractured finger and an undetected whiplash. I began suffering from unaccustomed headaches, backaches and loss of appetite. It was time, I decided, to close down. It took a month or so and Yvonne Williams and Jean Robinson stuck with me to the end. When I finally closed down, Jean was able to move straight into another job and Yvonne switched to one of my former clients who took over my office and stock. I came out with my capital intact – a substantial five figure sum. Checking back I realised I had acted for over thirty different companies at one time or another.

CHAPTER 18

Pilgrims, Spiritualists and Lyons

With the closure of my business I needed some new outlet, and at the end 1980, Alex Cummings offered me the job of Chief Reporter on the local weeklies of which he was now Editor. I started work on 19 January, 1981, and Sylvia and I found ourselves back where we had started when I returned from war service in 1946, myself as Chief Reporter and she as women's page feature writer. Life had turned full circle. It was also the start of fifteen enjoyable years.

A clinical masseuse finally traced my headaches, backaches and lost appetite to the whiplash sustained in that car crash. She referred me to a chiropractor but first we had a holiday planned in Greece. It was an almost fatal step.

Two days after our arrival I suffered, suddenly and dramatically, a perforated duodenal ulcer. I was saved by a nightmare three-hour ambulance journey to Piraeus and an emergency operation. I came round at midnight with the surgeons enjoying a quiet post-operative fag! Conditions in the hospital were basic, the medical and nursing skills superb. Twelve days later we caught our scheduled flight home. It was a traumatic time for Sylvia also. Apart from worrying about me, she had to return to our holiday village to collect all our belongings and re-locate to a hotel near the hospital. There was one other outcome of the operation. For ten days, hooked to a spaghetti of tubes, I was unable to smoke. I have never smoked since; one way to give up, though not to be recommended.

Back home the chiropractor gradually got my spine back in alignment and the headaches disappeared. Once again alternative therapy came to my rescue.

At home industrial unrest continued and public surveys showed Mrs

Thatcher to be the most unpopular Prime Minister on record. People at the margins took to the streets. There were riots in Brixton and skinheads and Asians clashed in Southall. Unemployed demonstrators from Liverpool descended on London.

In the middle of it all Prince Charles wed Lady Diana Spencer in a marriage which was to end in tragedy of almost Shakespearian dimensions.

In December, 1981, the Far Left icon of the coalfields, Arthur Scargill, was elected President of the NUM and events took on a kind of inevitability.

Then the Falklands War erupted. By sending Argentinian troops in to capture the Falklands, General Galtieri saved Mrs Thatcher's political life and ruined his own. To assemble a fighting force at speed and despatch it 8,000 miles south towards possible defeat was a brave decision which displayed Mrs Thatcher's resolute character even if, in the end, the same single-mindedness all but annihilated her Party.

The war claimed three British ships and inevitable casualties. But it was all over in two and a half months and Mrs Thatcher, who had only recently had to resist calls for her resignation, was now on a pedestal which would carry her to victory in the next General Election.

By October, 1982, the House of Lords had upheld the injunction against the NUJ. All penalties were revoked and membership was re-instated although the guilty verdict remained on record. Wryly, although still writing her women's feature, Sylvia was by now 61 and past the official retirement age. We had continued to pay her Union contributions, however, so that her membership remained unbroken. For both of us the final act came on 17 November, 1983, when we were simultaneously made Life Members of the Union.

Several journalists, who had ceased to pay their contributions during the dispute, never returned. The Branch was decimated and the weeklies' Chapel all but ceased to exist. It was a traumatic time for the Union exacerbated by the Government's anti-Union legislation. It would be another twenty years before members began drifting back in any numbers locally.

With the weeklies still losing money the owners, Southern

Newspapers, bought up a rival give-away and amalgamated the whole lot into a new freesheet series, the Advertiser which made its appearance in March, 1983. It confirmed the staffs' earlier concern about their futures. A number now left with acceptable redundancy payments. I stayed on for a couple of months to help with the transition and then I, too, left – two months short of my 64th birthday and just in time to qualify for redundancy pay. The invigorating age of hot metal journalism, when newspapers were virtually the unrivalled purveyors of news, was coming to an end. As I departed, computerisation was already taking over and in a short time eliminated print rooms, foundries, stone subs, bust headlines, em measures, the smell of molten alloy and the clatter of newsroom typewriters.

It was no surprise when the Conservatives retained power in the June '83 General Election.

Looking back on my own life I realised it had been marked by a long trail of closures dating back to the abandonment of the Bentham Road Mission Hall. The Intermediate School had followed. Later the *Sussex Daily News* and the *Brighton and Hove Gazette* disappeared, although the *Evening Argus* survived, converted to a daily. Even two of the regiments I had been posted to in the war were disbanded. *The Star* lasted until 1960 before giving up, Southern Television surrendered its licence to Television South and finally the *Times/Herald* weekly series had died. All these closures were, I hoped, the result of evolutionary progress rather than my baleful influence!

Sylvia and I had now reached the time of life when we could spend more time with our daughters and grandchildren and watch events from the sidelines. Our eldest daughter, her marriage over, embarked on a degree course at Southampton University and subsequently became a primary school teacher and married again. Our second daughter qualified as a social worker, ending up in Social Services child care and then going steadily higher. She too, divorced and married again. Our youngest daughter rose to human resources management with one of the big banks. She too remarried, only to be widowed in her late 40s. Three of our grandchildren were already at grammar school. Life was pretty good.

Unexpectedly, more freelance assignments now came my way. At the beginning of 1984 I was approached by the National Bus Company – yet to be privatised – to contribute to their staff newspaper.

At the same time Mrs Thatcher was preparing for her pivotal battle with the National Union of Mineworkers and its new leader Arthur Scargill. The confrontation began in March, 1984, when the union turned down a 5.2 per cent pay offer coupled with a programme of twenty pit closures. Within three days over one hundred and fifty pits stood idle. Significantly, however, twenty-one in Nottinghamshire and Derbyshire carried on working, objecting to the fact that no strike ballot had been held. Violence quickly built up, with police and picketing miners being injured in pitched battles. Arthur Scargill, leading from the front, seemed hell bent on using his troops as battering rams to bring down the Government and establish his dreamed-of Socialist Republic. He believed his union was still an all-powerful force that could bring the country to a standstill. But coal was losing ground to other forms of energy. Mrs Thatcher had also meticulously planned for battle, building up large reserves of coal and ensuring the confrontation would begin in the spring, coinciding with the warm-weather rundown in coal consumption. In time there were splits in the miners' ranks and by November a number began drifting back to work.

My 65th birthday arrived and the start of another five year cycle. It coincided with an offer from Southern Television to carry out preliminary research for a series of countryside programmes that eventually emerged under the title of 'Country Ways'.

My first report was submitted a month after my birthday. The assignment lasted twenty months and encompassed some fifteen different areas, stretching from West Sussex in the east to the Vale of Pewsey in Wiltshire and the Bride Valley in west Dorset. So I was able to explore the rolling countryside of southern England, with Sylvia in tow, and be paid for the privilege.

I was also approached by an advertising agency that had taken on the account of a locally based engineering company. Part of the deal was the production of a four-page staff newspaper. They needed someone to take it off their hands. The company occupied four factory sites spread across Hampshire, Wiltshire and Somerset and that meant more countryside expeditions gathering information.

Over the next eighteen months I produced six issues but the company had an old fashioned approach and relied heavily on one specialist product. It was no surprise to me when the business was taken over and closed down.

Meanwhile the miners' strike drifted on until February, 1985. By then only a little over 50 per cent were still on strike. The end came in March when the Union executive faced the inevitable and called off the strike. Arthur Scargill led the remaining miners back to the pithead. It was a sad humiliation for a proud workforce.

The strike had gained nothing. It had divided mining villages, set brother against brother and generated a bitterness that was to last for years. The Union was a broken force, with the Nottingham and Derbyshire miners setting up a rival organisation. Arthur Scargill, the coalfields' icon of a year before was now a shadow, his dream a shattered illusion.

Insensitively, Mrs Thatcher claimed 'a famous victory' and continued her policy of marginalising the unions. Perhaps it was no co-incidence that, where strikes had dominated the news headlines in pre-Thatcher days, they were now replaced by stories of rioting and hooliganism leading later to surging crime and drugs figures. Had the new culture simply replaced one problem with several others?

The privatisation of the National Bus Company in the spring of 1985 led to a management take-over of the Wilts and Dorset part of the organisation and I switched to producing the new company's staff newspaper. Here, too, was a widely scattered workforce spread across three counties from Romsey in the east to Salisbury and beyond to Pewsey and a two-bus depot in the Wiltshire village of Hindon. Sylvia and I were touring the countryside yet again in search of more news items. It was pleasant enough but, in all cases, I made sure the clients benefited professionally and got value for money.

One 'Country Ways' area I covered, the western end of the South Downs Way, which included East Marden village where my father was born, had special personal significance. I entered my name and address in the visitors' book in the church along with my father's details and was surprised two months later to receive a letter from Canada.

The writer, Bruce Baker, living in Calgary, had married a Doris Hounsome, whose forebears also came from East Marden. He had been researching the family tree at a distance for some years and, visiting England, had called at the village church and spotted my entry. This was how I discovered that three of my father's cousins had emigrated to Canada all those years ago.

We met Bruce and Doris twice when they visited England and we became good friends before her death. Bruce had traced the Hounsome family back to the mid–18th century. Our meetings led me to begin to research my own family tree and history.

Then came another interesting link. My name appeared in the local newspaper in connection with a family history inquiry. It was spotted by a Thomas Hounsome who proved to be the grandson of the Thomas Hounsome I had visited as a boy with my father in Brighton.

Thomas, in turn, told his daughter Lyn Lancefield and her husband Rex who lived not many miles from me. They had both worked in local government Records Offices and had also been researching the family history. Given their expert knowledge and access to records, they had made even greater progress than Bruce.

I put Bruce Baker in contact with Rex and Lyn to compare notes and made further efforts myself to track down more of my father's family. It wasn't easy. Even today I know almost nothing of some members.

One person whose details I was desperate to discover was Robert Hounsome Allen. Help came from my childhood acquaintance, Winnie Cleaver, daughter of Aunt Hilda, in Petersfield. It was she who produced the letter Mollie Allen had sent to Hilda, informing her of Robert's death on the Somme. Through her, too, I finally contacted one of Robert's cousins, Alan Webb, who filled in the story and sent me photographs of Aunt Mollie's family and of Robert himself in civilian clothes and in army uniform. At last my namesake began to take physical shape.

I had another surprise visitor at this time, an unknown second cousin, Brenda Woods (later Brenda Horwill). She was the grand-daughter of one of my mother's brothers and had been researching the Woods history. She had reached back to the 1770s. So here again I suddenly had a family tree provided by another's efforts.

Hardly had my 'Country Ways' assignment come to an end than I was called in to help BP with its community relations in the Isle of Purbeck, on the southern shores of Poole Harbour, where it was developing its extensive Sherwood oilfield.

Small deposits of oil had been found in south-east Dorset since Victorian times but the first real breakthrough came in 1974 when a new reservoir, the Bridport field, was found 3,000ft below the Purbeck lowlands centred on Wytch Farm. It was still a modest find producing some 1,000 barrels a day through remote 'nodding donkey' wellheads and causing little local disruption.

The Sherwood reservoir was of a different order. A further 2,000ft below Bridport, it extended under the western side of Poole Harbour itself and ran 2.5 kilometres out into Poole Bay.

It was the largest onshore field in Western Europe. It was also sited beneath an environmentally and ecologically sensitive area, partly owned by the National Trust, marked by a scattering of special scientific sites and famous for its rare fauna and flora. Local planners and villagers were also worried about the effect of development work on the tranquillity of the area and on village life.

Concerned at the reaction BP, developers of the field, decided to issue a quarterly community newspaper. Its purpose was to explain the basic facts of the oilfield and to give progress, construction, extraction and processing plans, ecological and environmental safeguards and consequential labour and business opportunities. My job was to produce the bulk of the copy for the newspaper. Six issues were produced between the summer of 1987 and the summer of 1990, although the last was never issued. By then the major part of development had been completed.

It was a massive operation requiring the sinking of some fifty wells across nine sites. Miles of underground pipeline connected the wellheads to a new gathering station where oil and gases were separated and processed. The oil was carried via a fifty-six-mile underground pipeline to a terminal at Hamble on Southampton Water. A parallel pipeline carried methane gas to feed into British Gas's trunk system at Christchurch. Another pipeline carried liquified petroleum gas to a railhead for onward transmission by rail to Avonmouth near Bristol.

Millions of pounds were spent to meet the concerns of environmentalists and conservationists. Pipelines were diverted to avoid sensitive areas and wildlife habitats, a special service road was built and the gathering station itself was designed to remain hidden below the treeline in a pine forest.

Archaeologists were called in to carry out surveys ahead of pipeline laying, resulting in the discovery of important sites and artefacts. Schools and other institutions benefited financially and educationally. My contribution led to my being commissioned to provide features for various other BP publications.

The beginning of 1986 brought the last major trade union confrontation of Mrs Thatcher's reign. Rupert Murdoch switched his News International empire to Wapping without first agreeing manning levels with the print unions. Some 2,000 printers struck and 5,000 militants manned the picket line.

In the end they had to accept defeat. It was the culminating point in the changing nature of the newspaper business. It marked the end of the print unions' stranglehold and the beginning of the flight from Fleet Street, the industry's traditional home. In time all major newspapers would depart to more accessible parts of London.

The Labour Party was still at loggerheads with itself despite the efforts of its leader, Neil Kinnock, and at the General Election of June, 1987, Mrs Thatcher won an unprecedented third term. But she was beginning to lose her sure touch, epitomised by her insistence on replacing the old style Council rate with a new community charge, known as the 'Poll Tax'.

Demonstrators took to the streets and the opposition grew. Her government was also split over membership of the European Community. It ended with her forced abdication and her replacement by the shadowy John Major. The smart money was on a Labour victory at the next general election in April, 1992, but Major caused an upset by winning despite the fact that, as Chancellor of the Exchequer, he had taken the pound into the ERM at too high an exchange rate.

Now he paid the penalty. On what became known as 'Black Wednesday', Britain expended millions of pounds trying to fend off the speculators but was still forced out of the ERM. It was a disaster from which the Tories and their reputation for financial rectitude were to take years to recover.

Shortly after Black Wednesday my BP commission came to an end. By now oil was flowing from the Sherwood reservoir and, with development work completed, it quickly faded from public notice. So well disguised are the various installations that visitors and residents alike now enjoy Poole Harbour and the Purbeck lowlands without realising that a large scale oilfield lays beneath their feet.

For me that, more or less, was it. Sylvia and I were both now in our 70s. I wanted her to give up her weekly women's feature also but she insisted on carrying on. It was a mistake.

CHAPTER 19

The End of the Line...
and the Scourge of Alzheimer's

Now, at last, I was able to return to genealogical matters. For me it was more than simple curiosity. For almost as long as I could remember, I had carried that irrational, niggling lack of self-belief, never mentioned and deeply hidden. It dated back to those impressionable days of my youth and had inhibited my confidence at decisive moments so that I missed out on the big chances. Now I discovered my heritage and I experienced an irrational release of old tensions.

Behind me stretched a direct ancestral line going back to the mid-1500s and beyond to the thirteenth century and the original family name of de Hundesham ('home of the hounds'). From these beginnings my ancestors had risen from their lowly position to become farmers and country craftsmen and to occupy historic houses. They had never reached aristocratic heights but the line was direct, ancient and pure-blooded. At last I could bask in true self-belief.

Later I chanced on a booklet written by Mary Tyfield about her village of Conford near Liphook in Hampshire. Flicking through it I found an ancient section of the Hounsome family tree. I contacted Mary and made another friend and another source of information. To her and to Lyn and Rex and Bruce Baker I am indebted for enabling me to share the results of their efforts.

I am indebted also to Alan Webb, The Manchester Museum Committee of the King's Regiment, Michael Stedman's 'Manchester Pals', Tameside Local Studies Library and the Commonwealth War Graves Commission for enabling me to flesh out the story of Robert Hounsome Allen from his days as a young schoolteacher till the time of his untimely death on the Somme. I was back where the story began.

But there was still the denouement.

In October, 1993, my sister Eva died at the age of 84. A year later, in October, 1994, I reached my 75th birthday, the start of another five yearly cycle and another turning point. There were trying times ahead.

In the spring of that year I noticed Sylvia was experiencing minor short-term memory problems. Our GP arranged psychiatric tests and a brain scan but, because of staff changes, we were never given the results. Optimistically, I assumed that there was no problem; just a touch of old age. The signs were so mild that Sylvia continued with her women's feature for another six months before voluntarily giving up. Life continued much as before.

Four months after my birthday my other sister Ethel died, leaving me as the only sibling survivor. Twenty days later her husband Leslie also died.

In 1996 everything was consigned to the back burner. On a further visit to our new GP I was given the shattering news that Sylvia was suffering from Alzheimer's. It was news I could barely hide as I took Sylvia home. I never did have the courage to tell her.

The condition was slow to develop. We did the round of social engagements and had one more holiday in Majorca. Only then did a certain quirkiness appear to slightly puzzle acquaintances. I had to act normally because Sylvia was unaware of any abnormality. But by April, 1997, the condition had advanced sufficiently to qualify for the modest lower level of Attendance Allowance to provide some home help.

Coping with Sylvia's condition meant detaching oneself from the outside world. There were important events taking place of course. I remember Election Night in May, 1997, and the excitement and anticipation when Tony Blair's 'New Labour' demolished the Conservatives. What grabbed the public emotions even more was the death of Princess Diana in a Paris road crash and the continuing scrutiny of the lives and role of the Royal family.

In October, 1999, I reached 80 and Sylvia's deterioration became more rapid. Looking after her was the sole focus of my attention. Alzheimer's is an awful, so far incurable condition that attacks the brain, destroys the personality, slows the metabolism and, given time, turns intelligent beings into stumbling zombies bereft of dignity.

By April, 2000, paranoia, hallucination and incontinence had set in and the real nightmare began. There were times when she no longer recognised me, was convinced her father was still alive, had aggressive moments and tried to wander off in search of some imaginary address where she thought she lived. I frequently had to call in our daughters for help, neighbours even became involved and there were visits from Social Services and a community psychiatric nurse.

By mid-July, 2000, it became too much and Sylvia was admitted to a psychiatric ward. She remained there for twenty-two days for assessment. From now on I found myself caught in a bewildering whirlpool of psychiatrists and social workers, hospital visits and day centres, the ramifications of the Mental Health Act, arcane medical terms and an idiosyncratic and inadequate funding system. There were encounters with overstretched staffs in faraway offices making arbitrary decisions and sending out contradictory letters of domiciliary and residential care demands. Being trapped in the system and trying to find logical answers sometimes felt like driving round the M25 with all the exits blocked off.

In September, 2000, Sylvia was again admitted to hospital. She remained there for four weeks, after which I had her back home with me under Mental Health Act Section Release. I managed to keep her with me over the Christmas holiday but on 27 December, exhausted and demoralised I had, reluctantly, to agree to her return to hospital, pending a vacancy in a residential home. She was admitted in February, 2001. I was bereft to the point of tearful outbursts and consumed by guilt. It wasn't supposed to end like this.

That May's General Election produced another massive victory for Tony Blair. But, as with so many aspects of life in Britain, Labour philosophy had changed. It had taken the Party eighteen years to rise again from near annihilation. In that time a new generation had reached maturity having experienced only Thatcherism, with trade unionism banished to the sidelines and nationalisation a discarded policy. Many on the left who now dreamed of a new millennium gradually came to question the new regime. The trade unions were disappointed if they expected a wholesale cancellation of Conservative constraints, there seemed little enthusiasm for a return to nationalisation, and the gap between the very rich and the persistent poor showed little sign of closing. Meanwhile it was the Tories' turn to stumble into the wilderness in search of a new raison d'etre. Thus, somehow, democracy manages to maintain a healthy equilibrium.

Where I would have once been excited by these changes in the political landscape they now seemed irrelevant in 2001. I was more concerned with trying to salvage something from the past. Every afternoon I would take Sylvia out to the New Forest for tea. I would talk to her about our life together, even if she did not understand. We would return in time for me to sit with her for her evening meal.

The hallucinations intensified. She would often introduce me to fellow residents as her 'father'. She ceased to recognise our daughters and grandchildren. 'Who's that lady?' she would ask.

The nightmare continued for almost two more years, her personality slowly disintegrating although, right to the last, she struggled to maintain her former determination and joie de vive. 'Can't we have some fun?' she would ask in her more lucid moments. Leaving her I would weep tears of anguish and frustration and pray that she would not live long enough to become a zombie.

Then on 18 December, 2002, after a brief illness due to a severe renal infection, she died peacefully and mercifully in her sleep only a few hours after I had unsuspectingly kissed her goodnight. She had died aged 81 in accordance with her own time scale and 127 days short of what would have been our diamond wedding anniversary, a final Very Nearly occasion. We had the funeral service on Christmas Eve.

Four weeks later Percy Roberts, my one-time junior reporter colleague, died while on holiday in Africa; one more among the growing list of relatives, friends and celebrities who have passed on.

So the phantom figures have come and gone around the magic shadow show; the stars and the nonentities, the virtuous and the villains, those whom one loved and those one respected. Meeting them has been an enduring experience. If I have taken wrong turnings at times, have lacked the ultimate degree of self-belief and shunned ambition's hard edge, I have few regrets.

As A.E.Smith, my old English master, predicted all those years ago, I never found great wealth but I have had an interesting life; and if Sylvia has gone she has left me a legacy of three daughters, six grandchildren and to date three great-grandchildren, all of whom I love dearly. These are my riches.

If Robert Hounsome Allen has been my guardian angel, my alter ego, I hope he has not been disillusioned. Perhaps, to some degree, I have by proxy, experienced the kind of life with which he could identify and of which he was so futilely robbed.

Robert Hounsome died in the early hours of Thursday 24th March 2005 in Poole Hospital, Dorset. His passing was the result of a car accident that took place on 31st December 2004. He was 85 years of age.

As well as being a thoughtful and moving autobiography and an important historical document for the subsequent generations of his family, I believe this book also acted as a therapeutic and cathartic experience for Robert whilst he wrote it. Having nursed Sylvia, his wife of almost sixty years, through such a traumatic and debilitating illness and ultimately losing her, he went on to devote his time and attentions to reflect and comment and come to terms with his life, its ups and its downs. What you have read is the result of that experience.

Securing the publication of the completed manuscript then became an increasing concern for Robert who worried that he might never achieve his final ambition and be able to hold this book in his hands with the pride and satisfaction he so deserved. Passing away before seeing this book in print, therefore, seemed at first to be a cruel reminder of nature's indiscriminate unfairness and a concluding illustration of Robert's noted observation that every five years brought a major change, events influenced 'as if manipulated by a guiding spirit'. But on reflection, I believe Robert, wherever he is, would smile knowingly at the irony of the situation, and point out that it was just the final example of how he believed his life had been lived. Just another Very Nearly occasion.

However, it must be said, on behalf of everyone who knew him and especially on behalf of his family, that Robert was never considered and will certainly never be remembered as a 'very nearly man' as he called this book, reflecting his own characteristically modest approach to his achievements. Instead, Robert Hounsome will be remembered as a 'very great man' who will be sadly missed by all who knew him. Another great-grandson was born on 4th August 2005. He has been named after Robert. As one cycle ends, another begins.

Carlo Ortu
Grandson
December 2005